WORLD WAR I AND
SOUTHERN MODERNISM

WORLD WAR I & SOUTHERN MODERNISM

DAVID A. DAVIS

University Press of Mississippi / Jackson

www.upress.state.ms.us

The University Press of Mississippi is a member of
the Association of American University Presses.

First printing 2018

∞

Library of Congress Cataloging-in-Publication Data

Names: Davis, David A. (David Alexander), 1975– author.
Title: World War I and southern modernism / David A. Davis.
Description: Jackson: University Press of Mississippi, [2018] | Includes
bibliographical references and index. |
Identifiers: LCCN 2017025973 (print) | LCCN 2017028091 (ebook) | ISBN
9781496815422 (epub single) | ISBN 9781496815439 (epub institutional) |
ISBN 9781496815446 (pdf single) | ISBN 9781496815453 (pdf institutional)
| ISBN 9781496815415 (cloth : alk. paper)
Subjects: LCSH: American literature—Southern States—History and criticism.
| Modernism (Literature)—Southern States. | American literature—20th
century—History and criticism. | World War, 1914–1918—Literature and the
war. | World War, 1914–1918—Participation, African American. | American
literature—African American authors—History and criticism. | American
fiction—Women authors—History and criticism.
Classification: LCC PS261 (ebook) | LCC PS261 .D36 2018 (print) | DDC
810.9358404—dc23
LC record available at https://lccn.loc.gov/2017025973

British Library Cataloging-in-Publication Data available

Dedication

For Kris

CONTENTS

ACKNOWLEDGMENTS

This book began with the help of Fred Hobson at the University of North Carolina at Chapel Hill. The debt that I, and scores of other scholars of southern literary studies, owe to him will never be repaid. I can only humbly offer my thanks. I am forever grateful for his guidance and advice, as well as for the input of other colleagues—William L. Andrews, Joe Flora, Minrose Gwin, and Trudier Harris. I am also grateful to friends who encouraged this project. A partial list would include Lucas Carpenter, Elizabeth Fox-Genovese, Barbara Ladd, Noel Polk, John T. Matthews, James L. Peacock, Harry Rusche, Ron Schuchard, Linda Wagner-Martin, Harry Watson, and many others. A complete list would be prohibitive to publish.

My peers at Chapel Hill, my colleagues at Wake Forest and Mercer, and my friends in the Society for the Study of Southern Literature have provided good company, wise counsel, moral support, and enthusiastic cheerleading. Many of them have listened to my questions, some have offered advice, and others have read drafts. For their help and support, I would like to thank Bryan Giemza, Andy Leiter, Tara Powell, Harry Thomas, Amy Weldon, Robert West, Andreá Williams, Andy Crank, Jon Daigle, Rian Bowie, Colleen O'Brien, Dean Franco, Trevor Dodman, Doug Thompson, Mary Ann Drake, Rick Wilson, Andrew Silver, Anya Silver, Gary Richardson, Mary Alice Morgan, Rich Fallis, Gordon Johnston, Jonathan Glance, Deneen Senasi, Mary Raschko, Chester Fontenot, Lake Lambert, Michael Kreyling, Susan V. Donaldson, Jay Watson, Katie McKee, Eric Gary Anderson, Ben Wise, Robert Jackson, and Sarah Gleeson-White.

Three people over the past several years have invested special energy and expertise in this project. Maria Hebert-Leiter critiqued early drafts and made me believe that this book could be done. Michael Dowdy showed me directions I had not explored. My friend and colleague Sarah Gardner patiently offered goodwill and good advice.

Portions of this book were previously published in the *African American Review* and the *Mississippi Quarterly*. I am grateful to these publications for permission to reprint.

My family has contributed more to this book than they realize. My mom, Linda Smith, encouraged me to follow my interests, regardless of the costs. My sons, Lucas and Ayden, taught me the meaning of joy. And my wife, Kris, gives me a reason to be.

WORLD WAR I AND
SOUTHERN MODERNISM

INTRODUCTION

WORLD WAR I AND SOUTHERN MODERNISM

*World War I changed everything. It was a great shock
to the whole country, but the war broke open a frozen
culture like the southern world.*
ROBERT PENN WARREN, "MAD FOR POETRY"

William Faulkner's first novel, *Soldiers' Pay*, is the story of a mortally
wounded soldier returning from combat in France to Georgia to die.
Although not of the same caliber as his later masterpieces, the novel illustrates many of the elements of content and technique that Faulkner would
incorporate into his style and that many other southern writers of the same
generation would also use, including elements of experimentation, an
awareness of the discontinuity between the South's ruralism and America's
growing urbanism, and a critical attitude toward the region's past. It is not
coincidental that this pivotal text concerns the effects of World War I on
the South. The war changed the region by exposing provincial southerners
to modernity, which had a galvanic effect on southern writing for the next
generation, leading to the development of southern modernism.

When America entered World War I, the South lagged behind more
developed parts of the world. While areas of western Europe and the northeastern United States developed industrial economies, urban cultures, and
progressive political systems, the South remained an impoverished agricultural region within an industrializing and urbanizing nation. By clinging
to a dominant ideology that valorized the lost cause,[1] a set of economic
practices that exhausted the land, and a rigid system of social structures
that marginalized women and degraded African Americans, the South at
the beginning of the twentieth century had become socially and economically detached from the more modern parts of the United States. Despite
New South boosterism, the South in 1916 was a domestic colony of the

United States that produced cotton and poverty. The South, which H. L. Mencken called the "Sahara of the Bozart" in 1920, contributed meagerly to the nation's cultural production in the first years of the twentieth century.

But between 1920 and 1940, a period sometimes called the Southern Renascence or the Southern Renaissance, southern writers contributed disproportionately to American modernist literature. Dozens of writers emerged during this period, including William Faulkner, Elizabeth Madox Roberts, Allen Tate, John Crowe Ransom, Jean Toomer, Zora Neale Hurston, Richard Wright, and many others. One must wonder if this change in southern writing had a precipitating cause. I argue that World War I played a pivotal role in the emergence of southern modernism. Although the southern social structure continued to develop slowly during the first half of the twentieth century, southerners came into contact with more modernized cultures outside the South during the war, and wartime modernization altered the South's economy, the attitude of many white southerners to the lost cause, the role of African Americans in Jim Crow culture, and women's roles outside the home. After the war, southern writers incorporated aspects of modernist literary technique into their depictions of southern society, they developed a more critical perspective on the region, and they depicted the effects of modernity on the South in their writing.

Radiating Modernism

Modernity is a relative term. Changes in ideas, technology, and social practices; contact with divergent cultures; inventions and discoveries; conflicts and disasters; demographic shifts; and economic fluctuations inevitably alter the way people live in a given time and place. Neil Smith explains in *Uneven Development* that spaces develop at variable rates relative to their economic productivity, their natural resources, their political systems, their cultural values, and other issues. All of these factors can impede or propel processes of modernization, leading to differences in the rates of modernization in one territory relative to another territory. At the beginning of World War I, not all nations were evenly developed and not all regions within nations were evenly developed, and this variability of modernization is crucial to understanding southern modernism and how the war contributed to modernism radiating into the South.

When used in connection to literary modernism, the term "modernity" refers to a rapid and tumultuous period of development in the late nineteenth and early twentieth century when the conditions of everyday life in some areas of western Europe and the northeastern United States changed radically.[2] Charles Baudelaire coined the term in the essay "The Painter of Modern Life" to describe "the ephemeral, the fugitive, the contingent" atmosphere of urban Paris in 1864 (13). The crucial component of modernity is that life in a city constitutes a fundamentally different experience than rural life. Modern cities, the first metropolises, emerged in the late nineteenth century, when advances in industrialization led to expanded networks of trade, rapid flows of population, developments in infrastructure and technology, rigid divisions of labor, and a proliferation of consumer goods. These changes in everyday life, in turn, led to changes in political structures, ideological systems, labor organizations, and artistic movements. In *Paris, Capital of Modernity*, David Harvey claims that "modernism, after 1848, was very much an urban phenomenon" both because the social processes of modernity took place primarily in cities and because artists and writers tended both to congregate in cities and to depict the processes taking place in cities (25). Considering the critical roles that Berlin, Chicago, Dublin, London, New York, Madrid, Paris, Rome, and Vienna played in modernist cultural production, this claim seems completely plausible.[3] Indeed, of all the theories about modernism, the idea that it developed in global metropolises seems to be the most durable. In Malcolm Bradbury and James McFarlane's landmark collection *Modernism 1890–1930*, Bradbury states that "when we think of Modernism, we cannot avoid thinking of these urban climates, and the ideas and campaigns, the new philosophies and politics, that ran through them" (96). Most studies of modernist writers and artists focus on cities, either directly or indirectly.[4] To the extent that modernism is a cohesive and coherent movement, it appears to be a primarily urban movement, which makes the South's relationship to modernism inherently problematic.

The term "modernism" in literary criticism often refers to the avant-garde texts, such as Joyce's *Ulysses*, Pound's *Cantos*, or Eliot's *The Waste Land*, that, in their radical departures from literary convention, reflect, distort, and reinforce the social disruptions taking place in the context of modernity. Yet, as Michael Levenson explains in *Modernism*, the movement was not limited to these avant-garde works. It encompassed a much more expansive range of writers and artists who responded to the "oppositional culture" of modernity in a variety of ways, not all of which challenged literary conventions (8). Modernist literature exposes many fundamental contradictions of modernity. "[Modernism] was a celebration of a technological age and a condemnation of it," Bradbury and McFarlane write, "an excited acceptance of the belief that old regimes were over, and a deep despairing in the face of that fear; a mixture of convictions that the new forms were escapes from historicism and the pressure of time with convictions that they were precisely the living expressions of those things" (46). Modernism is not an exclusionary category, limited only to a select segment of writers, but a broad set of literary responses to the social disruptions of modernity. The defining element of a modernist text is the disruption of existing structures, which may be construed as social, economic, cultural, or literary, and the disruption may inspire responses that defend tradition, attack tradition, or in some cases both. The disruption reveals the tradition because, as Susan Stanford Friedman observes, "tradition comes into being only as it is rebelled against" (510). Southern writers more often wrote from the margins of modernism, frequently opposing disruption and defending tradition as they created it, but they clearly recognized changing conditions in the region.

Virginia Woolf arbitrarily pinpointed the disruption as occurring "on or about December 1910" ("Mr. Bennett," 32). Her provocative comment raises important questions about when, where, and how modernism emerged and spread. Stephen Kern, Peter Osborne, and David Harvey have theorized that modernity represents a disruption in the experience of space and time when the boundaries of temporality and spatially began to blur, but that disruption did not happen instantaneously in all places.[5] The disruptions of modernity concentrated in some areas and diffused through others, evolving over time through a dynamic process that was experienced differently in relation to a population's exposure to disruption. Modernism radiates outward from centers of disruption into marginal zones as flows of population, infrastructure, and commerce progress outward and inward. Under normal circumstances, modernity spreads as a function of social progress and economic innovations, but in some cases major events occur that alter the normal process of modernization. This is the crux of my argument. The South, a region at the margins of modernization, encountered modernity as an onrush of disruption during World War I, and the ensuing emergence of modernism represents a distinctive response to modernity. In the South, modernism preceded modernity.

Southern modernism illustrates the distinction between proximal modernism and distal modernism. Modernity spread unevenly because rates of urbanization and industrialization varied. In the early twentieth century, only several cities in western Europe and a few in the United States could be considered sites of modernity, where signs of disruption and discontinuity were highly evident. These cities became sites of proximal modernism, where artists, writers, and intellectuals clustered and where the most experimental works of modernism were produced. Paris, Berlin, Vienna, and London were the most intense proximal sites of modernism, and many of the most radical movements, such as surrealism, expressionism, vorticism, and imagism, were located in these and other European cities. In the United States, New York was the most obvious site of proximal modernism. The causal relationship between intense modernization and modernist writing in proximal zones is fairly evident. David Harvey underscores this relationship in *The Condition of Postmodernity*, arguing that "the modernism that emerged before the First World War was more of a reaction to the new conditions of production (the machine, the factory, urbanization), circulation (the new systems of transport and communications), and consumption (the rise of mass markets, advertising, mass fashion) than it was a pioneer in the production of such changes" (23). Not all creative works produced in modern cities were radical, of course, but the majority of radical works were produced in modern cities. The clearest example of proximal modernism is futurism, the movement associated with Filippo Tommaso Marinetti that began in Milan and spread to several other cities across Europe. The futurists adopted an aesthetic that venerated newness, speed, and technology, and many futurist works are radical in their form, such as Giacomo Balla's painting *Abstract Speed + Sound* and Umberto Boccioni's sculpture *Unique Forms of Continuity in Space*. These works attempted to represent perception rather than reality, suggesting that the forms of experience in a modernist context were different from those in a nonmodernist context. The futurists' ideas influenced many other proximal modernists who produced nonrepresentational works.[6]

Modernism radiated beyond these proximal sites, but the modernist work produced beyond the cities tends to be ambivalent about modernity and less experimental. Distal modernism is work produced by writers and artists outside the immediate context of modernity who are responding to the disruptions of modernity radiating beyond the proximal zones: modernism without modernity. It typically betrays an apprehension of modernity while reflecting rural living conditions, and it tends to blend representational forms with nonrepresentational influences, sometimes as a deliberate reaction to the influence of nonrepresentational works. Distal modernism is more likely to be conservative and more likely to represent a transitional phase in the social and economic development of a population. In America, the work of writers and artists associated with regionalism—as opposed to modernist cosmopolitanism—illustrates the characteristics of distal modernism.[7] Robert Frost's poetry, which was contemporaneous with the experimental work of Pound and Eliot, shows a rural sensibility and frequently uses settings on New England farms to articulate responses to changes in modern life. The visual art of Thomas Hart Benton, Grant Wood, and the American Scene painters use a similar method in painting, combining rural scenes with elements of expressionism. Among European writers, these characteristics can be found in the works of D. H. Lawrence, Hugh MacDiarmid, and Knut Hamsun, and the same dynamics appear in areas on the margins of modernity, such as South American Modernismo, Japanese proletarian literature, and, eventually, postcolonial literature emerging from Africa and South Asia.[8] Marshall Berman uses the phrase "modernism of underdevelopment" to describe an alternative form of modernity that he locates in Saint Petersburg, Russia, a city developed by governmental authority rather than industrialization, and he contends that Petersburgers created a "warped and weird" modernism that represents the inherent discontinuities between their city and modernity, and that this dynamic may provide a clue to the literature of other developing areas (181, 286). There is a truth here: as challenging as proximal modernism may be, distal modernism, with its competing dynamic energies, may be even more complicated.

This does not necessarily mean that geography is literary destiny. As modernity increased networks of trade and commerce, flows of population and capital, and systems of infrastructure and communication, modernism radiated outward from the proximal zones into distal areas. In some cases, rural individuals, such as Ezra Pound, relocated to urban places and reincarnated themselves as modernist artists. In other cases, modernist works followed systems of distribution, such as radio, mass reproduction, and film, far beyond proximal zones to influence aesthetic perception beyond the cities. These multitudinous points of contact created new disruptions and distinctive experiences of mediated, detached modernity. Some areas remained remote even as modernity flourished in metropolitan cities, and to distinguish these places from sites of proximal and distal modernism, they can be designated as latent zones. Like the waves that push outward when a stone is dropped into a pond, modernism radiated outward from proximal sites at the center, along networks of dissemination to distal zones at the margins before dissipating at latent margins.

World War I amplified the radiation of modernism. Like dropping a boulder into a pond, it greatly and rapidly extended the range of disruption. The war and modernism are both effects of modernization, and it is not coincidental that the war took place directly within the proximal zone in the space between Berlin and Vienna on the east and Paris and London on the west, but the war's impact was not limited to the proximal zones. It radiated outward into the distal zones far beyond the battlefields. Tim Armstrong explains in *Modernism: A Cultural History* that the war left in its wake "a disrupted temporality in which the dynamic relation between past, present, and future which we saw as intrinsic to modernity is forced to coexist with elements of 'frozen' time: a lost past; a traumatic present; a blighted future" (19). In addition to amplifying modernism, the war altered the complexion of modernity, making many of the disruptions that previously seemed to improve the quality of everyday life seem destructive and dangerous. Modris Eksteins argues in *Rites of Spring: The Great War and the Birth of the Modern Age* that modernism spread and flourished as a consequence of the war, which made real in the imagination of many artists the tremendous capacity for machines to create and to destroy.[9] By the end of the war, modernity permeated western Europe and the northeastern United States, and writers, artists, and intellectuals from these regions produced modernist cultural products. The war, clearly, was a massive disruption on the lives of everyone connected with it and, thus, was a crisis of modernity.

The war had a major impact on modernization in the United States. When the war began, some northeastern US cities were already proximal sites of modernity. Manufacturing had replaced agriculture as the leading sector of production for the US economy, and large segments of the population left rural areas to settle in cities such as Chicago and New York, which became centers of intellectual and cultural creativity. The rise of manufacturing involved the development of mass production and corporate bureaucracy, which changed the fundamental nature of labor for hundreds of thousands of people. At the same time, new inventions flooded the marketplace, generating a consumer economy, and networks of electrification, communication, transportation, and sanitation made the pace of daily life seem faster, more regulated, and less labor intensive. A number of American politicians, responding to the rapid changes, adopted the notion that social structures could be regularized and made more egalitarian and that government could be more efficient and promote the public good. Progressive laws made education accessible, regulated corporations, protected workers, and provided for the public welfare, and as America's domestic policy became more intrusive, its foreign policy became less isolationist. America's involvement in World War I was both a product of the changes taking place in the nation and an important part of the process of modernization. It signaled that America was an international, industrial power, and the jingo-istic campaign to make the world safe for democracy attempted to spread the ideals of progressivism across the Atlantic.

The South modernized slower than the Northeast, and by the beginning of World War I, the unevenness between the regions was glaringly apparent. Leigh Anne Duck argues in *The Nation's Region* that, by the beginning of the twentieth century, the South was "anachronistic," because it was tem-porally and culturally disconnected from the more progressive parts of the United States (7). The differences between the conditions of everyday life in the South, which continued to be agricultural, semifeudal, segregated, and insular, and the industrializing, urbanizing, progressive North were remarkable. The disparity between the regions created inevitable tension that complicated the ongoing process of national reunification follow-ing Reconstruction. Natalie Ring explains in *The Problem South* that "the national tendency to identify economic, racial, and social problems in the South worked to highlight the importance of modernization and the advance of civilization." The South functioned as an obstruction to the nation's overall development, and policy makers "attempt[ed] to rehabilitate and reconstruct southerners involv[ing] efforts to improve the economic welfare of cotton growers, develop a healthy labor force by eliminating such diseases as malaria and hookworm, stabilize the 'race problem,' and educat[e] the southern populace in the hope of creating a more prosperous body of democratic citizens" (6). The causes of the South's delayed develop-ment, however, did not yield easily to policy initiatives, so the gap between the regions was expansive by the time America entered World War I.[10] Before World War I, the South was far from a site of modernity.

World War I introduced social and cultural disruption into the South. When America mobilized for total war for the first time in the twentieth century, the war effort required essential labor and material resources located in the South. Because the region's climate allowed year-round train-ing, most soldiers in the American Expeditionary Force trained at newly constructed camps in the South named for southern Civil War generals, such as Fort Benning, Fort Gordon, and Fort Bragg. Training brought northerners and southerners into contact on a large scale for the first time since the end of the Civil War and militarized the South for the first time since the end of Reconstruction. Meanwhile, labor shortages in northern factories lured more than a million white and black workers to the North. The relative shortage of men in a traditionally male-dominated social sys-tem allowed women significantly greater personal agency. The population shift of northerners into the South and southerners into the North allowed for the diffusion of new social, political, and economic practices into the region. Because of proximity to resources and access to low-wage labor, factories that produced textiles, steel, refined petroleum, and consumer goods began to appear in the agricultural South, diversifying the region's economy. The shortage of wartime labor and the encroachment of new technology caused many southern landowners to invest in agricultural machinery, thus starting a process that displaced and dispossessed the region's vast unskilled labor force and shifted the region's economic base from agrarianism to agricultural-industrial manufacturing, until the Great Depression intervened. The South's initial engagement with modernity was rapid, temporary, and disruptive.

For many of the same reasons that the South lagged behind the proximal zones in modernization, southern writing often deviates from the currents of proximal modernist literature. Southern modernism is more likely to be conservative both in form and content, it tends to be placed in a rural context, and it tends to have a negative apprehension of modernity. In all of these features, it is a form of distal modernism. Leigh Anne Duck notes that "southern literary modernism is noteworthy for its temporal collisions, moments in which the region's and the nation's multiple temporal forms convulsively intersect" (8). These moments of intersection signify modernity disrupting southern tradition. Because of World War I, southerners experienced the effects of modernity often before the region actually modernized: they experienced cities before they urbanized, they worked in factories before they industrialized, they used new technologies before the South had electrical or communication infrastructure, and they made contact with populations that held more progressive ideologies before they liberalized. Southern modernists, thus, often have a more critical and detached perspective on modernization than their counterparts, and their literature has a certain set of characteristics. Southern modernism tends to self-consciously portray the differences between agricultural ruralism and industrial urbanism, it tends to depict modernity as an external disruptive force, it tends to be conflicted about nationalism, it tends to critique but not directly challenge race relations and gender dynamics, and it tends to engage in a limited amount of experimentation with literary form.

Many literary critics have spent their careers defining and revising the parameters of modernism. A disproportionate amount of modernist criticism focuses on proximal modernism, the experimental works such as *Ulysses* or *Mrs. Dalloway* and movements such as vorticism and imagism that challenged the aesthetic mainstream, but this focus overlooks many other works written at the same time and in response to the same social circumstances. More recently, a critical movement identified as "new modernism" has "extended the designation 'modernist' beyond such familiar figures as Eliot, Pound, Joyce, and Woolf . . . and embraced less widely known women writers, authors of mass cultural fiction, makers of the Harlem Renaissance, artists from outside Great Britain and the United States, and other cultural producers hitherto seen as neglecting or resisting modernist innovation" (Mao and Walkowitz, 2). Frequently, less expansive definitions of the term "modernist literature" don't encompass distal modernism and exclude many southern writers. With a few exceptions, most obviously Faulkner, southern writers were less experimental than their contemporaries, but their works reflect the effects of social disruption in a more conservative aesthetic form. In many cases, southern writers responding to disruption attempted to retrench rhetorically by reverting to linear narrative and formal poetry, but while these forms are conventional, they are no less modernist than the deliberately fragmentary forms that Pound and Stein used. Because southern modernists tend to be more conservative in their responses to disruption, they are sometimes not recognized as a component of American modernism. The new modernism, however, offers a space for more expansive considerations of modernist literary production, but, so far, the new modernists have not turned their attention to writers from the US South and considered the circumstances of production in that region. To make matters more complicated, critics' use of the term "Southern Renascence" implies that the outburst of cultural production by southern writers sprung sui generis from the South separate from modernity and modernism. The term "southern modernism," however, more accurately places southern writing in context with the social and cultural disruptions radiating from Europe and the Northeast.

The number of writers and intellectuals from the South who rose to prominence by the mid-twentieth century suggests that they were responding to broad cultural changes emanating from outside the region. One could argue, of course, that the work produced by southerners during this period represents not necessarily a reified modernism but, instead, a suppressed southern intellectualism that had not been capable of expression earlier, which is one common explanation for the term "Southern Renascence." This position has merit, especially since it allows that not all southerners between 1864 and 1918 were intellectually bereft, but it does not account for the fact that southern modernists were engaged with the same problems, themes, motifs, and techniques as their northern and European contemporaries. The connections between southern modernism and post–World War I transatlantic modernism strongly suggests that they were responding to similar circumstances. But because southern modernism differs from the typical characteristics of proximal modernism, studies that examine the South's culture between the turn of the century and World War II tend to make several problematic assumptions about southern modernism.[11] In "Why the Southern Renaissance?," for example, C. Vann Woodward explores the most commonly stated social causes for the movement, including the rise of industrialism in the South, increasingly liberal attitudes toward race and religion, and immigration from North to South—all sources of social disruption connected to World War I—but he eventually discounts all these explanations and concludes that the task of pinpointing a cause for the emergence of modernist writing in the South is virtually impossible. Michael O'Brien takes an even more drastic position in "A Heterodox Note on the Southern Renaissance," arguing that too much has been made of Tate's comment about the backward glance, that World War I had little significant impact on the region, and that the Southern Renaissance is merely ordinary cultural output finding a broader audience.

Other critics have suggested that World War I did have an impact on southern writing, although the impact in their estimation is insignificant. Louis D. Rubin Jr. remarks that "after the First World War, the South did begin to produce memorable literature, stories and poems of great moral and spiritual intensity, of tremendous intellectual depth" (*Writers of the Modern South*, 6). Rubin notes that the emergence of modernist literature by southerners coincides with the end of World War I, but he does not necessarily see a causal relationship between the two events. His position represents the conventional wisdom on the emergence of southern modernism. Lewis P. Simpson describes southern modernism as a "culture of alienation" resulting from a "large expression of discontent with the emphasis modern societies place on machines and consumption as a debasement of the humanity of man" (*The Dispossessed Garden*, 65). Richard King, meanwhile, dates the emergence of southern modernism later, after 1930, when "the writers and intellectuals of the South were engaged in an attempt to come to terms not only with the inherited values of the Southern tradition but also with a certain way of perceiving and dealing with the past" (14). Daniel Singal argues that the New South Creed, which he describes as a fusion of "Cavalier mythology onto the framework of Victorian belief in morality and industrial progress," acted as an intellectual barrier, "effectively block[ing] the arrival of intellectual Modernism in the region through the First World War" (9).

Most critics have disregarded World War I's impact on southern writing because the conflict did not take place in the South, so they overlook the war's disruptive impact on the region. Although no World War I military campaigns were fought in the South, conflicts between industry and agriculture, urbanism and ruralism, cosmopolitanism and provincialism, localism and globalism, and traditionalism and progressivism were taking place there during the war, and the effects of these disruptions would resonate through the work of southern writers over the following generation. Focusing on these disruptions illustrates how a war fought an ocean away could impact a distant region, and it demonstrates that southern writing takes place in a dynamic context that responds to changes taking place both inside and outside the region.

World War I led to the emergence of a distal form of modernism by southern writers. During the war, many southerners were exposed to sites of proximal modernity, and the war precipitated several delayed social changes in the South. After the war, southern writers produced works that showed an apprehension of modernity, that were placed within a rural context, and that incorporated some experimental techniques with traditional forms. This pattern extends across an enormous range of writers, from William Faulkner to Zelda Fitzgerald, all of whom portray the region's complicated engagement with modernity in the war's wake. Contact with modernity raised an interrelated set of issues for southerners about regional identity, segregation, agricultural economy, and domesticity, and the ways that southern writers represented these issues in their writing constitutes a distinctive form of distal modernism. By examining how the war impacted the South and how southern writers—and in some cases nonsouthern writers writing about the South—represented those impacts, we can see how modernism radiated into the South.

METAPHORS FOR MODERNITY

One of the essential characteristics of southern modernism is the literature's awareness of modernity as a disruption of southern tradition, and the war often figures in these texts as a metaphor for modernity. In southern modernist literature, the war typically takes place outside the text, either before the events of the plot or as a set of events that influence the plot but do not take place directly within the narrative, and this dynamic reflects the relationship between the South and modernity, a phenomenon originating outside the region that disrupts everyday life within the region. To demonstrate how the war led to the emergence of southern modernism, I examine how exposure to proximal sites of modernity, both directly and indirectly, created a form of distal modernism in the work of southern writers. This book follows the radiation of modernity through the region, beginning with southerners' initial contact with sites of proximal modernity, then the war's effects on white veterans' regional identity, black soldiers and segregation in the South, the war's impact on women in the South, and changes in the southern economy as a consequence of the war.

Some important qualifications need to be made here. First, this argument does not reduce southern modernism only to writing about World War I. Many, if not most, works of southern modernism make no direct mention of the war. The objective is to explain how the war led to the emergence of modernism in southern literature, not as the sole cause for social and cultural disruption but as a primary, perhaps even crucial, initiating cause. Books that directly portray the war make these disruptions apparent, but the changes to southern tradition and the often contradictory responses to these changes resonate throughout southern literature between 1918 and 1940. The same disruptions that Faulkner depicts in *Flags in the Dust*, for example, are evident in *The Sound and the Fury*, but the war's impact is less apparent in *The Sound and the Fury*. Once we identify the causes and the effects of social disruption in the South, then its resonance in literature is more easily discernible. Second, this does not suggest or imply that modernism would never have reached the South if not for the war. In fact, it likely would have, but it would have happened more slowly and in the works of relatively fewer writers as, over time, southerners were exposed to modernity. More to the point, modernity did not spontaneously emerge in the South. With the exception of an anticipatory vanguard, it emerged relatively later there than in some other areas, but it was part of the same process of urbanizing, industrializing modernization that changed everyday life in many parts of the world during the twentieth century.

Exposure to sites of proximal modernity through interregional contact was the initial disruption that led to the emergence of southern modernism. In the fifty years between 1865 and 1915, interregional contact was limited largely to the region's border areas. The South's rural agricultural paradigm discouraged significant population shift by tying families to the land, and, at the same time, the abundance of inexpensive labor deterred technological development. Mules, plows, and sweat were the mainstays of the southern economy until World War I. But, as chapter 1 illustrates, the war instantiated interregional contact on a major scale as southern farm boys joined the American Expeditionary Force, which brought northerners into contact with southerners, brought southerners into contact with northerners, and brought Americans into contact with Europeans. William Faulkner's first novel, *Soldiers' Pay*, portrays the impact of modernity on a provincial southern town, and works by F. Scott Fitzgerald and John Dos Passos demonstrate the effects of interregional exchange in the military on northerners' perceptions of the South.

Chapter 2 examines the war's impact on white male southerners who served in Europe, many of whom felt conflicted about their national identity during the war. Raised by the sons and grandsons of Confederate veterans, white southern males of the 1914 generation were more likely to identify as southerners than as Americans, but serving in a regionally unified American army led by a southern-born commander in chief against a foreign enemy forced many white male southerners to reconfigure both their identity and their ideology. William Alexander Percy, the scion of a patrician Mississippi family, regarded the war as an opportunity to demonstrate his fitness to his family's mantle of honor. In his autobiography, *Lanterns on the Levee*, he romanticizes the war and defends the traditional southern order. Paul Green, a native of rural North Carolina, had a different response to the war. Interacting with northerners, experiencing combat, and living in France hastened his ideological conversion from traditionalism to liberalism. His changing attitudes are apparent in his poems and in his pacifist play, *Johnny Johnson*. Donald Davidson, stalwart defender of agrarian principles, regarded the war as a tangible example of mechanization's destructive power, which he sees as a threat to southern tradition. In his long poem *The Tall Men*, he lauds the courage of the soldiers who fought face-to-face as their forefathers had fought, but he condemns the encroachment of modernity, which, in his opinion, makes men spiritually flaccid.

Many African Americans, including W. E. B. Du Bois, saw the war as an opportunity to make the case for racial equality and full citizenship. Black soldiers in American uniforms fighting and dying for freedom in the trenches of Europe would, presumably, make an incontrovertible case for civil rights earned through sacrifice. With the exception of minor concessions, such as the creation of a segregated officers' training camp, however, the black experience in wartime approximated the black experience in peacetime. The army, in fact, modeled labor battalions, the service assignment for 80 percent of black soldiers, after southern chain gangs. Following the war, African American writers pressed the case for civil rights, using military service and violence on the battlefields of Europe and the fields of the South as recurring tropes, but in this case, the war disrupted southern tradition less than they desired. Chapter 3 discusses three African American authors' portrayals of black southern soldiers fighting for freedom and equality. Victor Daly's *Not Only War* depicts the complexity of interracial relationships and the color line for the American Expeditionary Force in France. In Walter White's *The Fire in the Flint*, an idealistic veteran returns from France to fight for freedom in Georgia. Claude McKay's novel *Home to Harlem* suggests that black Americans are people without a nation.

The women's suffrage movement, meanwhile, capitalized on World War I in some tangible ways, culminating in the passage of the Nineteenth Amendment to the US Constitution, which granted women the right to vote in national elections. The Nineteenth Amendment symbolically recognizes the greater social and political agency of women in the United States as a result of the war. In the South, arguably the most repressive region in the nation for women, the relative absence of men in many capacities created new opportunities for women to earn their own income and to live independently. African American southern women writers supported the war movement, demonstrating a profound sense of social responsibility and patriotism. White southern women writers, meanwhile, describe the war as a period of changing gender roles that weakened the masculine foundations of southern society and temporarily expanded women's roles. Chapter 4 examines how several women writers portray changing domestic roles in the wake of the war. Elizabeth Madox Roberts portrays the war as a cataclysmic event for Jocelle Drake, who loses her brother and lover but gains self-reliance, in *He Sent Forth a Raven*. Ellen Glasgow makes the connection between the war and the encroachment of modernity explicit in *Vein of Iron*, the story of a Virginia family coping with the domestic uncertainty of a foreign war. The connection between social modernity, sexual agency, and artistic modernism figures prominently in Zelda Fitzgerald's *Save Me the Waltz*.

The war also disrupted the region's economy, introducing mechanization into the South. During the war, global cotton markets were upset, causing cotton prices to plummet while European markets were blockaded, then to skyrocket with wartime demand, before declining steadily with postwar overproduction through the 1920s and 1930s. At the same time, millions of people left the South or joined the army, creating a labor shortage, which led some farmers to invest in mechanization. During and after the war, textile, steel, and oil industries developed in the region and manufacturing and financial centers emerged in Atlanta, Birmingham, Charlotte, Houston, Nashville, and New Orleans, diversifying the economy. Industrialization and urbanization, the primary elements of modernity, did not displace rural agriculture as the region's dominant mode of production, but they caused enough change to threaten the traditional southern way of life. Chapter 5 analyzes the representation of economic disruption in several texts set during the war. In *Barren Ground*, Ellen Glasgow portrays a small farm accommodating the wartime labor shortage by investing in mechanization to increase production. Southern intellectuals debated the impact of these changes. In *The Mind of the South*, W. J. Cash describes the South's conversion to industrialism as an extension of lost cause ideology, but in *I'll Take My Stand* (attributed to Twelve Southerners), the Southern Agrarians indict industrialization as a threat to the region's agrarian tradition. William Faulkner explores the destructive effects of postwar mechanization on the Sartoris family in *Flags in the Dust*.

Southern modernism is modernism. Too often, southern writers are marginalized in studies of modernism, and elements of modernism are omitted in studies of southern literature. By examining the ways that the war impacted the South and the ways that southern writers depicted the war, this book will demonstrate that the processes of modernization that instantiated modernism in proximal zones also affected distal zones. Southern literature is a particularly useful illustration of how modernism and other forms of cultural development radiate through space because southern modernism is largely a response to a specific component of modernity, World War I. Southern modernism, thus, is eruptive, manifesting in the work of many writers within the same area in a short period of time and influencing the work of writers from across a broad social spectrum. Several decades of social and intellectual isolation eroded as southerners came into contact with modernity in Europe and the Northeast and as social structures in the South developed during the war. Although the trenches were an ocean away, World War I was fought in the South.

1

THE FORWARD GLANCE

Modernity, Southerners,
and Interregional Contact

In December 1918, William Faulkner returned to Oxford, Mississippi, disappointed. The previous spring, after the US Army rejected him for military service, he concocted a scheme to get into the war. He left home for the first time and went to live with his friend and childhood mentor Phil Stone, who was a student at Yale University. After Stone's graduation, they faked British accents and identification papers and enlisted in a Royal Air Corps unit training near Toronto.[1] Faulkner made satisfactory progress in his training, and if the war had lasted a few weeks longer, he would likely have been deployed to complete his training as an aerial observer in Great Britain. Like many young men of his generation, he had visions of soaring gallantly over the battlefield, locked in mortal combat with an airborne enemy. But the war ended too soon for him, and after nine months away, he went home.[2]

Although the war did not fulfill Faulkner's aspirations for glory, it had an enormous impact on his creative development. When he returned to Oxford, he invented one of his first and most enduring fictional characters, the exaggerated persona who would eventually be known as "Count No 'Count." Even though he never completed training, he wore a British pilot's uniform with insignia indicating that he had served overseas, and he continued to wear the uniform for several weeks after his return. He told stories of fantastic aerial acrobatics (including one tale in which he claimed to have crashed an airplane upside down into a hangar), he affected a slight limp, and he insinuated that he had a steel plate in his head.[3] During the war, Billy Falkner transformed into William Faulkner, becoming more worldly and intellectual in the process. As a British war veteran manqué, he felt different from, and in some ways superior to, the ordinary citizens of Oxford, most of whom had never left northern Mississippi except to visit

Memphis. Living outside the South expanded his frame of reference, and being involved in the war effort broadened his range of experience, exposing him to more modern places and making him more critical of the provincial South.

The differences Faulkner felt as a result of his experience outside the South during the war eventually led him to eschew the derivative late-Victorian poetry he had scribbled and to begin writing in a new narrative style. In his introduction to *The Portable Faulkner*, Malcolm Cowley writes:

> When the war was over—the other war—William Faulkner went back to Oxford, Mississippi. . . . [H]e was home again and not at home, or at least not able to accept the post-war world. He was writing poems, most of them worthless, and dozens of immature but violent and effective stories, while at the same time he was brooding over his own situation and the decline of the South. Slowly the brooding thoughts arranged themselves into the whole interconnected pattern that would form the substance of his novels. (vii–viii)

The South at this time was not necessarily declining by its own standards, but relative to other societies, compared to the North and to Europe, it was delayed, a realization that inspired Faulkner's literary project. His case demonstrates in microcosm the war's impact on the South. Modernity was a foreign element, a condition of societies outside the South, and it disrupted everyday life in the South.

World War I, for Faulkner and many southern writers of his generation, was a contact zone, which Mary Louise Pratt defines as "a social space where cultures meet, clash, and grapple with each other, often in contexts of highly asymmetrical relations of power" ("Arts of the Contact Zone," 34).[4] The war caused southern culture to meet and clash with modernity in ways that defined and disrupted established cultural practices, and this is one of the primary ways that the war contributed to the development of distal modernism in the South. Pratt has in mind circumstances such as colonialism or slavery, in which one social group exerts hegemony over another, but the idea can be extended to other situations in which the power relations are less obviously unequal. At the time of World War I, the South was part of the United States, but many southerners continued to harbor separatist inclinations, and northerners often conceived of the South as a space of national alterity, as America's national other.[5] Power relations between the regions were inherently unequal because the North produced significantly more of the nation's gross national product, it dominated the cultural and political mainstream, and it was the nation's capital-intensive core. The South was the nation's dependent periphery, a less-developed region that provided low-skill labor and raw materials for the northern economy. The war blurred boundaries between the core and the periphery, bringing northerners and southerners into contact on a large scale in ways that impacted modernist literature.

Contact between southerners and nonsoutherners during World War I was one of the crucial processes that led to the development of distal modernism by southern writers. In this chapter, I will describe the dynamics of contact during the war, as a foreign conflict initiated a rapid sequence of domestic exchanges, and analyze the ways that interregional contact affected how writers represented the South. Interregional contact affected how writers from outside the South portrayed southerners, as illustrated in the work of F. Scott Fitzgerald and John Dos Passos, and as William Faulkner's first novel, *Soldiers' Pay*, demonstrates, it changed the way southerners imagined the South. Over the course of decades, Allen Tate developed a theory of how World War I affected southern writing, and his extended thought process is both an explanation and an example of the impact of interregional contact on southern modernism.

THE CRISIS OF CONTACT

World War I was a pivotal moment in America's modernization. The generation before the war reshaped the nation demographically with waves of European immigration and economically with a drastic increase in manufacturing, but the nation continued to be a reluctant international power. By the time Woodrow Wilson was inaugurated in 1913, the United States was the richest nation in the world, as Vincent De Santis explains in *The Shaping of Modern America*, and manufacturing dominated the nation's economic and social structure, driving the development of modern, industrial cities. America was modernizing but still isolationist, so the war caused a crisis in American foreign policy. President Wilson, a native southerner, was a committed isolationist, who, even as the war ravaged America's key trading partners in Europe, campaigned for reelection in 1916 on the slogan "He kept us out of war" (Leuchtenburg, 20). But America could not remain uninvolved, and within three months of Wilson's second inauguration he requested a declaration of war, at the same time outlining a plan for peace—the Fourteen Points—that has become a model for American global interventionism. The war forced America out of its isolation, and, as Daniel Rogers argues in *Atlantic Crossings*, it propelled an era of transatlantic political progressivism that catapulted America into the forefront of urban development and modernist social programming.

Although America was politically isolationist before the war, its northeastern cities had become thoroughly cosmopolitan because of the millions of European immigrants who arrived between the end of the Civil War and the beginning of World War I. Immigration reached its peak in the decade before the war, and the large immigrant population, specifically the enormous German population in the Midwest, caused serious anxiety during the war. Some people wondered if immigrants were sufficiently American to be loyal citizens. Randolph Bourne interrogated the notion of a unified, assimilated nation in the essay "Trans-National America," published in the *Atlantic Monthly* in 1916 amid the debate about immigrant loyalty. He noted that the American melting pot had not, and should not, yield a homogeneous nationalist identity, and he asked a remarkable question that puts the consequences of American modernization into clear terms:

> Let those who feel the inferiority of the non-Anglo-Saxon immigrant contemplate that region of the States which has remained the most distinctively "American," the South. Let him ask himself whether he would really like to see the foreign hordes Americanized into such an Americanization. Let him ask himself how superior this native civilization is to the great "alien" states of Wisconsin and Minnesota, where Scandinavians, Poles, and Germans have self-consciously labored to preserve their traditional culture, while being outwardly and satisfactorily American. Let him ask himself how much more wisdom, intelligence, industry and social leadership has come out of these alien states than out of all the truly American ones. The South, in fact, while this vast Northern development has gone on, still remains an English colony, stagnant and complacent, having progressed scarcely beyond the early Victorian era. It is culturally sterile because it has had no advantage of cross-fertilization like the Northern states. What has happened in states such as Wisconsin and Minnesota is that strong foreign cultures have struck root in a new and fertile soil. America has meant liberation, and German and Scandinavian political ideas and social energies have expanded to a new potency. The process has not been at all the fancied "assimilation" of the Scandinavian or Teuton. Rather has it been a process of their assimilation of us—I speak as an Anglo-Saxon. The foreign cultures have not been melted down or run together, made into some homogeneous Americanism, but

have remained distinct but cooperating to the greater glory and benefit, not
only of themselves but of all the native "Americanism" around them. (253)

Bourne's assertion that southerners are the most distinctively American
would likely have seemed startling to a southerner in 1916, but the fact
that it hinges on the point that the South is the region that has been least
affected by modernization is provocative.[6] His point raises questions about
southerners' place in America's nationalist structure, and he implies that
southerners are most American because they have been least affected by
modern flows of population. Over the ensuing few years, however, the war
would expose southerners to modernity and would disrupt their notions of
regional and national identity.

In the same way that the war brought American political isolationism
to an end, it brought southern isolation to an end, crumbling the invisible
intellectual and social barrier between North and South. Because the South
had lagged in industrial development into the early part of the twentieth
century, the region's economy still depended upon agriculture, specifically
the export of cotton. Southerners, who sold large quantities of cotton in
markets in both Great Britain and Germany, initially opposed America's
entry into the war. They supported the policies of President Wilson, who
advocated neutrality, thus keeping international markets open. But they
also supported his decision to enter the war when German submarine
activity threatened both the shipment of cotton to Europe and American
lives.[7] Most Confederate veterans, now long in the tooth, also supported
the newly unified American military. Thomas L. Connelly and Barbara L.
Bellows in *God and General Longstreet* describe a scene of a quarter of a
million people cheering as elderly Confederate veterans marched through
Washington carrying signs that read "Send us if the boys can't do the job"
(4). The atmosphere of the war, the refocusing of animosity toward a foreign enemy, the conscription of young men from all regions into a national
army, and America's rampant wartime patriotism signaled the end of the
South's regional isolation.

The marching Confederate veterans signify the erosion of lost cause ideology, southerners' revision of their defeat in the Civil War. The lost cause
proposed that the war was fought over the states' right to secede, that African
Americans were loyal and happy slaves, and that the South lost because of
the North's "overwhelming numbers and resources," as General Robert E.
Lee stated in General Order no. 9. Southerners clung to this legitimating
ideology, as Gaines Foster explains in *Ghosts of the Confederacy*, vilifying

northerners as enemies, condemning northern social practices, sanctifying the fallen Confederacy, and asserting a strong regional identity. Thus, a state of antagonism existed between North and South, at least in the minds of southerners, that impeded contact between the regions between the end of the Civil War and the beginning of World War I. Although a group of progressively minded southern boosters, including Atlanta *Constitution* publisher Henry Grady, attempted to market the idea of a "New South"—one free of sectional animosity, racial violence, and rampant poverty—as a means of attracting northern investment in the South, the region continued to suffer from cultural isolation into the beginning of the twentieth century.[8]

The literature southern writers produced between 1876 and 1916 reflects the region's self-imposed isolation and delayed cultural development. On one hand, southern writers continued to defend and romanticize the Old South, creating a moonlight-and-magnolias myth of the southern plantation primarily for consumption by northern readers, epitomized by the work of Thomas Nelson Page and Joel Chandler Harris. On the other hand, southern writers and the northern magazines that published their work bought into the myth of the New South, a region that was able to reconcile with mainstream America and the modern era. Meanwhile, northern writers, as Nina Silber argues in *The Romance of Reunion*, created a competing myth of reconciliation between the victorious North and an idealized South. In other words, northerners created a mythical South, and southerners created a mythical North at the same time that they mythologized the South.

These myths persisted because southerners and northerners had had limited interregional contact before World War I. Before the emergence of broadcast media, most Americans based their perceptions of other regions on print culture and stage performance, so the dominant images of the South in the American imagination came from literature and minstrel shows. These perceptions were amplified because Americans were unlikely to travel outside their own regions on exhausting, expensive, time-consuming railroads without a significant inducement.[9] The most common inducement was jobs, and the asymmetrical relationship between the southern and northern economies provided few reasons for northerners or immigrants to move to the South. The growth of manufacturing presented some attractive opportunities for southerners to move to the North, yet many were reluctant to move. James Gregory documents in *The Southern Diaspora* that by the turn of the twentieth century approximately one million southerners had relocated outside the South, some to find more promising farmland in the West and some to find work in northeastern manufacturing hubs. During the war, the floodgates opened, so by 1920, 2.7 million southerners had relocated outside the region, and the process of outmigration continued for the next several decades (13). The war changed many southerners' attitudes toward the South, as evidenced by the numbers of white and black southerners who left, but the war also affected the southerners who remained in the South.[10]

At the same time that the war opened the North to southerners, it brought thousands of northerners to the South, creating a massive interregional contact zone. Katherine Du Pre Lumpkin, for example, explains that Camp Jackson, which was built near Columbia, South Carolina, a few months after the war began, changed the city's population. "Our streets were filled with soldiers," she writes, "and not just Southerners. Northerners by the thousands, officers and men, overran the town" (198). Thousands of northerners came to the South for military training, where they had their first encounter with the region. They interacted with southerners on a large scale, training with southerners in the army, spending their leave in southern towns, and dating southern girls. The contact between northerners and southerners exploded the northerners' regional stereotypes of the South and dissolved much of southerners' lost cause enmity toward Yankees. The interregional contact destabilized traditional regional identity, changing the attitudes of northerners toward southerners, of southerners toward northerners, and of southerners to the South.[11] The war ended southern isolation, eroded the lost cause, and unified the nation, at least temporarily.

These were major disruptions in the southern way of life, but interregional contact had another major consequence for the South. It brought the region into contact with modernity before the region actually modernized. For many southern writers, contact with people from urban, industrialized areas generated a sense of regional self-consciousness. In the "The New Provincialism," Allen Tate commented that "with the war of 1914–1918, the South reentered the world—but gave a backward glance as it stepped over the border: that backward glance gave us the Southern Renascence, a literature conscious of the past in the present" (*Collected Essays*, 545). Southerners, according to Tate, were relatively unaware of their cultural stagnation until exposure to social and artistic developments taking place outside the South awakened them from their collective dogmatic slumber, precipitating a rush of new literary and intellectual production by southerners responding to modernity. While not all southern writers wholeheartedly embraced the massive social and cultural changes that accompanied modernization, even the staunchest defenders of traditional southern society, such as John Crowe Ransom and Donald Davidson, recognized modernity's significance.

These attitudinal changes revolutionized southern writing. Although most white southern writers before the war romanticized the Old South, the literature of southern modernism after the war tended to regard the South's history critically. Some writers became more experimental and innovative in their technique, even openly antagonizing the tradition of southern letters, and a number of new voices from previously marginalized segments of society, namely female southerners and African American southerners, joined the mainstream of southern modernist literature. Daniel J. Singal, in *The War Within: From Victorian to Modernist Thought in the South, 1919–1945*, explains:

> [W]hen a new generation of southern intellectuals emerged after [World War I], theirs was a task of deliberately and rapidly catching up. Modernism, they soon discovered, was an accomplished fact in most of the western world, of which the South had become a backward province. To escape that backwardness, they would have to assimilate a veritable galaxy of new ideas with unusual speed, recapitulating as they did the experience of their northern brethren during the previous half century. Far more self-conscious than the northern pioneers of modernism had been, and operating, one might say, with the script already written, they were to follow a smoother and straighter path. As a consequence, by the time the United States entered the Second World War modernism had been firmly installed as the predominant style of literary and intellectual life in the region. (9)

What makes southern modernism remarkable, and what often differentiates it from other types of modernist writing, is the irony inherent in it. The South was not modern, especially when compared to the North and Europe, the other territories involved in the war. When southern writers engaged with modernism, they were encountering a set of conditions that were not yet endemic to the region, so they were showing the effects of contact during the war.

It is not coincidental that southern writing exploded after World War I with the publication of such works as Jean Toomer's *Cane* (1923), the run of the *Fugitive* (1922–1925), Ellen Glasgow's *Barren Ground* (1925), Elizabeth Madox Roberts's *The Time of Man* (1926), William Faulkner's *The Sound and the Fury* (1929), Thomas Wolfe's *Look Homeward, Angel* (1929), and many other works. The outburst of literary production attracted a great deal of attention. H. L. Mencken, possibly the most influential American critic of the time, described the South in 1917 as "almost as sterile, intellectually, culturally, as the Sahara Desert" (136). But by the end of the 1920s his criticism no longer applied. Herschel Brickell, a New York book reviewer, rejoined in 1927 that Mencken's "dreary desert has become an oasis," and he pointed out the recent works of authors such as Faulkner, John Gould Fletcher, Elizabeth Madox Roberts, Frances Newman, and James Branch Cabell (289). He explained that the new literary awakening in the South had its roots in a number of coinciding social disruptions:

> Just what causes are behind the present flowering of southern talent it is not easy to discover. The industrial revolution of the last few years has broken up old patterns of life, bringing a shifting of values; much new blood has come into the section, especially in the cities, introducing a needed leaven of liberalism; dozens of southerners of the oldest stock have taken to wandering up and down the earth with the rest of America; there has been a change in the general attitude toward the Negro because of his exodus to northern and western industrial centers. (290)

Brickell's list of reasons is especially notable because all of the disruptions he mentions emanate from outside the South. To a great extent, the South experienced modernity indirectly.

In the years before the war, a few southern writers anticipated the effects of interregional contact, specifically writers from places bordering the North or the Midwest, where they had contact with modernizing areas. Kate Chopin, for example, set her stories and her novel *The Awakening* (1899) in Louisiana, where she spent most of her married life. But by the time she began writing, she had returned to her hometown, Saint Louis, and her works blend elements of local color fiction coming from the South and naturalism coming from the Midwest. James Weldon Johnson, similarly, grew up in Jacksonville, Florida, but he lived outside the South—in Latin America and New York City—for several years before he began writing. Samuel Clemens grew up in Missouri but spent most of his career in the North, and even Thomas Dixon, the notorious retrograde southern racist, began writing after living in New York City. This pattern is consistent with the dynamics of modernist radiation. Contact with intellectual and social currents from outside the South often led to literary innovation, and southern modernists combined elements of local folk culture with social disruptions and, in some cases, with experimental techniques in a distinct form of distal modernism. What makes World War I so significant to the emergence of southern modernism is the vast scale of contact that took place during the war.

Many southerners were ambivalent about their contact with modernity. To them, it was a foreign element, associated with cities, immigrant populations, factories, progressive politics, and beam-and-girder aesthetics. Southern writers tended to represent a comparatively provincial landscape—rural, nativist, agricultural, politically conservative, and aesthetically primitive—out of sync with modernity. Some southern writers, particularly Allen Tate and William Faulkner, incorporated innovative modernist techniques into their depictions of the South to highlight the temporal discontinuity between the regions. They were not necessarily "antimodern"—in the sense that T. J. Jackson Lears uses the term in *No Place of Grace* to describe the efforts of cultural elites to resist modernist collectivization.[12] Instead, they produced modernist works about nonmodernist conditions, which is the hallmark of distal modernism. Mary Louise Pratt borrows the term "transculturation" from ethnographers "to describe processes whereby members of subordinated or marginal groups select and invent from materials transmitted by a dominant or metropolitan culture" ("Arts of the Contact Zone," 34). Southern modernism is a form of transculturation in which southerners, members of a peripheral region within the United States, employ the ideas and materials of the nation's metropolitan core to produce a form of writing that combines elements of both groups.

As southerners made contact with modernity, many of them developed a new perspective on southern history. They also faced disquieting issues not directly associated with their region's past, such as the issues of Darwinism, Marxism, and mechanization, which modernist writers from the North and Europe were exploring in aesthetically startling works. Southern intellectuals, many of whom had been largely sheltered from such issues by their orthodox academic and religious institutions, now were exposed to these complex social issues and puzzling art forms, which further challenged their deeply inculcated values. W. J. Cash makes a point about the type of confusion southerners faced when America joined the war: "the world in which they had lived was not and would not be again the old fixed, certain, familiar, and easy world they had known before 1914. Strange new ideas and faiths and systems were sweeping through the Western lands, and all the old ideas and faiths and systems were under attack, in danger, crumbling or even vanishing in places. Everywhere were doubt and change and chaos and flux and violence" (293). Compared to northern writers, southern writers faced an even more unsettling prospect when they encountered modernity for the first time. Not only did they have to face the inherent uncertainty of a world in flux, they also had to contend with the burden of southern history.

WORLD WAR I, NORTHERN WRITERS, AND THE SOUTH

During World War I, northern soldiers invaded the South. As the American military hastily mobilized, training camps were constructed across the South, and most recruits in the American Expeditionary Force spent several weeks in the South, creating the largest interregional contact zone since the end of the Civil War.[13] For northerners, the experience of living in the South humanized southerners and overturned many preconceived notions of the South based on myth and local color fiction. Before the war, southerners in American literature were categorically different from northerners, but after the war, the representation of southerners became less different, marking southerners as a contingent part of mainstream American culture.

Northern writers in the period between the end of Reconstruction and the beginning of World War I tended to portray white southerners negatively and black southerners not at all. As Nina Silber argues in *The Romance of Reunion*, northern writers "cultivated specific types of images and promoted a specific version of reunion that was best suited to Yankee needs" (6). Before World War I, the South was an imaginary construct in American literature, a landscape on which prejudices and desires were projected. Consider, for example, Henry Adams's assertion that "the Southerner had no mind; he had temperament. He was not a scholar; he had no intellectual training; he could not analyze an idea, and he could not even conceive of admitting two" is one of the most often cited regional antipathies (57–58).[14] Another example is Henry James's representation of Basil Ransom, an attorney from Mississippi practicing law in New York City in *The Bostonians* (1886).[15] James portrays Basil as steeped in southern tradition and unwilling to admit the possibility of social progress even as he woos the progressively minded Verena Tarrant. James uses the trope of interregional marriage to contrast the modernizing North with the provincial South. Notably, when James wrote *The Bostonians* he had not visited the South, so he based his depiction of southerners entirely on regional bias. He appears to be capitalizing on what Charles R. Anderson in "James's Portrait of the Southerner" calls "southern conservatism," the impression among northern reformers that southerners, bound in the tradition of chivalry and social order, were unwilling to or incapable of permitting social progress (311).

Northern writers who had contact with the South during World War I produced more complex portrayals of southerners. Some of these works continue to capitalize on regional differences, but they place the differences within a relatively equitable dialogue of cultural exchange. F. Scott

Fitzgerald's Tarleton stories, for example, draw upon stereotypical images of southerners from local color fiction, but his stories place northerners and southerners in proximity to each other, often in romantic relationships, and they portray the South as slowly and awkwardly encountering modernity. His stories demonstrate how interregional contact during World War I disrupted northern perceptions of the South.

Fitzgerald had a number of personal connections to the South that made him curious about and sympathetic toward the region even before the war. He was born and raised in Saint Paul, Minnesota, but his father came originally from Maryland, where he had abetted southern spies during the Civil War. Fitzgerald admired his father's manners, his graciousness, and his romantic stories of the South. John T. Irwin suggests that Fitzgerald is a southern writer by proxy, which may be a slight overstatement, although he clearly had a well-established interest in the South.[16] In spite of this interest, Fitzgerald might not have ever had contact with the South if not for World War I. He did not live there either before the war or after it, but his experience there during the war inspired his work and literally changed his life. He enlisted in the army in 1917, and he wrote and revised the manuscript that would eventually become his first novel, *This Side of Paradise* (1920), while stationed at Camp Taylor in Kentucky, Camp Gordon in Georgia, and Camp Sheridan in Alabama.[17] In Montgomery, Alabama, he met Zelda Sayre, a beautiful, unconventional southern woman who captivated him, and their intense, dysfunctional relationship inspired many of his stories and novels. He wrote two stories about the South during World War I while courting Zelda, "The Ice Palace" (1920) and "The Jelly-Bean" (1920), and a third story written a few years after their marriage, "The Last of the Belles" (1929), and these stories complicate the conventional romance of reunion.[18]

"The Ice Palace" draws heavily upon local color stereotypes and lost cause iconography. It describes the courtship of a vivacious southern woman, Sally Carrol Happer of Tarleton, Georgia, by a recently demobilized US Army lieutenant, Harry Bellamy, from a northern state, perhaps Minnesota. The story plays on regional distinctions, especially climate, contrasting the steamy, languid South with the frigid, inhospitable North. Sally Carrol finds her hometown and the eligible bachelors in it "ineffectual and sad," so she accepts Harry's invitation to visit his home in March (51).[19] But she finds the frosty northern spring unwelcoming, as suggested by the metaphorical ice palace, a clear, cold structure constructed entirely of frozen springwater. When Sally Carrol, symbolically, gets lost in the ice palace and nearly freezes, she comes to a realization: "she couldn't be left here to wander forever—to be frozen, heart, body, and soul. . . . She liked warmth and summer and Dixie. These things were foreign—foreign" (68). Echoing the term "foreign" underscores the cultural separation between the regions and suggests that the regions are categorically distinct.

In this story, published just after World War I, the lost cause continues to separate the regions. When Harry visits Sally Carrol in Tarleton, she takes him to "one of her favorite haunts," the Confederate cemetery (52), and she attempts to explain the lost cause to her Yankee suitor:

> "[The Confederate soldiers] died for the most beautiful thing in the world—the dead South. You see," she continued, her voice still husky, her eyes glistening with tears, "people have these dreams they fasten onto things, and I've always grown up with that dream. It was so easy because it was all dead and there weren't any disillusions comin' to me. I've tried in a way to live up to those past standards of noblesse oblige—there's just the last remnants of it, you know, like the roses of an old garden dying all round us—streaks of strange courtliness and chivalry in some of these boys an' stories I used to hear from a Confederate soldier who lived next door, and a few old darkies." (54)

Fitzgerald's cliché description of the lost cause uncritically romanticizes the South, playing into regional stereotypes.[20] But he stops far short of celebrating the South. On one occasion, Harry, who, like Fitzgerald, appears to have intertwined the myth of Old South with the beauty of the modern southern belle, makes a distinction between the South of myth and the South of reality. He says of contemporary southerners, "they're sort of—sort of degenerates—not at all like the old Southerners" (62). Harry's attitude represents northern attitudes toward the South in the early twentieth century, which, after years of consuming local color fiction, absorbed the moonlight-and-magnolias mythology of the Old South as romantic, yet tragic, and regarded the New South as emasculated and virtually irrelevant. Harry, crucially, was not stationed in the South during the war, and he had spent only a few days in the South—two days in Asheville, North Carolina, where he met Sally Carrol, and a couple of days visiting her in Tarleton.

Fitzgerald complicates the image of the South in the northern imagination in "The Last of the Belles," which he wrote several years after the war. In the story, Andy, a former lieutenant once stationed at Camp Henry Lee in Tarleton, Georgia, remembers his experience in the South and his infatuation with Ailie Calhoun, a friend of Sally Carrol Happer. His initial impressions of the South mimic those of Harry Bellamy, meaning he fixates on the heat and the beauty of the women. He even alludes to local color fiction, lost cause mythology, and the cult of gyneolatry when describing Ailie Calhoun:

> There she was—the Southern type in all its purity. I would have recognized Ailie Calhoun if I'd never heard Ruth Draper or read Marse Chan. She had the adroitness sugar-coated with sweet, voluble simplicity, the suggested background of devoted fathers, brothers and admirers stretching back into the South's heroic age, the unfailing coolness acquired in the endless struggle with the heat. There were notes in her voice that order slaves around, that withered up Yankee captains, and then soft, wheedling notes that mingled in unfamiliar loveliness with the night. (450)

Andy and a series of army officers court Ailie until they are shipped to New York to prepare for debarkation, but the war ends before their shipment. When they return to Tarleton for demobilization, Ailie realizes that her working-class northern beau, Earl Schoen, fails to meet her matrimonial standards. So Andy, Earl, and the other soldiers return to their homes with memories of the South but no southern bride—their collective romances of reunion unfulfilled.

Andy, however, returns to Tarleton six years later to visit Ailie and the site of the army camp, but he finds everything changed, especially Ailie: "The modulations of pride, the vocal hints that she knew the secrets of a brighter, finer antebellum day, were gone in her voice; there was no time for them now as it rambled on in the half-laughing, half-desperate banter of the newer South. And everything was swept into this banter in order to make it go on and leave no time for thinking—the present, the future, herself, me" (460). Ailie symbolically demonstrates that the modern South had lost much of its romantic luster and its lost cause mythology. In a sense, the changes that began when northern soldiers came to the South during World War I spoiled the romantic notion of the South that northerners idealized. Andy, returning to the abandoned site of the camp, feels alienated and disenchanted in the landscape of the New South, so he returns to the North disillusioned with the modern South. Fitzgerald's depiction of the South's response to modernity overcomes the romance of reunion to depict a more complicated, nuanced version of the region. His changing representations of the South indicate that interregional contact affected both southerners' perceptions of the North and northerners' perceptions of the South. The war as a contact zone affected all who were involved in it.

John Dos Passos presents a complex version of World War I and regional identity in *Three Soldiers* (1921). The three soldiers in the title constitute a composite portrait of American regional identities: Dan Fuselli, an ethnic Italian from San Francisco; Chrisfield, a farm boy from Indiana; and John Andrews, an intellectual music composer from Virginia.[21] As conscripts in the American war machine, as Dos Passos characterizes it, they are amalgamated into a common identity as dehumanized cogs.[22] Under the regimen of training the soldiers endure, their personal identities dissolve. In the novel's first part, the soldiers discuss their backgrounds and hometowns, and Chrisfield remarks on the range of regional identities: "You're from the [West] Coast, this feller's from New York, an' Ah'm from ole Indiana, right in the middle" (22). Later in the text, regional variations play a less significant role in the contact zone of the war, which implies that in the context of the novel the common identity of oppressed soldiers has more significance than individual civilian identity.

Yet Dos Passos does make oblique references to the South that reflect conflicting American attitudes toward the region. When the new recruits are discussing their impending voyage to France, their conversation reveals the effects of their indoctrination into an ultramilitaristic, patriotic mindset. As a group of soldiers discusses their zeal to destroy the Huns and kill the Kaiser, one comments: "They ought to torture him to death, like they do niggers when they lynch 'em down south" (25). The quotation is not attributed to any specific person, but it demonstrates that Americans at the time of the war, regardless of their region of origin, associated the South with racial violence. But the fact that the speaker, who has been programmed to associate the Kaiser with death and brutality, wishes to lynch the Kaiser as an extreme form of bloodthirsty torture clearly indicates that southerners were considered excessive in their cruelty, perhaps even crueler than the Germans who were portrayed as bayoneting children in Belgium. This suggests that mainstream American attitudes toward the South were deeply ingrained and that only a prolonged period of mutual exposure would serve to alter those perceptions.

Dos Passos considered Andrews, the Virginian, the most autobiographical of the characters in the novel. While critics do not ordinarily associate Dos Passos with the South, his mother came from Virginia, and to the extent that he claimed any place in America as home, he considered himself closest to Westmoreland County, Virginia.[23] He was born in Chicago, grew up in Europe and on the East Coast, and went to school at Choate and

Harvard. He never identified himself as a southerner, and he certainly was not inculcated with the myth of the lost cause. He had a relatively disinterested attitude toward American regional antagonism, which makes him a revealing indicator of American attitudes toward the South. From his cosmopolitan perspective, identity had only a minor relationship to geography. Andrews, in fact, claims New York City as his second home, and he never in the course of the novel attempts to tell about the South in a substantial way. Dos Passos and his doppelgänger Andrews represent a new, or at least different, type of southern identity: one that bears only a nominal relationship to the South, one that is well suited for the type of interregional and international exchange that takes place during the war, and one that largely escapes the burden of southern history. He may be the prototype of the modernist southerner.

He is also an anomaly. Andrews is a southerner living outside the South permanently, so his particular case distorts the dynamics of the contact zone. Unlike a typical southerner, nothing impedes him from amalgamating with modernity. The more important issue for him is escaping the war. His case, though, illustrates the issues that southern writers must navigate as they encounter modernity through the war. Contact with southerners during the war changed the way northerners represented southerners, but contact with northerners changed the way southerners represented the South. Southern writers were forced to simultaneously negotiate modernity and the southern past, seemingly contradictory topics, and to reconcile these issues into a new form of literature that infused both. But the issue at stake was more complicated than simple cultural borrowing because of the asymmetrical power relations at play.

THE RETURN OF THE SOUTHERN SOLDIER

William Faulkner's first novel, *Soldiers' Pay* (1926), illustrates how interregional contact during World War I contributed to the development of modernism in the work of southern writers. In the book, Donald Mahon, a mortally wounded pilot, returns from Europe to his home in rural Georgia, but because of his experience in the war he no longer belongs to the community. *Soldiers' Pay* is not Faulkner's best novel, his most ambitious novel, or his most experimental novel, but it shows unmistakable characteristics of southern modernism. The relationship between the social changes represented in the book and the aesthetic forms Faulkner employs is not coincidental. While the war did not present a direct military threat to the South,

it did present a cultural crisis by bringing southern communities into contact with more modern communities outside the South, which led to the
fragmentation of cohesive southern communities. The contact violated
established norms, causing "a radical readjustment in the sense of time and
space in economic, political, and cultural life" that David Harvey claims
leads to the "crisis of representation" known as modernism (*The Condition
of Postmodernity*, 260).

The book opens with a train ride from a port of debarkation in the
North, through New York State, and across the Midwest. Mahon, wounded
in the face, sits uncommunicative and virtually invisible on the train, and
the other soldiers find his presence unsettling, partly because of his disfig-
uring wound and partly because of his uniform. He wears a British pilot's
uniform, and most of the soldiers are reluctant to speak to him because
they assume that he is not American. Julian Lowe, a frustrated pilot cadet
from California, sees Mahon's uniform and his wound and "wonder[s] what
a British officer in his condition could be doing traveling in America" (21).
A black porter from the South, however, sees past Donald's uniform to an
unspoken regional identity.[24] When Private Joe Gilligan refers to Donald as
"a lost foreigner," the porter corrects him. "Lost?," the porter says; "He ain't
lost. He's from Gawgia," which shocks the other soldiers. "Gilligan and Lowe
looked at each other. 'Christ, I thought he was a foreigner,' Gilligan whis-
pered" (22). The book's opening jumbles the spatial boundaries of region
and nation. It takes place in transit, thus not in any localized place, and
the people on the train mostly represent a heterogeneous mix of regions.
Mahon, wearing a British uniform and uncommunicative, is unplaced,
except for Faulkner's suggestion that the porter, like Deacon in *The Sound
and the Fury*, has an extrasensory perception for southerners.

Spatial identity took on peculiar significance in the military because
allies and enemies were determined by nationality. Within a military unit,
soldiers come from all parts of a country, which diminishes the importance
of region as a point of identification, but a citizen of one nation serving in
the military of another nation greatly complicated military nationalism, a
theme that Ernest Hemingway also explores in *A Farewell to Arms*. For the
soldiers, Donald's southern identity is of less consequence than his British
uniform, which marks him as a friend but also as an other. Margaret Powers,
a young war widow, also mistakes Donald for British, but Gilligan tells her
"he ain't no foreigner"; his spatial identity does not matter for the moment.
"Whatever he is," Gilligan says, "he's all right. With us, anyway. Let him be
whatever he wants" (29). Multiple contact zones develop on the train, and

the instability of spatial identities indicates the inherent fragility of an identity predicated on insularity. Contact itself has a tendency to redefine identity construction, as evidenced by the distinction between provincial porter and cosmopolitan soldiers. The train becomes an extension of the trenches, because the distinctions of military and civilian are more significant than any other identity category.

In contrast, Mahon's hometown epitomizes cultural isolation. Faulkner describes the town as ill prepared for modernity:

> Charlestown, like numberless other towns throughout the south, had been built around a circle of tethered horses and mules. In the middle of the square was the courthouse—a simple utilitarian edifice of brick and sixteen beautiful Ionic columns stained with generations of casual tobacco. Elms surrounded the courthouse and beneath these trees, on scarred and carved wood benches and chairs the city fathers, progenitors of solid laws and solid citizens who believed in Tom Watson and feared only God and drouth [sic], in black string ties or the faded brushed gray and bronze meaningless medals of the Confederate States of America, no longer having to make any pretense toward labor, slept or whittled away the long drowsy days while their juniors of all ages, not yet old enough to frankly slumber in public, played checkers or chewed tobacco and talked. A lawyer, a drug clerk and two non-descripts tossed iron discs back and forth between two holes in the ground. And above all brooded early April sweetly pregnant with noon. (108)

The inevitable creeping of time has barely altered this town since 1865. The insular community clings to lost cause icons and traditions, and it shows no signs of modernity. Faulkner indicates that Charlestown represents a typical rural southern community. In *The Narrative Forms of Southern Community*, Scott Romine asserts that cohesive southern communities are coercive because they are based on stable structures. Hegemonic communities inherently resist change, and the community's reaction to Mahon demonstrates how communities responded to modernity.

Initially, Mahon's return has little impact on Charlestown. Faulkner describes it as "hardly a nine days wonder even":

> Curious, kindly neighbors came in—men who stood or sat jovially respectable, cheerful: solid business men interested in the war only as a by-product of the rise and fall of Mr. Wilson, and interested in that only as a matter of dollars and cents, while their wives chatted about clothes to each other across Mahon's scarred oblivious brow. (145)

Distance insulated the South from the war's most traumatic effects, at least for a while. During the war, the citizens of Charlestown, as in most southern towns, participated in gratuitous displays of patriotism, marched their sons off to war, endured rationing of essential supplies, and followed events in the newspaper. Most southerners did not perceive the structural changes taking place in their society during the war as they obliviously carried on with their lives: planting cotton, going to church, and talking about the weather. Because the actual fighting took place "over there," to quote the refrain of a popular song, most southerners could not relate to Mahon's experience. They refer to him as "one of them airy-plane fellers," speculate about his inevitable death, and gossip about his hometown sweetheart, Cecily Saunders, and the two outsiders who escorted him home, Margaret Powers and Private Joe Gilligan (107). They resist disruption by ignoring it.

As more soldiers return, however, evident changes disrupt the community. At a dance to celebrate the soldiers' return, a group of young men have a peculiar reaction to Private Joe Gilligan. In seeing him, they become aware of their provincialism: "They greeted him with the effusiveness of people who are brought together by invitation yet are not quite certain of themselves and of the spirit of the invitation; in this case the eternal country boys of one national mental state, lost in the comparative metropolitan atmosphere of one diametrically opposed to it. To feel provincial: finding that a certain conventional state of behavior has inexplicably become obsolete over night" (194). As citizens of "one national mental state," these country boys, much like their oblivious fathers, have identified themselves as southerners rather than as Americans, thus separating themselves from the rest of the nation. But a contact zone develops at the dance, exposing the provincial young southerners to the worldly northern soldier. While little direct influence takes place on this particular occasion, it reveals how exposure changes attitudes about spatial identity. The dance is a microcosm of interregional contact because it illustrates who the presence of a regional other leads to a critical apprehension of the regional self. Faulkner suggests that the war is responsible for creating an atmosphere of openness between the regions as the entire nation faces "the hang-over of warfare in a society tired of warfare" (194). At the end of the war, even provincial young southerners belonged to an international collective of alienation, the lost generation, the international contact zone of modernity.

A smaller subset of southerners experienced personal loss as a result of the war, and their experiences signify a shift in cultural values that underscores the modernist sense of alienation. Following the Civil War, a cult of reverence deified the Confederate soldiers who died in combat with overt displays of regional piety, including elaborate pageants held in memory of the Confederate dead and ubiquitous monuments erected in their honor. No such cult, however, venerated the dead soldiers of World War I. Because the conflict concerned geopolitical issues that had a tenuously tangential effect on southerners and because the influenza pandemic of 1919 distracted the region's attention at the time of demobilization, the civic compulsion to celebrate the soldiers' sacrifice immediately after the war was diminished. The people who suffered a loss in World War I were often left to grieve alone. In a conversation between Mrs. Burney, whose son Dewey was killed in the war; Margaret Powers, whose husband Dick was killed in the war; and Donald's father, for example, unspoken thoughts of the grief dominate the exchange. Margaret remembers "(Dick, Dick. . . . How ugly men are, naked. Don't leave me)," while Mrs. Burney grieves, "(Dewey, my boy)," and Donald's father, unwilling to openly admit Donald's inevitable death, subconsciously accepts his son's fate: "(This was my son, Donald. He is dead)" (177–80). Faulkner emphasizes the mourners' isolation by placing their thoughts in parentheses, which separates their feelings from the dialogue and underscores their sense of alienation, but their common experience of loss constitutes another form of contact. As an outward sign of a society tired of warfare, the lack of public mourning following World War I contrasts with the cult of the Confederate dead, which implies that southerners drew a sense of solidarity from their defeat in the Civil War. The casualties of World War I were not uniquely southern dead, however, so southerners who lost loved ones in the war shared an international experience of mourning. This form of common experience made the South less cohesive and less coercive.

The South placed strict emphasis on social order with coercive mores determining the relations between genders, but those relations began to change as a result of the war. Faulkner focuses attention on gender roles in the novel by contrasting the traditional southern belle with the modern new woman. Before World War I, southern women were trapped by what W. J. Cash calls the "cult of gyneolatry," the dual impulse to idolize feminine virtue and strictly regulate feminine behavior. This patriarchal standard dictated customs of courtship and marriage and prevented women from seeking financial or legal independence from their male benefactors. During the war, however, a number of women challenged southern gender codes. In *Soldiers' Pay*, Faulkner dramatizes the tension between southern femininity, represented by Donald's fiancée, Cecily Saunders, and modern femininity, represented by war widow Margaret Powers. Faulkner portrays

Cecily as vapid and foolish, a template for Temple Drake in *Sanctuary*. Her parents apparently forced to her to agree to marry Donald before his enlistment, which indicates that she is obedient to patriarchal control, but she has had an ongoing, widely known affair with a town boy, George Farr, since Donald enlisted. When Donald returns wounded, she at first yields to pressure from her parents and agrees to go through with the wedding, then she changes her mind and elopes with George Farr. Cecily, as the incarnation of the southern belle, lacks the inner strength and virtue that southern men admired in southern women, which brings the entire construct of southern womanhood into question.[25]

Margaret Powers is an independent, resourceful, sexually liberated modern woman.[26] Originally from Alabama, Margaret escapes from the patriarchal South during the war. She explains to Joe Gilligan, "I lived in a small town and I had got kind of sick lazing around home all morning and dressing up just to walk downtown in the afternoon and spending the evenings messing around with men, so after we got in the war I persuaded some friends of my mother's to get me a position in New York" (158). She met and married Dick Powers, but their marriage lasted little longer than their honeymoon, after which Dick deployed to France and died in action. After living on her own in New York, holding a job, and surviving a husband, Margaret gains an insightful perspective on the cult of gyneolatry and southern men's obsession with feminine virtue: "Men are the ones who worry about our good names, because they gave them to us," she says, "but we have other things to bother about, ourselves. What you mean by a good name is like a dress that's too flimsy to wear comfortably" (101). Margaret makes her own decisions about who to marry and who to love. After Cecily elopes, Margaret marries Donald as an act of charity, allowing his family a moment of relief from his visible suffering. When he dies, she leaves Charlestown to live independently, indicating that she is beyond the coercive bonds of southern community. Her modern, urban-influenced gender ideas conflict with southern tradition.

Faulkner's Charlestown is a community in flux, changing in both obvious and subtle ways, and he represents this evolution through experiments with modernist literary techniques.[27] While living in New Orleans and writing *Soldiers' Pay*, Faulkner read the work of many other modernist writers including F. Scott Fitzgerald, T. S. Eliot, Ernest Hemingway, and James Joyce, and he incorporates elements of their writing styles into the novel.[28] For example, as Joseph Blotner documents, he embeds cultural artifacts, such as popular songs, into his text as Fitzgerald did to establish setting and atmosphere (*Faulkner: A Biography*, 429). One of the most obvious borrowings occurs in chapter 7 of *Soldiers' Pay*, where Faulkner copies Joyce's method of assembling a multitude of interior monologues as in the overture to the "Sirens" chapter of *Ulysses*. Faulkner also incorporates stichomythic dialogue—exchanges of short sentences without embedded character identifiers—in some sections, similar to Hemingway's technique in *A Farewell to Arms*. Additionally, he experiments with stream of consciousness, which would eventually become his trademark, but the passages tend to be too brief to adequately develop the technique's intended effect. Faulkner's experiments in *Soldiers' Pay* demonstrate the growth of an immature but ambitious writer exploring new forms.[29] Faulkner's technique and his narrative both demonstrate the effects of the contact zone in the South and the juxtaposition of modernity and provincialism.

Faulkner's willingness to embrace new literary forms and seek out artistic influences from outside his otherwise limited scope of experience signals a shift in southern writing. Rather than modeling his early prose after the local color sketches and moonlight-and-magnolias mythology, such as his great-grandfather's novel *The White Rose of Memphis*, that dominated southern literature until World War I, Faulkner rejected these trite apologist forms for new literary techniques to better reflect the uncertainty and disillusionment of the modern world. In a sense, he imported the modernist narrative to the South, but he intentionally maintained a southern voice in his work, demonstrating the characteristics of distal modernism. While visiting Paris in 1925, he considered forgoing his southern identity for that of a cosmopolitan modernist artist as many of the writers of the lost generation did, but he chose to follow Sherwood Anderson's counsel to explore the imaginative life of his own postage stamp of land. By making this decision, he unified the two essential elements of his career as a prose writer: literary modernism and the South. He may have intuited that the South's entry into the modern world would be inherently painful and dramatic and that he could harness the experimental spirit of modernist prose to describe the experience of southern alienation.

World War I constituted for Faulkner a literary threshold that, once crossed, could not be recrossed. While many of the modernist writers he emulated in his first novel were searching for new methods to express and describe their apprehension of modernity, Faulkner likely recognized that aspects of modernization—such as the erosion of religious faith, the development of assembly-line killing machines, and the dissolution of nationalist identities—affected the South almost as directly as they affected the

North and Europe. While composing *Soldiers' Pay*, he wrote a short, unpublished essay, "Literature and War," that discusses four contemporary works about the war.[30] He takes issue with Rupert Brooke's glorious representation of heroism in battle, he applauds the gory realism of Siegfried Sassoon's poetry and Henri Barbusse's novel *Le feu*, and he comments on the veracity of R. H. Mottram's novel *The Spanish Farm*, which depicts the impact of warfare on a small home-front community.

The Spanish Farm may have influenced the thematic structure and content of *Soldiers' Pay* more than any of the other works Faulkner read while writing the novel (Millgate, "Faulkner on the Literature of the First World War," 391). *The Spanish Farm* demonstrates that the scope of war's cultural impact is not limited to the battlefield, that massive dramatic changes can take place far removed from actual combat, and that lingering social consequences can be as conducive to literary development as fighting in the trenches. In *Soldiers' Pay*, Faulkner describes only a brief scene of combat of the "slogging up the Arras" style he admired in Sassoon and Barbusse, which may bespeak his lack of actual experience in the trenches. But he did represent combat in some of his earlier short stories, such as "Ad Astra," and he was clearly fascinated with battle, as Donald Kartiganer argues in the essay "So I, Who Never Had a War." The relative lack of combat scenes in a book about war implies that the events that take place at home when the fighting has passed are as important as the fighting itself. In the South, interregional contact was a front of the war.

Much of the literature of southern modernism depicts southerners struggling to reconcile southern tradition with modernity and negotiating the difficult transition from the myth of the lost cause to the reality of the modern world following World War I. This war, like its predecessor in the 1860s, exposed many of the region's social, cultural, and economic weaknesses, but unlike the Civil War it left the region's writers and intellectuals better prepared to analyze those weaknesses artistically. Faulkner's awkward fumbling in *Soldiers' Pay* eventually led to the fruition of southern modernist literature in *The Sound and the Fury* and *Absalom, Absalom!* The South's encounter with modernity after its half-century-long intellectual isolation signaled the beginning of a dynamic period in the history of southern literature. Interregional contact fragmented some of the coercive structures that made southern communities cohesive, and the literary representation of the disruptions taking place within the South's social structure demonstrate a conflict within the mind of the South over the role of the region's past in its future.

Allen Tate's New Provincialism

One of the southern writers most self-consciously aware of the complicated cultural negations to be made in the war's wake is Allen Tate. Over the course of his career, he wrote frequently about the relationship between World War I and southern modernism. He recognized the impact of contact with northerners on southern writing, both because southerners borrowed new ideas and techniques from northern writers and because southerners became more critically aware of the South. His observations are especially interesting because he did not serve in the military during the war, but he understood the aesthetic ramifications of the contact zone as an intellectual construct. As a young writer in the 1920s, he was drawn to literary modernism, which led him to leave the South for the North. His experience in the North, however, led him to identify strongly as a southerner, so he understood the dynamics of contact personally, and he was able both to extrapolate the dynamics to a regional scale and to diagnose the initiating agent that led to the emergence of literary modernism in the South. His evolving ideas about southern modernism help to construct a model of distal modernism.

Tate was nineteen years old and draft eligible in 1918, and he planned to enlist if he was not admitted to college. He was frail and sickly and suffered respiratory problems, so he probably would have been rejected, but his admittance to Vanderbilt made the point moot. When he enrolled in the fall, however, he had an unexpected experience with the war because the campus had become an encampment. A unit of the Student Army Training Corps had moved onto campus, and "soon the peaceful tree-lined campus was overrun by five hundred boys wearing ill-fitting uniforms of tunics, breeches, and puttees. The Gothic dormitories became barracks, reveille was called out at 7:00 a.m., and a strict 9:00 p.m. lights-out policy was instituted" (Underwood, 31). For the first few months of Tate's college career, military discipline replaced traditional academic culture, and even fraternities were temporarily disbanded. Vanderbilt returned to normal after the armistice was signed in November, but Tate's initial encounter with intellectual culture included an unintentional and vicarious experience with the military. In addition, Tate's most important mentors, John Crowe Ransom and Donald Davidson, were both World War I veterans who returned to Vanderbilt after the war.

Ransom and Davidson recognized Tate as a precocious and talented writer, and they invited him to join the off-campus group of writers and intellectuals who eventually became known as the Fugitives. Although Ransom and Davidson were older, well educated, and war veterans, they regarded Tate as the most modernist member of their group. "The role Tate played within the Fugitives," Daniel Singal comments, "was that of young rebel, casting himself as the solitary Modernist marooned among provincial conservatives" (234). His modernism manifested in predilections for experiments in form and difficulty in imagery, using techniques that he imitated from T. S. Eliot and Hart Crane. After graduating from Vanderbilt, Tate went to New York, where he lived among the Greenwich Village writers at the epicenter of American modernism—Hart Crane, e. e. cummings, Malcolm Cowley, John Dos Passos, and Edmund Wilson, among others. He found the city fascinating initially, marveling at the technology and enjoying the seamless fusion of modernity and modernism. In time, though, he became self-conscious of his southernness, and he grappled with the attributes of his identity that marked him as different from the other New York writers.

In 1926, as feelings of urban ennui set in, Tate wrote "Ode to the Confederate Dead," in which he meditates on his feelings of ambivalence about modernism and the South. In the poem, the speaker gazes upon a cemetery where "Row after row with strict impunity / The headstones yield their names to the element." The graves lead the speaker to contemplate the emotional connection these dead felt to the cause for which they gave their lives. He imagines them giving their lives for the South, sacrificing themselves by marching into gunfire in rows as straight and even as the ones in which they are buried. Echoing Sally Carol Happer in Fitzgerald's story, he marvels at their commitment, and he questions whether or not he believes in anything with the same conviction, but he walks away from the cemetery convinced only that he, too, will eventually die. This introspective, alienated pose is characteristic of Tate's mature poetry and criticism. Singal observes that his "modernist self-consciousness stood irrevocably between himself and the region he sought. His fate was to be perched on the precise balance point of ambivalence between the two cultures" (252). Singal here makes a trenchant observation about the contradictory dynamics of distal modernism: Tate was intellectually divided between his fascination with modernity and his allegiance to the South. He spent much of his career attempting to mediate his intellectual conflicts, and his developing ideas about southern modernism can be traced in a series of essays he wrote over a period of decades.

Tate offers his own interpretation of his ambivalence in "Ode to the Confederate Dead" in his first essay about southern modernism, "Narcissus as Narcissus." He explains that the poem is about the experience of solipsism, a profound state of modernist alienation. One of the symbols in the poem is a "blind crab," which, as Tate explains, symbolizes "the nature of the moral conflict upon which the drama of the poem develops: the cut-off-ness of the modern 'intellectual man' from the world" (*Collected Essays*, 253). But, in the poem, the modern intellectual man is cut off from a specific segment of the world, the South. Tate's oppositional configuration between the South and modernity implies that they are irreconcilable, that modernity inherently antagonizes southern tradition, and, perhaps, that modernity threatens to overtake the South. If the modern intellectual man is cut off, then it would be impossible for him—in this case, Tate—to commit to an ideal, so the notion of a dedicated southerner vanishes in the modern world.

Facing this imaginary conundrum, Tate forced himself to commit to southern identity, even knowing that this option is foreclosed. The unavailability of southern identity, however, is an essential component of the equation for him. Tate's mother raised him on apocryphal stories of their family's roots in antebellum Virginia, so he felt an atavistic connection to the myth of the lost cause. In the 1930s, he attempted to resuscitate his southern identity by force, an approach that he suggests in his contribution to the Agrarian manifesto, *I'll Take My Stand*.[31] Tate wrote biographies of Stonewall Jackson, Robert E. Lee, and Jefferson Davis, and he wrote a novel that reimagined his own family history, *The Fathers*. His efforts to connect to a reified southern identity, one that reinstantiated the Old South in the modern world, were vain, which he clearly understood. But the efforts themselves were crucial to Tate; they were the crux of his world view, which yoked together—by violence—the South and modernism.

Because of his self-conscious awareness of both the South and modernity, Tate was ideally positioned to analyze the emergence of southern modernism. He addressed the issue in "The Profession of Letters in the South," an essay he wrote for the *Virginia Quarterly Review* in 1935. In this essay, he echoes H. L. Mencken's assertion that the South has no literary tradition. "It must be confessed," he writes, "that the Southern tradition has left no cultural landmark so conspicuous that the people may be reminded by it constantly of what they are. . . . We have just enough literary remains from the old regime to prove to us that, had a great literature risen, it would have been unique in modern times" (*Collected Essays*, 268). He goes on to admit that the South's dearth of literary tradition distinguishes it from the North, and he argues that southern literature is a casualty of southern history. "The great Southern ideas were strangled in the cradle, either by the South herself (for example, by too much quick cotton money in the Southwest) or by

Union armies" (*Collected Essays*, 270). His explanation is that southerners have not had sufficient time or energy to devote to creating a literary or intellectual culture, because southern intellectuals were too invested in politics. His argument is specious on its face, of course. During the nineteenth century, black and white and male and female southerners all contributed to a literary tradition, but many of their contributions were marginalized, ironically, often for political reasons, which effectively separated the South from the nation's intellectual mainstream.[32]

Tate's argument is less interesting for its veracity than for the logic behind it. He bases his argument on the notion that the South, having no indigenous tradition of its own, imported its literary culture, and he quotes John Crowe Ransom's worry that southern writers were "becoming merely 'modern' writer[s]" (*Collected Essays*, 278). Tate responds that "the arts everywhere spring from a mysterious union of indigenous materials and foreign influences," an equation that allows for the possibility of southern modernism that incorporates southern influence with modernist influences radiating from outside the South (279). Rather than make this point, however, he launches into a rant about the plutocratic northern publishing industry, and he concludes with a veiled threat that the period of southern literary production would be brief. "The Southern novelist has left his mark upon the age," he warns, "but it is of the age. From the peculiarly historical consciousness of the Southern writer has come good work of a special order; but the focus of this consciousness is quite temporary" (281). Southern writers, he predicts, will inevitably be drawn into politics once again. His ominous, preposterous prophecy did not come to pass, but his idea about combining indigenous material with outside influence has merit as a possible theory of southern modernism worth developing.

Ten years later, Tate revisited the topic in another essay for the *Virginia Quarterly Review*, "The New Provincialism," which disavowed much of the earlier essay and constructed a more durable theory of southern modernism. He rejects both the label "regionalism" and the label "nationalism" as inaccurate literary descriptors, preferring instead to use the term "provincialism" to describe the geographical frame of a work of literature. Region, he explains, is limited in space, and "the provincial attitude is limited in time but not in space" (*Collected Essays*, 286). In the wake of World War I, according to Tate's theory, limitations of space dissolved, both within and between nations, which effectively brought all writers into the same temporal context. His theory suggests that contact in war has eradicated spatial divisions, forging a global contact zone and rendering the notion of regionalized literature moot. The emergence of provincialism is a radical change because, in the past, individuals belonged primarily to localized, tribal units, their "village, valley, mountain, or sea-coast" (289). Diminishing physical barriers led to the development of "a world regional economy," a phrase that presages Immanuel Wallerstein's world-system theory, but Tate does not necessarily see this as a cultural advance (289). "Provincialism is that state of mind in which regional men lose their origins in the past and its continuity into the present," he writes, "and begin every day as if there had been no yesterday" (289).

Tate, a committed traditionalist, worries that provincialism is antithetical to southern literature. Looking back to the period between the world wars, he laments that southern literature rooted in history, such as his novel *The Fathers*, had no market because northern critics are biased toward books that portray the South as "backward and illiberal, and controlled by white men who cherish a unique moral perversity"; so, in his opinion, southern literature of this period focused on social agitation at the expense of history and tradition (*Collected Essays*, 292). He lumps southern writers after 1918 into two groups: traditionalists and sociologists. The traditionalists he lists include Stark Young, Elizabeth Madox Roberts, Caroline Gordon (his wife), Ellen Glasgow, and William Faulkner, "who is the most powerful and original novelist in the United States and one of the best in the modern world" (292). He does not bother to list the sociologists, but Erskine Caldwell would likely be at the top of the list. He fears that provincialism will eventually vanquish tradition, so his assertion that "with the war of 1914–1918, the South re-entered the world—but gave a backward glance as it stepped over the border: that backward glance gave us the southern renascence, a literature conscious of the past in the present" is a veiled warning (292). Ominous or not, his notion about provincialism allows for the formulation of a theory of distal modernism based on contact between literary influences from outside the South combining with indigenous southern experience during World War I.

In the 1959 essay "A Southern Mode of Imagination," Tate revisited the idea of southern modernism once more and reconsidered some of his earlier pronouncements. His warning about the eradication of southern literature is replaced with the grandiose assertion that "with the exceptions of Hemingway and Fitzgerald, the region north of the Potomac and Ohio Rivers has become the stepsister of American fictions" (*Collected Essays*, 555), and he proposes to explain, chauvinistically, how southern writers came to dominate American literature at midcentury. He notes that "with the end of the first World War a change came about that literary historians have not yet explained" and that relations between the North and South had thawed, creating a new era of good feeling between the regions after World War I (558). The key to understanding the emergence of modern southern writing, according to Tate, is the "southern mode of discourse," a rhetorical stance in which the author imagines him or herself speaking to an audience as an orator on a stage rather than as a participant in a conversation. Southern discourse, he claims, "is about the people who are talking" (560). The ideal southern author of the period between 1865 and 1914 is Cicero Cincinnatus, an imaginary planter-soldier from Roman history who blends oratory with action, a figure similar to Davidson's vision of Lee in the mountains.

"The pertinent fact for any approach to the modern literary Renaissance," Tate writes, "is that the South was more isolated from 1865 to about 1920 than it had been before 1865" (*Collected Essays*, 565). The key issue for him is to explain how the South became less isolated after World War I. Clearly, this issue preoccupied him for much of his life, as his repeated attempts to explain it demonstrate. In this final effort, he considers social change as a literary catalyst, but he hastily dismisses the notion, scoffing that social change "may produce a great social scientist, like the late Howard W. Odum, of North Carolina," but it will not necessarily be a great writer like John Crowe Ransom or William Faulkner (566). He focuses on *Huckleberry Finn*, which he calls "the first modern novel by a Southerner," and he admits that modern southern writers have switched from the isolationist rhetorical mode to the conversational dialectical mode that had been associated with northern writing, synthesizing the forms into a distinct southern mode of imagination (567). His final conclusion about the emergence of southern modernism "is that the South not only re-entered the world with the first World War; it looked round and saw for the first time since about 1830 that the Yankees were not to blame for everything" (568).

Over several decades, Tate worked through the process of recognizing World War I as a contact zone. His southern chauvinism obstructed his ability to recognize the actual dynamics of the process for nearly a generation even as he was actively participating in the process, but he eventually came to realize that contact with the North changed southern writing by incorporating elements of southern culture with modern literary techniques. Expansive interregional contact during the war forced southerners to break with their defensive intellectual isolationism, to reimagine themselves as part of a complex matrix of American identity, and to encounter exciting new narrative techniques that could be adapted to southern narrative material. In short, World War I led to southern literary transculturation, an essential component of southern modernism. Eventually, he came to understand that southern narrative could coexist with modernist form and to develop a theory of southern modernism that points toward the importance of interregional contact.

Interregional contact is the dark matter of southern modernism, the barely visible and subtle process that radiated modernism into a distal region beyond the proximal zones of urbanization and industrialization. Contact changed the way people imagined the regions. As a result of interregional contact, nonsouthern writers developed more nuanced representations of the South and southern writers developed more critical representations of the South. Faulkner's description of southerners' perception of themselves as part of a larger nation and Tate's grudging realization that exposure to other perspectives enhanced southern writing are important indicators of interregional contact, and the fact that both of these writers were noncombatants who went on to become standard-bearers for southern modernism is also important. Their development as writers indicated that the war affected the South broadly, even altering the experience and perspectives of people who did not actually serve in combat. Those who served in combat, meanwhile, had a more profound experience of modernity—one that left them disillusioned and, like many members of the lost generation, searching for meaning.

2

THE SOUTHERN SOLDIER IN THE AMERICAN ARMY

Sectionalism, Nationalism, and Modernity

Between America's declaration of war in 1917 and the demobilization of the army of occupation in Germany in 1919, nearly a million southerners served in the military, accounting for almost a quarter of America's enlisted personnel and a higher demographic proportion than any other region of the United States. For southern farm boys turned doughboys, the prospect of military service was both exhilarating and unsettling. Along with the many challenges of recruitment and military training, white southern soldiers faced the additional task of reconfiguring their national identity. Even after the turn of the century, many white southerners conceived of the South as an occupied nation and regarded the federal government as an enemy agency. The election of Woodrow Wilson, a native southerner, in 1912 mitigated that sentiment but did not eliminate it. Wilson, in fact, hoped that the war might finally ease sectional animosity, so he ordered that all units in the American Expeditionary Force should be geographically mixed. As he explained to Virginia governor Henry C. Stuart: "There should be intermingling of troops from all the States. We should submerge provincialism and sectionalism and party spirit in one powerful flood of nationalism, which would carry us on to victory."[1]

While southerners enlisted in large numbers and contributed to the Allies' victory in significant ways, the powerful flood of nationalism that Wilson predicted proved to be problematic.[2] A scene from Faulkner's *Flags in the Dust* illustrates the tension in the South between allegiance to the lost cause and allegiance to the United States. When Bayard Sartoris takes refuge on the Macallums' farm, he shares a room with Buddy Macallum, who, like Bayard, had served with the army in Europe.[3] Buddy offers to show Bayard a medal he won for bravery, but he warns Bayard that they will have to look at it when his father is not around. "Why?" asks Bayard; "Don't he know you got it?" Buddy answers, "He knows. . . . Only he don't like it because he claims it's a Yankee medal. Rafe [Buddy's brother] says pappy and Stonewall Jackson aint never surrendered" (368). Buddy's father regards the US Army as a foreign force, and he is obviously conflicted about his son's role in the American Expeditionary Force. Because Congress enacted mandatory conscription when America entered the war, many southerners who, like Buddy, felt ambivalent about both the war and the United States were forced into service.

These southern soldiers found themselves in an awkward situation. Those who identified as southerners more than as Americans found themselves conscripted to fight for a virtually foreign army against a completely foreign enemy in an absolutely foreign country. Many isolationist southerners believed that America should not intercede in the war. In fact, when Wilson ran for reelection in 1916 using the slogan "He kept us out of war!," he carried a vast majority of the vote in the South. Yet when America finally declared war on Germany, public sentiment in the South ran heavily patriotic, at least on the surface. Beneath the surface, however, within the hearts and minds of several white southern writers who served in the American Expeditionary Force, including William Alexander Percy, Paul Green, and Donald Davidson, a set of antagonistic forces created an ideological crisis that played out in their literature. Serving in a national army exposed them to modernity and forced them to repress their sectional identity and embrace patriotic nationalism, at least temporarily. During the war, many white male southerners self-consciously questioned their regional identity, leaving them torn between the legacy of the lost cause, their tendency to view the United States as an occupying enemy, and their sectional identity on the one hand and their sense of patriotism and duty, their impulse to homogenize with the rest of the nation, and their emerging sense of nationalism on the other. Their postwar writing shows them wresting with these antagonistic forces, and the tension they reflect between rural regionalism and urban nationalism is one of the characteristics of distal modernism.

THE BIRTH OF A NATIONALISM

Even before America entered the war, sectional identities were changing. Woodrow Wilson's election in 1912 was a watershed in the course of sectional animosity. Although he served as Governor of New Jersey, Wilson was born in Virginia and raised in South Carolina and Georgia, and southerners claimed him as their native son. Election returns show that he polled a majority in only one state outside the South, Arizona, which means that he ascended to the White House as a direct result of political support in the South.[4] At his inauguration, a former Confederate—chief justice of the Supreme Court Edward Douglass White Jr. of Louisiana—administered the oath of office, and rebel yells and cries of "Dixie!" were heard among the crowd.[5] With a sizable representation in the Democratic majorities in both houses of Congress and a southerner in the White House, the region influenced the national agenda, and the new administration enacted a number of policies that supported the objectives of southern politicians: promoting investment in southern industry, securing the place of southern crops at the market, and codifying white supremacy. In the years immediately before the outbreak of the war in Europe, the South as a political entity seemed poised to begin the process of peacefully homogenizing with the remainder of the United States and shifting from a separatist region to a part of the American nation-state.

Progressive southern politicians and business leaders promoted the idea of ideological reunification as a means of improving social welfare and economic prosperity in the South. While they had a certain degree of success in pressing their agenda, many other southerners, especially rural southerners, continued to feel at best ambivalent about America and at worst openly hostile.[6] Since the end of the Civil War, white southerners developed a distinct separatist identity as a nation within the United States that was, as Liah Greenfeld remarks, "no longer American" (476). Southern sectionalism was a quasi-nationalist identity predicated upon three key tenets: distinctiveness between southern culture and northern culture, the perpetuation of white supremacy, and lost cause revision of the Civil War. In *Still Fighting the Civil War*, David Goldfield explains that "white southerners elevated defeat into a heroic Lost Cause, their fallen comrades and faltering leaders into saintly figures, their crumbled society into the best place on earth, and their struggle to regain control over their lives and region into a victorious redemption. Memory offered salvation; they could not allow the past to slip into the past" (20).[7] Not all white southerners, of course, adhered to the lost cause, but it was prominent enough to be a prevailing attitude. In order for white southerners to begin to conceive of themselves as Americans first and southerners second, the grip of the lost cause would have to be loosened.[8]

The opening of hostilities in Europe in 1914 had a mixed impact on southern sectionalism and the ideology of the lost cause. Sentiment in the South ran strongly on the side of the Allies, and some political leaders, ministers, and newspaper editors publicly denounced Germany. But isolationism in the South ran more deeply than support for England and Belgium.[9] Actually, southerners were most concerned initially about the war's impact on cotton markets. Because of the blockade of German markets and submarine activity in the Atlantic, much of the export crop of 1914 was a loss, and many farmers, unable to sell their crops that year, fell deeply into debt. Meanwhile, in response to the impending threat of war, the federal government began a program of national military preparedness—even while Wilson promised that the United States would not get involved in the war unless absolutely necessary. Although most white southerners sided with the Allies, they were uneasy about the prospect of growing the national military. Already economically unstable, southerners were reluctant to see large amounts of money invested in potentially unnecessary preparations. George Tindall comments that "a deep suspicion permeated the rural South that preparedness was a scheme for the profit of munitions makers and financial interests" (41). Part of that paranoia can be traced directly to sectionalism; in effect, white southerners regarded a strong American military as a potential threat both politically and economically. That is not to say that southerners expected to be invaded again, but since virtually all of the military's bases, training camps, shipyards, and munitions factories were located outside the South in 1914, southerners saw little direct benefit from increased preparedness.

By early 1917, the sinking of the *Lusitania* and the publication of the Zimmermann telegram rendered the debate over preparedness moot.[10] When America formally entered the war, a wave of martial patriotism swept the South, making southerners, as Dewey Grantham observes, "more self-conscious about their Americanism" (*Southern Progressivism*, 386). Southerners proudly waved the flag of the United States, often side by side with the stars and bars.[11] But George Tindall notes that the southern version of wartime nationalism was "a peculiar kind of 'Americanization' in the fires of patriotism," although he allows that "sectional loyalty receded at least temporarily before the universal cry for unity" (63). In some respects, the myth of the lost cause expanded to encompass the nation's entrance into war, as, for example, in the hyperbole of Representative Robert L. Doughton of North Carolina, who, in a speech to a northern audience, said that "the grandsons of the men who wore the gray and the grandsons of the men who wore the blue are now marching with locked shields and martial step to the mingled strains of Dixie and the Star Spangled Banner."[12] Doughton's rhetoric exemplifies a stereotypical southern bellicosity, but many white male southerners, like their counterparts on both sides of the Atlantic, saw the war as an opportunity to find glory, honor, duty, and patriotism. Southerners were willing to fight, both for their region and for their nation.

Nationalism, according to Liah Greenfeld, is a complex, abstract "emergent phenomenon" that depends upon an array of factors, including economic development, racial and ethnic identity, population migration, common history and language, geography, and political organization. The process is highly dynamic, and changes in any of its factors can ripple through the entire process. A rise in literacy, for example, can lead to a greater emphasis on common language, especially within the political regime, which can in turn lead to an exclusionary construction of national identity. Nationalism, as an abstraction, is distinct from the nation-state as a political entity, so it is not unusual for citizens of one nation-state to identify as part of a different nation or for the population of an area within a nation-state to imagine themselves as a distinct nation. In a large nation-state such as the United States, some areas develop unevenly, so one region may have a different economic system, population base, history, or political system than another. At the beginning of the twentieth century, many white southerners imagined themselves as part of a distinct nation within the American nation-state, so they imagined themselves to have competing nationalist identities, namely American and southern. White southerners, who held absolute political control over the region, recognized themselves as having a different economy, history, culture, and political system than the rest of the United States. Benedict Anderson argues that imagination is a crucial element of nationalism, because a nation "is an imagined political community" (6). If white southerners believed that they were members of a separate nation, then they essentially were.

The war highlighted the complicated dynamics between region and nation, and the multinational conflict involved the processes of globalization.[13] Increasingly, scholars have focused on the region, rather than the nation-state, as the fundamental unit of ideological affiliation, which has drastically changed understandings of the South as a distinct space. The collection *Look Away* shifts the paradigm of southern identity into a hemispheric relationship. "If we are to avoid modernity's fetishization of the nation-state and the imagined community," Jon Smith and Deborah Cohn write, "we need to return . . . to a prenational vision of North and South. In such a modified reading, the U.S. South comes to occupy a space unique within modernity: a space simultaneously (or alternately) center and margin, victor and defeated, empire and colony" (9). Destabilizing the idea of nationalism in this way opens up new interpretations of southern identity.

Smith and Cohn offer the notion of "uncanny hybridity," claiming that the US South is both First World and Third World and thus a locus for post-colonial analysis. Nationality and modernity are both dynamic processes, so they are always unstable. Looking at southern identity in a hemispheric context yields one set of perspectives, and looking at it in a transatlantic context, the perspective most relevant in the context of World War I, yields another. Either way, the characteristics that are most evident are that southern identity involves a legacy of defeat and a resistance to progress. Leigh Anne Duck explains that regionalism, such as the assertion of a southern identity, signifies a tension between two spaces developing unevenly. The slower-developing space will use regionalism to justify maintaining a pattern of traditional social structures that are inconsistent with modernity (179). Southern modernism, therefore, is something of a contradiction: antimodernist modernism. The terms "regionalism" and "sectionalism" are often used interchangeably, but "sectionalism" more accurately highlights the relationship between the region and the nation.

This relationship between the nation-state and the section is inherently precarious and potentially violent. Ernest Gellner explains: "Industrialization and modernization proceed in a notoriously uneven manner. Just as notoriously, it is the early stages, the first few generations, of these processes which cause the greatest disruption, the greatest misery and which provide the maximum opportunity for political revolution and for the rethinking and redrawing of political loyalties" (166). The unevenness of this process can create major ideological fractures in nationalism, and one could reasonably contend that the Civil War was partly a product of uneven development, between the industrial North and the agrarian South. World War I was also a product of nationalist development, as rapidly industrializing European nation-states fought for raw materials. Eric Hobsbawm labels World War I the beginning of the "apogee of nationalism," which lasted until the end of World War II because it was a period in which economic advancement led nations into sustained military conflict (*Nations and Nationalism*, 131).

Conflicts over industrialization and nationalism were difficult for southerners to process. According to Jeanette Keith in *Rich Man's War, Poor Man's Fight*, some rural southerners were highly suspicious of the war movement, which they believed was guided by monopolistic corporate interests. At the same time that southerners enlisted in large numbers, they deserted from the military and evaded the draft in large numbers, often because they did not see how the war involved them on either a personal level or a nationalist level. To the extent that southerners imagined themselves as a separate nation, they did not see themselves as Americans, which forced them to reconfigure their nationalist ideology in order to fight and die for a nationalist cause. Liah Greenfeld contends that "the adoption of a new, national identity is precipitated by a regrouping within or change in the position of influential social groups. This structural change results in the inadequacy of the traditional definition, or identity, of the involved groups—a crisis of identity, structurally expressed as 'anomie'—which creates among them an incentive to search for and, given the availability, adopt a new identity" (16). World War I was a crisis for white southerners, not only because of the combat, which they saw on a relatively small scale, but also because it caused them to recognize the inadequacy of the lost cause ideology and to accept, at least tentatively, the mantle of American patriotism.

In a 1917 address to a reunion of the United Confederate Veterans, Woodrow Wilson spoke to surviving members of the last army to invade the United States about patriotism and American nationalism. He acknowledged that memories of the lost cause had brought the Confederate veterans together to celebrate "those days when the whole nation seemed in grapple," when "heroic things were done on both sides," and when men fought "in something like the old spirit of chivalric gallantry."[14] Yet he urged the Confederates to forget their sectional animosity, saying that "there are some things that we have thankfully buried, and among them are the great passions of division which once threatened to rend this nation in twain." He goes on to suggest that the South's defeat was part of a grand design. "We now see ourselves," he said, "part of a nation, united, powerful, great in spirit and purpose, we know the great ends which God, in His mysterious Providence, wrought through our instrumentality. Because, at the heart of men of the North and of the South, there was the same love of self-government and of liberty, and now we are to be an instrument in the hands of God to see that liberty is made secure for mankind." Charles Reagan Wilson uses this speech to conclude *Baptized in Blood: The Religion of the Lost Cause, 1865–1920*, arguing that this moment represents the end of sectionalism as a major ideological barrier between the North and the South. President Wilson gave his address on the same day the first Conscription Act since the end of the Civil War went into effect. As he was speaking, lines of young men in the North and the South were waiting to register for the first American military draft since the end of the Civil War. But while the irony and symbolism of this occasion cannot be overlooked, the tension between sectionalism and nationalism within the hearts and minds of the

Confederate veterans who were present to hear Wilson's speech and, more importantly, within the hearts and minds of their grandsons who were at the same moment enlisting was more complex.

While Wilson's speech to the Confederate veterans represents a significant moment in the ideological reunification of the United States, it has been long overshadowed by the impact of D. W. Griffith's *The Birth of a Nation*. The film, based on Thomas Dixon's novels *The Clansman* and *The Leopard's Spots*, outlines a template for how southerners achieved US nationalism within the context of the lost cause.[15] Released in 1915, the film takes advantage of Wilson's election and the sense of sectional reconciliation he represented, and several intertitles in the film quote from Wilson's *A History of the American People*,[16] a title that implies the eventual success of nationalism.[17] The film's opening intertitles blame abolitionists for the sectional animosity that divided the nation and led to the Civil War. The key issue in the film, and some might argue the key issue that maintained the cult of the lost cause, concerns the color line. The film suggests not only that national reconciliation is possible and desirable but also that division would never have occurred if not for a small group of agitators who contravened natural racial hierarchy by opposing slavery. In this way, the revisionist logic of the lost cause asserts that North and South have no quarrel outside the debate over racism and slavery. The film, instead, asserts that northerners and southerners should reunite under a common banner, in this case the flag of the Ku Klux Klan, to vanquish their mutual enemy. An intertitle during the film's climatic action, a racial uprising, asserts: "The enemies of North and South are united again in common defense of their Aryan birthright."[18] The film, thus, fetishizes race as the key to national unity.[19]

Race is a common factor in configurations of nationalism, and it has obvious resonance for white southerners. As the United States became more nationalistic, Barbara Ladd observes, white southerners became increasingly anxious about race (*Nationalism and the Color Line*, 20). Because white supremacy was a crucial aspect of southern identity, the prospect of destabilizing racial hierarchy was more disturbing to white southerners than unifying with the United States. The connection between race and nationalism is not unique to southerners, however. Etienne Balibar argues that "racism is constantly emerging out of nationalism" because a nation requires an oppositional entity to define itself against (37). Under the lost cause, southerners defined themselves against northerners and blacks. They could reconcile with the regional opposition but not the racial one. Leigh Anne Duck contends in *The Nation's Region* that southern

racism is crucial to US nationalism because, in the same way that southerners defined themselves in opposition to northerners, Americans have
defined themselves as a liberal nation in opposition to the South. These
oppositions fluctuate in response to many factors, some of which are exacerbated by uneven development.

Considering the highly fluid historical context, *The Birth of a Nation's*
impact on nationalism is not surprising. It was released on the fiftieth anni-
versary of the surrender at Appomattox, by which time northern attitudes
toward southerners had softened even as southerners continued to cleave
to the lost cause. Meanwhile, as a result of increasing waves of immigration into northern industrial centers, including the anticipatory waves of
the Great Migration, northerners developed increasingly nativist attitudes,
and the war in Europe, especially the German submarine campaign in the
Atlantic that targeted American shipping, made Americans more bellicose
and jingoistic than usual. Griffith's film capitalized on all of these sentiments with a cinematic spectacle that appealed to patriotic, if racist, ideals.
Because the film easily fit the myth of the lost cause, white southerners were
quick to admit the film's portrayal of Reconstruction and the rise of the
Klan as fact. Many northerners were equally willing to sanction the film's
interpretation of history. In "Dixon, Griffith, and the Southern Legend,"
Russell Merritt states that "most of the audience that came out of the
Tremont theatre [in Boston] that night in 1915 [when the movie opened]
believed Griffith's story was historically true" (26). The fledgling NAACP
protested the film vehemently and numerous racially progressive leaders
boycotted the film, but, considering the film's overall impact, its opponents
were a relatively small, if vocal, minority.[20]

The Birth of a Nation prepared northerners and southerners for the
process of sectional reunification. By portraying the Civil War as a violent
misunderstanding between racial brothers, the film generated a rhetoric of
national unity and patriotism that both northerners and southerners could
employ. White southerners, drawing upon the image of a united Anglo-
Saxon army, could, when America joined the war in Europe, envision themselves fighting alongside northerners against a common enemy. The only
alteration necessary in the southern psyche required the transposition of
Germans for blacks as the threatening entity. Southerners, thus, already
had a useable model for national ideological unification on hand when
America declared war on Germany, so they only had to find a common
enemy whom they and northerners could both hate. During the war, maintaining this sense of unity through animosity contributed to the success of

the war movement, but after the war, when the common enemy had been vanquished, maintaining nationalism proved to be more problematic.

Many southerners were able to negotiate their nationalist issues in the expediency of wartime, but the issues became more difficult after the war when they attempted to reintegrate with the South. An ideological disruption occurred in the South following World War I that mimics the experience of postwar disillusionment commonly associated with the Lost Generation of European and American intellectuals with only a few notable differences. As Charles Reagan Wilson explains, "the post-war era was one of disillusionment throughout much of Western society, as the world was not made safe for democracy or the lost cause" (179). The patriotic ideals upon which nationalism hinged proved to be false, and the decline of Wilson's physical health and political influence following the defeat of the League of Nations proposal signifies the waning influence of the South on national and international affairs. White southern writers responded to postwar uncertainty and instability in ways similar to their modernist counterparts in England, France, Germany, and the North. Southern modernism shows the battle scars of World War I in that it questions both American patriotism and lost cause sectionalism, questions the value of modernity, and questions the South.

THE DARK OF MODERNITY

William Alexander Percy, scion of an aristocratic Mississippi family, responded to modernity by retrenching into conservatism. Percy abhorred mechanization and cleaved to his family's reputation, so his peculiar critical temper reflects the despondency of one who sees his world "crashing to bits," as he writes in the foreword to his memoir *Lanterns on the Levee* (xx). Percy, whose namesake grandfather had been a colonel in the Confederate army and whose great aunt had bequeathed her family's estate to Jefferson Davis, had a strong familial affiliation with the lost cause. While he may have been one of the most urbane southern intellectuals of his generation, he identifies himself as a native southerner, and he opens his memoir by intoning: "My country is the Mississippi Delta, the river country" (3). Percy's memoir describes his childhood on the Delta, his patrician family, his education, and his service during World War I. For Percy, the war represented a crucial moment, perhaps the most pivotal moment in his life. Equating the Great War with the Civil War, he writes: "The North destroyed my South; Germany destroyed my world" (156). This bit of hyperbole reveals much about Percy's ideological affiliation, and he self-consciously constructs a tradition-bound southern identity in his memoir and his war poetry.

Many critics have noticed that Percy's war experience triggered a defensive conservatism. In *Tell about the South*, Fred Hobson asserts that World War I was "the most intense experience of [Percy's] life" and that after the war he saw his "world rapidly changing and [felt] the need to capture it while he could, before it disappeared completely" (284, 294). "Percy was a serious man," Richard King writes, "whatever else he was, and attempted to live by a tradition that had been created by the Civil War and destroyed by the First World War; or, perhaps more accurately, destroyed by the Civil War and re-created by the First World War" ("Mourning and Melancholia," 248–49). King implies that Percy conceived of himself as a last gentleman, a living vestige of a version of the South that may have never existed or may have existed only in Percy family legend. James Rocks notes that "Percy's is not the fragmented sensibility we associate with the post–World War I temperament, for he holds on to the memory and the values of the past. But in his struggle to integrate the inner self and the outer world he reflects the kind of dialectical process we find in so much modern literature, particularly of the South" (815). Percy attempts in *Lanterns on the Levee* to capture a version of the South that he feared would vanish in the wake of modernity.

Percy was an upper-class aesthete. Born into a family who traced their lineage, dubiously, to the lords of Northumberland, he lived in the dark shadow of his grandfather, a family deity whose Civil War exploits formed a Percy family catechism, and of his father, Leroy Percy, who represented Mississippi in the US Senate. Heir to wealth and prestige, he studied at the University of the South, spent a year after graduation traveling in Europe, and then studied law at Harvard. When Percy returned to Greenville after his education, however, he felt himself to be an outsider, and he felt that his family regarded his chosen ambition—to be a poet—as superfluous and precious. He felt, frankly, that "in a charitable mood one might call me an idealist, but, more normally, a sissy" (*Lanterns on the Levee*, 126). This act of self-naming simultaneously places Percy inside and outside the southern planter class, making his identity as a member of the Percy family problematic in his mind. For him, service in the war offers a realistic opportunity to verify his masculinity and, thus, to establish his credentials as a Percy by defending the family's honor. Not long after Percy's return to his family home in Greenville, his father lost a bid for reelection to the Senate to James K. Vardaman, whom Percy characterized as a ruthless, venal, white-trash demagogue. Vardaman's public and principled, yet viciously racist, opposition to America's entrance into the ongoing war in Europe fueled Percy's obsession to enlist, seeing his service as an opportunity to defend his father's honor, discredit the lower-class usurper, and demonstrate his masculinity.

After his father's political defeat, Percy went to Europe, and in the summer of 1914 he climbed Mount Etna in Sicily to see the sunrise. His Italian guides told him that the last person they had taken to the top of the volcano was Austrian Archduke Franz Ferdinand, who, uncannily, was assassinated the day before Percy's climb. As Europe tumbled into war, Percy returned to Greenville, but his obsession with glory pulled him back toward Europe, and he seized the opportunity to join the war effort. He writes:

> Safely back home, I wondered why I had left [Europe]. I was miserable. Men were fighting for what I believed in and I was not fighting with them; men were suffering horribly for my ideals and I was safe at home applauding and sympathizing. I tried the usual opiate—travel—and my private opiate— writing poetry. But I was shot through with discontent and probably self-disappointment.... Physically I was not made for a soldier, nor spiritually, for that matter.... But ... for me, feeling as I did, not to have enlisted was inconsistent and shabby. (158)

Percy volunteered to join Herbert Hoover's Commission for Relief in Belgium, where he distributed supplies to civilians in German-held territories. When America entered the war, Percy left Belgium with intentions of joining the US Army. After a series of misadventures and a period of internment in Switzerland, Percy returned to Greenville once more, this time to enlist.[21]

By the time Percy returned to Greenville, the town, like the rest of the nation, buzzed with the excitement of war. Gratuitous, often meretricious, displays of American patriotism took place on every corner. "Women were knitting," he writes, "and beginning to take one lump of sugar instead of two, men within draft age were discussing which branch of service they had best enter, men above draft age were heading innumerable patriotic committees and making speeches" (169). The patriotism of this postdeclaration period greatly appealed to Percy. He appreciated the order of a society committed to a single aim, and for the moment, sectionalism was irrelevant, since he could supplant it with patriotism as an abstract, unifying ideology. With the rapid shift of allegiances in the region, modernity radiated into the South, and it converted the region's provincialism into patriotism. Note the enthusiasm in his tone when he comments that "[p]eople found themselves all of a sudden with an objective in common, with a big aim they could share, and they liked it immensely. You could sense the pleasurable stir of nobility and the bustle of idealism" (169). He joined the officers' training camp at Leon Springs, Texas, which "bulged with five thousand anxious, husky young Southerners who believed that if they failed to become officers the war would be lost and they might just as well have been born out of wedlock in New England" (173).

Percy joined the Ninety-Fourth Brigade, a unit stationed on the front lines in the Argonne Forest, where he served as aide-de-camp to General William P. Jackson. He hoped for combat, but he was disappointed at first. He wrote to his mother, "we carry our gas masks about, but it's only to give us a serious air. . . . I've resigned myself to losing all chances of glory, and what's more, of the deep human satisfaction of suffering and fighting with the men."[22] Percy's cavalier tone may have been intended to mollify his mother, but his obsession with glory has more to do with his father. As a self-described "sissy," he felt a sense of inadequacy with regard to his father, an attitude reflected in the self-effacing subtitle to his memoir, *Recollections of a Planter's Son*. Benjamin Wise argues that, although Percy is often identified as a quintessential southerner, he felt more comfortable living outside the South, where he could enjoy "intimate relationships with men," so he was combination of provincial southern aristocrat and cosmopolitan homosexual man of letters (*William Alexander Percy*, 57). The tension between these two identities complicated many other aspects of his personality. Because of his extensive travels, Percy had an easier time negotiating the complicated shift from sectionalism to nationalism, but his sexuality made the issue of masculinity difficult. Because his father had been too young to serve in the Civil War and was too old to serve in World War I, Percy believed that proving his own manhood in combat was the most efficient means of earning status within his family by earning esteem through war.[23] In some respects, rather than making Percy more American, the war made him more southern.

During the Battle of the Argonne Forest, Percy's unit captured the German stronghold at Montfaucon-d'Argonne amid fierce fighting. Notably, Percy changes his narrative position in *Lanterns on the Levee* to describe this experience in combat. Rather than describing the events as first-person recollection, the stance he uses in most of the text, he inserts a selection of letters he sent to his parents before and after the battle, using an indirect narrative technique perhaps because he felt that that would more accurately reflect his response to combat. A letter to his father dated October 4, 1918, recounts the events of his first battle experience in fairly concrete language. He discusses the events objectively and only occasionally shifts into a moralistic tone, as when he claims that an "infantryman is the most to be pitied person in the world" (204). But a letter to his mother dated November 4 reveals him returning to his obsession for glory and his preoccupation with abstraction. He describes for her the "beauty" of battle as a truck convoy braves artillery fire to supply front-line troops and the "day of glory" when his unit enters a recently liberated French village, and he compares a peasant woman serving milk to American officers to "the wife of the king who poured the mead cup for the heroes" in *Beowulf* (208–11). Percy appears to intentionally play roles to suit certain contexts, a subliminal theme that recurs throughout his autobiography. On occasions when he knows the appropriate role, he appears to be comfortable and confident, but on other occasions he seems awkward and aloof. This sense of alienation and psychological fragmentation, underscored by his lingering melancholy, demonstrates one of the fundamental tensions of modernism. Percy, who clings to southern provincialism as the bedrock of his identity, realizes that modernity has altered the social structure that he intends to inhabit, and he finds the new social structure, much like the battlefields of France, foreign and uninhabitable.

Percy omits from *Lanterns on the Levee* a letter that complicates his role playing in relation to his father—a letter that may be his most revealing piece of writing. The letter, dated October 25, 1918, two weeks before the armistice, uses a surprisingly different syntax to describe no man's land, the demolished, violent space between the trenches. Consider the following sentence:

> In the mad welter of shell holes and filth and mud emerge, like prehistoric animals from the slime of creation, the wrecks of battles lost and won— shelters of elephant iron, for in the waterlogged land trenches could not be dug; concrete pillboxes torn apart till the iron ribs shattered in gigantic explosions, tanks fantastic and terrible, that had crawled to the roadside or into a shell hole to die (you could not believe they belonged to men till you looked inside and saw the skeletons still by the wheel and the guns); planes that crashed down doubtless into the midst of hurley-burley; shells of all sizes; exploded; duds, used and unused, helmets, coats, equipment, belts of ammunition, these were down broadcast over the loblolly and in and around and across the inextricable confusion, pattern without plan, ran the barbed-wire, a crown of thorns on the mangled landscape.[24]

For this letter, Percy sheds his compulsion for abstraction and writes in a visceral, experimental style that presages the trench novels of Ernest Hemingway, John Dos Passos, and Erich Maria Remarque. This letter may be the most modernist piece of writing Percy ever produced. It portrays combat as chaotic and destructive, not as glorious or heroic, which suggests that combat may have shattered the heroic masculine identity that he attempted to construct for himself. This letter also suggests a crucial difference between the ideological abstractions of nationalism and patriotism and the violent reality of modern warfare, which Percy attempts to sublimate by omitting this letter from *Lanterns on the Levee*. Distal modernism, unlike proximal modernism, could sublimate the conditions of everyday life, but the exposure to modernity still causes disruption within the distal social structure.

Two weeks after Percy wrote this letter, the war ended. He wrote to his mother on November 11, 1918, expressing his relief and elation over the Allies' victory. Perhaps revealing his true intentions for enlisting, he tells her, "I haven't got a captaincy . . . so I'll bring home no honors," but he catches himself and says, "I didn't go into it with the hope of getting any, and rewards given by other men have never impressed me" (*Lanterns on the Levee*, 213). Yet after a flurry of postwar promotions and decorations, he returned home with an impressive set of medals. When he met his mother and father in New York after his demobilization, in addition to insignia indicating his promotion to captain, he wore a Croix de Guerre, Ordre du Corps d'Armée, and Médaille du Roi Albert. If Percy did enlist in the army in hope of achieving glory, his uniform, at least, suggests that he accomplished his goal of becoming a hypermasculine warrior.

Percy intended to become a poet after the war, in spite of his father's disapproval. In the October 4 letter to his father, he mentions that he carried a copy of *The Oxford Book of Verse* into battle. In *The Great War and Modern Memory*, Paul Fussell notes that a number of British soldiers also carried *The Oxford Book of Verse* in their knapsacks, and the poems in it served as models for many of the trench poems written during the war (159–61). Percy may have used his copy for the same purpose, as his war poems tend to employ similar metaphors and imagery to describe the experience of combat. Characteristically, Percy's poems tend to be highly formal and traditional. His war poems are among the few poems that he does not set in antiquity and that do not meditate on aestheticism. But that is not to suggest that his poems demonstrate the raw, critical edge associated with the modernist work of Wilfred Owen, Siegfried Sassoon, and Edmund Blunden.

Instead, his poems have more in common with the late Edwardian poems of Rupert Brooke and John McCrae. Like them, he plays on common tropes—such as the soldier's grave, poppy fields, and swallows over the trenches—to juxtapose images of peacefulness and order with the chaos of combat.[25] Moreover, his war poems, rather than facing the gruesomeness of modern combat, valorize abstractions and ideals such as courage and glory. For example, in the elegy "For Them That Died in Battle," he writes: "How blossomy must be the halls of Death / Against the coming of the newly dead! / How sweet with woven garlands gathered / From pastures where the pacing stars take breath!" (*Collected Poems*, 196). His flowery, romanticized Valhalla has nothing in common with the brutal experience of trench warfare.

One of Percy's war poems, "The Farm Again," describes the experience of a southern veteran of World War I who feels a sense of unique guilt for surviving the war. Much like Tennyson's "Ulysses," the poem's persona glorifies his dead comrades and pines for the clarity and intensity of combat. In the poem, Percy blends southern imagery with Flanders imagery as he imagines fallen soldiers resurrected and "marching down the road / And whistling in the rain" as "They talk of Montfauçon, / Of Thielt and Chryshautem; / My cotton rows, it seems, / Are turnip fields to them" (*Collected Poems*, 197–98). Transposing the turnip fields of Flanders in which the bodies of the fallen soldiers were planted with the cotton fields of Mississippi connects Percy's southern identity with his identity as an American soldier, bridging both the Atlantic and the Mason and Dixon line in a single verse and collapsing sectionalism with nationalism. The tone of this poem reveals his sublimated survivor's guilt and his vainglory. Watching the phantom soldiers march through the turnip fields turned cotton fields, his persona says, "It's hard to stay indoors / With soldiers marching by. / And if you've hiked and fought / It's hard until you die." The speaker in this poem clearly feels disconnected from his postwar environment. But, whereas Donald Mahon in Faulkner's *Soldiers' Pay* and many other shell-shocked veterans were unable to reintegrate because of the horror of their combat experience, Percy's persona seems to prefer the masculine camaraderie and the singleness of purpose of wartime to the comparative social disintegration of peacetime.

Despite his attempts to sublimate the experience, Percy had difficulty reintegrating after the war. As Bertram Wyatt-Brown writes in *The House of Percy*, "for once in his life, [during the war] Will Percy was not the alienated observer," but "once the war ended and the noise of victory parades and cheers died away, [his] sense of isolation quickly reappeared" (216–17). Wyatt-Brown goes on to explain that the disconnect between his wartime clarity and his peacetime confusion stems, in part, from his identification with the lost cause: "Like Sarah Dorsey [his great-aunt who had bequeathed her home to Jefferson Davis] after the Civil War, his reaction to the great, shattering conflict of his life was to claim for the prewar years a legendary grandeur, of moral principle and uprightness to contrast against the tawdry present. Thus participation in the war did not shake his faith in the old verities but made him more aware of their obsolescence or unacceptability in the face of harsh reality" (216). For Percy, nationalism and sectionalism were interchangeable abstractions to be defended, quixotically, against the relentless approach of modernity. Herein lies the crisis of the war for Percy: he longed to maintain the appearance of traditional southern masculinity even when he recognized that modernity challenged that traditional construction. Where the war served as a means to that end, he found the experience valuable, but the actual experience of combat and the instability of modernity challenged his identity.

Percy published a collection of poems about the war in his book *In April Once*, where they appear alongside poems inspired by his visit to Sicily before the war and lyrical pieces chasing aesthetic quandaries. Percy's war poems stand out, but they share in the affected tone of the entire volume. William Faulkner, then an unknown struggling poet, reviewed the collection, and he perceptively diagnosed that Percy "suffered the misfortune of having been born out of his time." The poems about medieval knights and the fixation with beauty lead Faulkner to observe that Percy "is like a little boy closing his eyes against the dark of modernity which threatens the bright simplicity and the colorful romantic pageantry of the middle ages with which his eyes are full."[26] On this point, Faulkner is correct, but for Percy the knights of the Middle Ages, the soldiers of the Old South, and the soldiers of World War I shared a common quest: to defend reified Tradition. Curiously, considering that at the time Faulkner wrote the review he, like Percy, was obsessed with combat and was composing Swinburne-esque poetry, he comments that Percy's war poems "will tend more than anything else to help [the collection] oblivionward."[27] On this point, too, Faulkner is correct, for Percy now receives little regard as a poet. Instead, literary scholars look to his memoir, *Lanterns on the Levee*, as a record of one vestigial southern aristocrat fighting vainly against the dying of the light as the dark of modernity overtakes his Delta home.

BIOGRAPHY OF A COMMON SOLDIER

Before the war, Paul Green was an unreconstructed and unreflective southerner, and he was unprepared for what he would experience during the war. The poems he wrote about his experiences catalog his ideological shift from traditional sectionalism to nationalism, and his antiwar play, *Johnny Johnson*, illustrates that the war led him to liberalism. After the war, he became famous for his Pulitzer Prize–winning play *In Abraham's Bosom* (1926), his collaboration with Richard Wright on the dramatic version of *Native Son* (1941), and his symphonic dramas, such as *The Lost Colony* (1937), and he became a public intellectual who promoted desegregation before the civil rights movement. His experience in World War I had a pivotal impact on his ideological and artistic development, which illustrates the radiation of modernity into the South.

"When I was a boy," Green writes in the introduction to his autobiography *Home to My Valley* (1970), "the gaunt shadow of the Civil War hung like a spectre out of the Apocalypse over this land" (ix). At the turn of the century, Harnett County in eastern North Carolina, Green's childhood home, was a bastion of the lost cause, a place where he learned to fear God, revere Robert E. Lee, and pick cotton.[28] During the war, he encountered proximal sites of modernity. He visited New York, traveled in England and France, studied in Paris, experienced gruesome combat, and matured into a battle-tested leader—all before he finished his sophomore year in college. While it is impossible to speculate how Green's intellectual development would have differed had he remained isolated in North Carolina during his formative years, the impact of his experience with modernity is evident in the poems he wrote while a soldier.

While in training camp in South Carolina, Green began publishing poems in one of the Charlotte newspapers. The poems he wrote during this period reflect his feelings of naïve patriotism, and they reveal curious ideological overtones. For example, in the poem "They're Dying To-night," Green celebrates the Americans who had already committed themselves to fighting for the cause of liberty in France, but the poem's closing quatrain indicates that the US Army still bears sectional distinctions: "O North! O South! How fierce you fight / For the white ideal out here to-night— / And ye shall know when the battle's done / What the living gain when the dead have won." This verse suggests that the two regions have unified for a common cause, but his description of that cause, "the white ideal," offers many puzzling interpretations. The word "white" clearly has racial implications, which, considering that most of the American soldiers were white and that most of the English, French, and German soldiers were also white, seems self-evident, yet even that presupposition proves problematic. But the term "ideal" offers no obvious referent other than the usual abstractions of wartime, such as freedom, liberty, and so on. This poem suggests that Green still sees the United States as a sectionally divided nation, and he grapples with issues that were complicated for white southerners, namely region, race, and patriotism.[29]

After a terrible Atlantic crossing on the converted cattle ship *Talthybius*, during which Green wished that "a submarine would come and blow us all to hell," Green's unit arrived for final orientation in England before taking their posts in combat. His unit, the 105th Engineers, was posted along the front line near Ypres, which had been the site of fierce combat, leaving the landscape devastated. He wrote to his sister, "the poor tired earth has drunk enough blood within the last four years to be offensive in the sight of God."[30] Green spent much of his time under the blood-drunk soil of the battlefield, digging tunnels beneath no man's land with his unit. His work was incredibly dangerous, but he performed bravely. Within a few weeks he was promoted to sergeant major, and a few weeks later, as officers for his unit became increasingly scarce, he was brevetted second lieutenant and assigned to a field training program that allowed him to remain with his unit while training to be an officer.

Even as he moved through the ranks, Green identified with the common soldiers, including the soldiers in the opposing trenches. Green biographer John Herbert Roper explains that Green viewed the war as a class conflict in which the working classes of both sides were manipulated by the aristocracy into fighting to the death. He focused his anger on the "silver-spurred Prussian officers" who forced the "poor German boys" into the trenches at gunpoint.[31] Roper explains that Green saw parallels between Germany and the South, and he recognized the rigid, traditional social structure as a source of antagonism, so "he wanted nothing less than the defeat of the landed elites everywhere." According to Roper, "[t]he prospect that this war would herald the liberation of the lower classes of eastern Carolina and western Flanders, of the Mississippi Delta and the Slovakian Danube . . . literally gave Paul the rationale to fight" (*Paul Green's War Songs*, 136). He began to identify himself with the oppressed classes during the war, and he resolved to advocate on their behalf, which he would do for the remainder of his career as an artist and public intellectual. He saw the social hierarchy of his native South reflected in the militaristic hierarchy, which led him to develop a social vision expansive enough to allow for the possibility of social plurality.

His racial liberalism, however, developed more slowly. Like most white southerners, Green believed in white supremacy, but his racial views began to change during the war. On one occasion during training in South Carolina, several other soldiers made a game of flinging a young black boy into the air and catching him in a blanket, which went on until the boy was injured. Green wrote in his diary that he did not approve of the game, and he shunned some of the soldiers who played, but he said nothing outright about the incident (Roper, *Paul Green: Playwright*, 33). While in Europe, his attitudes continued to evolve. He admired the contributions of African American and African soldiers, who he believed fought as bravely as any white soldiers, but he had trouble with the prospect of interracial relationships that emerged as a consequence of the war. In his diary, Green described his consternation over the prospect that black American soldiers were becoming involved with white French women. "Many of the negroes are marrying French girls," he writes; "in some places the negroes represented themselves as the real Americans."[32] Eventually, Green would overcome his objection to racially mixed relationships; "by the bleak midwinter of 1919," Roper comments, "he was taking a stand on integration and miscegenation utterly different from other southern reformists" (*Paul Green's War Songs*, 42). Roper directly credits Green's exposure to black soldiers as the cause of his changing racial attitudes.

After the armistice, Green was stationed as a clerk in Paris. He took the sinecure position because it allowed him to experience the city. He wrote to his sister ecstatically, telling her that he had been reading new literature, seeing the city's museums, and meeting intellectuals. He read *The New Poetry* (1917), a collection of modernist verse edited by Harriet Monroe, which left him somewhat conflicted about modern literature. He wrote: "Although I like its freshness, I fear there is little worth in it. All this swarm of *Verslibrists*, this motley crowd of discordant street musicians, are poor ragged illegitimate children of the powerful Walt Whitman—nothing else. Still, I enjoy reading these verses; their jaggedness makes them hang in your mind."[33] In spite of his skepticism, he began incorporating their techniques into his poems about the city and absorbing proximal modernity.

While in Paris, Green also observed the dehumanizing effects of modernity: filth, degradation, and poverty. By this time, his exposure to new ideas and his innate sympathy had merged to produce the liberalism that would be his intellectual trademark, and his liberalism included an element of anti-modernism. Several poems he wrote while in Paris describe the inhumane conditions some Parisians endured, but these poems may be most interesting for their class awareness. In the poem "The Other Night I Saw a Little Ragged Girl in a First Class Metro Car," for example, he emphasizes the distinctions between social classes in a common setting, as a self-conscious girl tries to hide "her sabots and her ragged dress" from the judgmental eyes of "the jeweled women there / and officers in gold and braid" (Roper, *Paul Green's War Songs*, 71). In another poem he wrote while in Paris, provocatively titled "The Making of a Bolshevist," he describes the experience of a laborer, Nicolai, who is exploited and exhausted and "made to be a cog of the machine" until "his weary soul rebelled" (74–75). When a stranger, a communist agitator, whispers to Nicolai that "the trouble lay / With those who rule," he joins an apparent uprising, gets arrested, and ultimately is sentenced to death. Implicitly, Nicolai as a worker is an impotent agent who has been manipulated by both the bourgeoisie and the proletariat. Green's perception of urbanization in Paris coheres with Ernest Gellner's observation that the transition from an agrarian society to an industrial society requires a "turbulent readjustment" (Gellner, 40).

The crisis of modernity left Green feeling alienated and disaffected, and he developed an understanding of class structure that evolved into sympathy for African Americans in the South. He became interested in drama as a vehicle for social change and as a means for transforming his liberal attitudes into works of aesthetic and social art. In the 1920s, he committed himself to writing socially conscious plays for the New York stage. After a string of successful productions, he joined the Group Theatre.[34] For his second play with the Group, he collaborated with Kurt Weill, a composer recently exiled from Nazi Germany, to produce the antiwar play *Johnny Johnson*. Their joint production blended drama with music in a way that Green would later develop into symphonic drama, the mode of production for which he is most well known. *Johnny Johnson*, first produced in 1936, however, is a more typical proscenium production with an ideologically charged plot about an attempted mutiny on the front lines. While the play's commentary on the value of war and its overt religious and psychological symbolism are overly didactic, the play offers a fascinating insight into the effect of World War I on white, male southern ideology.

In the opening scene of the play, Green caricatures the South's ideological vacillation. The play opens in a small town in the South on a morning in 1917 where people have gathered to dedicate a monument to peace. As the town's mayor gives a pompous speech praising peace, a newsboy gives the mayor an announcement of Wilson's declaration of war on Germany, and instantly the community's aspect changes from peaceful to warlike, mimicking the region's whipsaw shift from sectionalism to patriotism. Yet, even as the community navigates the challenges of nationalism, it idolizes the lost cause.

Grandpa Joe, whom the scene notes describe as "an old man with a scraggly graying moustache dressed in a shrunk-up faded blue-and-gray uniform of 1865 on the breast of which is pinned a marksman's badge and . . . hold[ing] a bloodthirsty looking saber in his hand," acts as a living memory of the Civil War (*Johnny Johnson*, 4). As the mayor speaks of peace, Grandpa Joe rants about fighting at Chickamauga, interjecting sectionalism into a scene about nationalism. Only Johnny Johnson, the stone carver who crafted the monument to peace the town has gathered to dedicate, recognizes the town's ideological capriciousness and remains committed to pacifism after the declaration of war. Yet even Johnny's allegiance proves fungible when his sweetheart insinuates that refusing to enlist would be unmanly.

The army in the play is a microcosm of patriotic American nationalism. As his troop ship passes the Statue of Liberty, Johnny delivers a soliloquy in which he swears that he will not see the statue again until he has "helped to bring back peace and win this war which ends all wars" (57). His platoon includes a diverse cross section of American society. Among his comrades are Private Svenson, "a long horse-faced Swede" from Iowa; Private Goldberger, "a little squabby Jew"[35]; Private Kearns, "a huge square shouldered fellow about twenty years old, chewing tobacco"; Private O'Day "a short red-faced Irishman" from Boston; Private Harwood, "sandy-haired and blue-eyed, about twenty-one" from Texas; and an English sergeant (64–66). The men in the unit squabble among themselves, but Johnny, the only obvious southerner in the group, has a mollifying effect on them. He seems to be beyond regional or ethnic identifiers, and rather than representing the southern soldiers, Green means for him to represent the American soldier, as he explains in a letter. He writes that "there were several thousand Johnny Johnsons in the first world war army. In fact, according to the records, there were over three thousand of them in the American Expeditionary Forces alone. . . . Johnny represents the common man."[36] This platoon is a zone of interregional contact where the component parts of the nation amalgamate, and in an interesting maneuver that echoes Randolph Bourne's comments about American identity, Green depicts the southerner as the typical American, suggesting that the war obliterates sectionalism.

Johnny's exploits on the battlefield follow a convoluted modernist plot that combines elements of absurdity, religious mythology, political conspiracy, and Freudian psychoanalytic gibberish. He volunteers for a mission to find a German sniper hidden in a huge wooden statue of Jesus. Instead of killing the sniper, Johnny befriends him, and together they conspire to incite a bilateral mutiny. Johnny later infiltrates a meeting of the assembled

Allied High Command and uses a tank of laughing gas to force them to sign an order ending the war. After causing a momentary cease-fire, he is arrested and sent to a psychiatric hospital, where he is incarcerated for several years. The scenes that take place in the psychiatric hospital may be the most interesting in the play. The inmates mimic a meeting of Congress in which they debate the ratification of a treaty to form the League of World Republics, which they pass unanimously. Obviously commenting on the failure of the supposedly sane US Congress to support the creation of the League of Nations, this scene suggests that nationalism is an irrational aspect of modernity.

Green believed that activism, both artistic and political, could make a difference in public policy. One of his last war poems reveals that he felt the war to be a terrible loss but that he hoped that the lesson of the war would be heeded, which amplifies the play's ending. While working as a clerk in Paris, he wrote the poem "War Book" in the form of an accounting ledger. In the losses column, he listed "2.5 million killed / 26,000 factories destroyed / Thousands of miles of rich farming lands rendered unfertile / Thousands of broken hearts / Thousands of ruined homes / Hundreds of wrecked villages and cities." In the visibly shorter gains column, he listed "Alsace-Lorraine / Gain of self-confidence." He succinctly tallies the balance as "Unspeakable losses" (Roper, *Paul Green's War Songs*, 85). A rational, sympathetic person could not arrive at a different conclusion about the experience of the war. Yet Green, like his idol Woodrow Wilson, continued to believe that some value could come from the experience.[37] Wilson, in the wake of the war, hoped to use the advent of nationalism to promote peace through the League of Nations, and Green's liberal antimodern depictions of the war suggest that nationalism must be overcome for people to make social progress.

The Southern Soldier in the Modern World

Donald Davidson enlisted in the army as soon as America entered the war.[38] During the war, he experienced active combat, which he found profoundly affecting, and after returning to the United States he self-consciously identified with the generations of his southern forefathers who had fought Indians, Yankees, and adversity to settle his beloved Tennessee homeland. His war experience led him to question industrialism and the postwar modernization of the South. Lewis Simpson observes that "in 1917 Davidson was far from thinking about the necessity of another Southern secession, a spiritual and literary one, but in a few years he would be close to doing so. He would come to interpret his First World War experience as a revelation of the Truth of his homeland, or the America that is the South" (foreword to *The Literary Correspondence*, vii).

While in officers' training camp at Fort Oglethorpe, Georgia, Davidson had an unsettling encounter with nationalism. In the shadow of the Chickamauga battlefield, where the creeks ran red with rebel blood during the Civil War, he and the rest of the cadets, many of whom were native southerners, heard a speech by General John T. Wilder, who had commanded Union troops against the Confederate soldiers under General Braxton Bragg on that same battlefield. "With great pride the old General told of his part in that other war," Davidson writes. "He dwelt long and, it seemed to me, with vicious exultation upon the fact that his mounted infantry were armed with Sharps repeating rifles, and therefore did bloody execution upon the Johnny Rebs opposite him, who had only single shooters" (*Southern Writers*, 33). Davidson recognizes the painful irony that he had enlisted with the same army that had once slaughtered his kinsmen and countrymen. When General Wilder reached his climax—exclaiming that the doughboys should massacre the Germans with equal zeal—Davidson and many of his comrades sat in awkward silence. Wilder's speech left him facing a serious crisis of identity:

> The Blue and the Gray had merged in undistinguished khaki, and we were going to cross the Atlantic Ocean in the First World War of our century to fight an alleged enemy for reasons that we had to take on faith and actually did not in the least understand. As young southerners from South Carolina, Georgia, Tennessee we were inwardly disturbed at the crude equation set up by an old Union General. How could Lee, Stonewall Jackson, Jefferson Davis, or even Braxton Bragg be equated, as enemies to be slaughtered, with Kaiser Wilhelm, Hindenburg, and *Les Boches*? (*Southern Writers*, 34)

Thinking of himself as an enemy forced him to realize, perhaps for the first time, that he stood outside the mainstream of early twentieth-century American society, that he did not share in the broadly defined American dream, and that he greatly valued the traditions and history of the South. Unlike Percy and Green, the war made Davidson more self-consciously southern.

After the war, he found himself utterly disillusioned with America, and he vilified the northern industrial economic complex that invaded the

South after the armistice, which he saw as a clear and present threat to the southern way of life. Extending the lesson he learned at Chickamauga, he wrote: "We could hardly anticipate that the identical social and historical forces that in 1917 could send us to a foreign battle could also operate in civil life in the United States and actually demand that the South put General Wilder's equation into effect—in politics, in economics, in literature, in religion" (*Southern Writers*, 34). Like the doomed Confederates firing antiquated muskets at the federals, he saw the South as outgunned by the North's relentless industrial efficiency and the coming onslaught of modernity. He had much more difficulty than Green and Percy navigating the shift from sectionalism to nationalism, and after the war he reverted to an atavistic antimodern form of agrarianism. This reaction, however, is just as consistent with distal modernism as the responses of Percy and Green. Distal modernism tends to be reactionary and to align with ruralism, so Green's response, which shows influences of Marxism, is more anomalous than Davidson's reaction.

For Davidson, who had spent his entire life until this time in central Tennessee, the war was a major disruption. His unit saw fierce action at Moranville, including heavy losses from German shelling that lasted up to the signing of the armistice.[39] He describes his personal experience in the war as "novel, indeed astounding." He explains, "I had never traveled before; now I traveled: to Columbia, S.C., an old and sleepy town, suddenly beset by hordes of new officers, new soldiers. . . . Traveled—yes, to New York (my first sight), Long Island, across the Atlantic on the Cunarder *Aquitania*, across England, into France, and all that!"[40] Interregional contact made him more self-aware of the South, and traveling through New York and Europe exposed him to proximal modernity.

Davidson's war experience inspired "The Faring," a section of the long poem *The Tall Men*. Although he never wrote autobiographical narrative about his experience as a soldier, a sense of urgency rooted in personal trauma in his poetry and his politics discloses his internalized attitudes toward conflict. Davidson—fresh from college, thousands of miles from home, separated from his new wife and the infant daughter he had never seen, responsible for the lives of a company of men, and surrounded by senseless carnage and brutality—must have felt overwhelming psychological pressure. One of his closest friends from the army, a fellow officer named S. Toof Brown, says: "It was hard to realize then the thoughts which must have been constantly in Don's mind and the agony he must have suffered, particularly when at the front. Naturally, he spoke of [his wife and infant daughter] often, but his anxiety neither affected the performance of the job at hand nor did it reflect in his disposition."[41]

Davidson's poems about the war take a reactionary tone toward the progress of modernity in the South. He wrote to his publisher in 1927 to explain that, in *The Tall Men*, he intended to place "considerable emphasis on the heroic and the romantic, in contrast to the disillusionment which afflicts us in the chaotic modern world. The idea is to arrive at some basis for an attitude of acceptance, which, while resting on the past, would not wholly reject the present—a mood of positiveness rather than the gesture of defeat to be found, say, in *The Waste Land*."[42] Davidson makes a distinction between his version of modernism and Eliot's, and he characterizes distal modernism as combining elements of the past and the present. Although he intends to strike a positive tone, his preoccupation with clinging to traditional values belies his distaste for imminent change.[43] Louis Rubin suggests that this preoccupation had a negative impact on his poetic career:

> Davidson largely ceased to use the form of poetry as a vehicle for self-examination and began using it to celebrate a predetermined intellectual and social position, with the result that though his advocacy and evocation of that position was often eloquent indeed, his language thereafter lacked the element of tension between self and society, public and private identity, tradition and modern circumstance, that made for the creative resolution of poetry such as Tate's and Ransom's. (*The Wary Fugitives*, 162)

In the case of *The Tall Men* and much of his later social criticism, Davidson explores the tension between the South and modernity, but he ceases to explore his own relationship with society. He becomes, in effect, an imaginative ideologue, too involved in his own opinions to recognize change in his midst.

Although written years before *I'll Take My Stand*, *The Tall Men* previews the Agrarian agenda, the crux of Davidson's reactionary social ideology. In the opening lines of the poem, he idealizes the pioneers who will become his cultural standard: "It was a hunter's tale that rolled like wind / Across the mountains once, and the tall men came / Whose words were bullets. They, by the Tennessee waters, / Talked with their rifles bluntly and sang to the hills / With a whet of axes" (4). He contrasts these rugged individuals with his own generation, which has become weak and corrupt: "Something (call it civilization) crept / Across the mountains once, and left me here / Flung up from sleep against the breakfast table / Like numb and helpless driftwood. Through the trees / Where summer morning grows with a threat of drouth [*sic*] / I look back on the centuries (not quite two), / Rustling the morning paper and watching the clock" (5). He suggests that modernity has supplanted the pioneer spirit of the tall men, and he sees his own generation as pivotal, wavering between the values of his fathers and the values of the carpetbaggers. He identifies the corrupting agent as northern industrialism, and he describes the tension between values as a kind of warfare:

> Some sort of battle, would you call it, where
> Words pass for bullets, dabbed in a scribble of ink?
> Now here the hero sprawls while a little man
> Purrs in a patent tone of voice and a sleek
> Copyrighted smile. He has a Northern way
> Of clipping his words, and with an inevitable curve
> Of an arm in a business suit reveals cigars
> In the tribal code. (6–7)

This verse describes the modern conflict between traditional southern values and homogenized modern values. Nationalism, in Davidson's view, has the potential to eradicate southern identity. The enemy in his poem is not Germany, but modernity.

Davidson describes the clash of values in the modern age as the final battleground of the Civil War. The second section of *The Tall Men*, "The Sod of Battle-Fields," articulates the lost cause and glorifies the "men in gray," romanticizing the few old men who remember the war as "exultations made / Visible in the flesh that woke their banners" (19). He recalls the stories of Confederate heroes and the men of his own family who worshiped Lee, Jackson, and Longstreet, who told him of Fredericksburg, Chancellorsville, and Shiloh. He contrasts the Confederate heroes with base, cowardly Yankees who terrorize defenseless women and children under cover of night. In one passage, he describes eight drunk Yankee soldiers breaking into a farmhouse and menacing the family with their bayonets; a "little girl in a flannel nightgown" says, "'Shucks, I'm not afraid / Of you . . . You're nothing but a damn Yankee'" (21). He also celebrates the folk myths of extraordinary heroism by southern soldiers, such as the story of Jim Ezell, "a Forrest scout / And a Chapel Hill boy," who licked at least ten and maybe as many as fifty Yankee soldiers single-handed (22). Compared to these lost cause legends of cunning, courage, and conviction in his imagination, he views the modern generation with contempt.

Davidson chastises his own generation for growing facile and weak. In a passage echoing the tone of Eliot's "The Hollow Men," he says:

> The modern brain, guarded not only by bone,
> Afferent nerves, withering hair, and skin,
> Requires the aid of a mystical apparatus
> (Weights, levers, motor, steel rods, black boy)
> And pyramiding dollars nicely invested
> To float boredom up to the cool fifth floor
> And a tiled room. (28)

Here he describes the most insidious enemy the South has faced, the faceless specter of modernity. Louis Rubin explains Davidson's attitude toward the modern age as an assault on values: "The enemy the Tennesseans face now is not a hostile army, but the age of the machine, the pressure of materialistic industrial society which would strip the land of its beauty, create a wasteland of asphalt and concrete and steel, and rob the people of the old heritage of individuality and resourcefulness" (*The Wary Fugitives*, 166). Davidson imagines an imminent age when the sons of proud men allow themselves to grow weak. Their muscles atrophy because machines perform labor, and their souls turn to the worship of material items. He associates this vision specifically with urbanization, as more and more people were leaving their rural homes for the city, and he contrasts his vision of the corrupt modern city with a pastoral scene of agrarian beauty:

> Over the Southern fields green corn is waving,
> Husky and broad of blade. The ranks of corn
> Push from the stable earth. The pollen falls,
> A yellow life from shaken tassels, piercing
> The seed below. Pollen falls in my heart,
> A dust of song that sprinkles fruitfulness,
> Mellowing like the corn in Southern fields. (30)

In this time of domestic crisis, with pioneer virtues dissipating and the nation moving toward a corrupt modern age, a foreign event alters, at least briefly, the course of events.

Davidson portrays World War I as a crisis of modernity, and he dramatizes his own war experience in the persona of McCrory, a soldier from Tennessee. McCrory wears the wildcat insignia, for Davidson's unit, the

Eighty-First "Wildcat" Division: "A wildcat snarling, / Emblem of western mountains where tall men strode / Once with long rifles" (47). He imagines himself, carrying a rifle with fixed bayonet, as a tall soldier striding bravely into battle. He describes his unit's arrival at the front in grandiose terms. As his unit leaves the troop train in France, he says:

> Now they are going
> Somewhere in France on roads where Roman eagles
> Slanted to meet the Nervii or where
> Napoleon, flushed with greetings, galloped from Elba
> A hundred years before. The husky guns
> Rumbled at twilight from the Western Front.
> The slow column poured like moving bronze
> And something (call it civilization) struck
> In the latest battle of nations, somewhere in France. (49)

Davidson compares McCrory's experience to the campaigns of the great armies of history, and his use of the word *civilization* has significant portent. In this case, when he associates civilization with war, the word appears to have a positive connotation, but earlier, when he associates civilization with commerce, the word has a negative connotation. For Davidson, war reaffirms the virtues of a civilization—courage, honor, glory—and he castigates those at home dozing by the fire who will grow to hold their manhood cheap. Civilization and nationalism are thus contingent on their relationship to Davidson's notions of masculinity.

These ideas become more complicated after a German attack. In the middle of the night an artillery barrage begins, and McCrory orders his men down into the trench while he orders a responding barrage. During a lull between barrages, he looks over the parapet and "peered / While flares made blinding day along the front, / And there they were, the gray-green men, a line / Of forward wrenching shapes, careering, hurling / Lightnings and death about his head" (55). At the sight of the enemy advancing across no man's land, McCrory blows his whistle to signal his men to fire on the Germans. At length, the tall men repel the Germans, and as dawn breaks over the battlefield, he finds that he has been superficially wounded in the arm and that dead Germans and dead Americans litter the trenches. A tone of disillusionment enters into Davidson's poem, and he questions his reason for participating in the war: "I tell you, I have come a long way, I have come / From a world that was into a world that is, / Bringing the strongest part of all that I was / Into the moment when all strong things fade / Into a fog of questions" (56). He feels conflicted about the war in part because he realizes that this war does not directly affect him, which indicates that his American nationalism is relatively weak. He fights not to defend himself or his home or even his country but to defend a nation an ocean away from his home for purely political reasons. Under these circumstances, he begins to search for answers—"Ask the fog / For comfort? Ask for death! Ask fire to give / Water for parched tongues" (57).

When the armistice comes in Davidson's poem, no one at the front celebrates the victory. McCrory's soldiers—exhausted, cold, and hungry—say "Thank God, we'll build a fire at last," ask "When do we eat," and collapse into sleep (57). At the end of the war, he shares a different idea of heroism:

> Heroes are muddy creatures, a little pale
> Under two days' beard with gritty mouths that mumble
> Oaths like the Ancient Pistol; or opening cans
> Of messy beef with brittle bayonets;
> Or winding spiral leggings with eyes alert
> For cockle-burrs. (58)

This description of exhausted, dirty men contrasts starkly with his previous descriptions of larger-than-life characters. But, for him, it is not the men who have changed. They are still heroic, but the circumstances of heroism have changed. In this war men do not stand eye to eye and exchange blows. Instead, they wallow in mud while machines of deadly destruction commit cold, brutal acts of wholesale slaughter. Modern mechanization ended the era of the tall men, according to Davidson. Years after the war, he would explain his disillusionment with the war:

> It was a bad war, of course; but what made it extremely bad was the totally
> asinine way it was managed by most higher-ups concerned, on both sides.
> The soldiers of the line were splendid, always. But the generalship was
> ineffably stupid; how can we ever explain such holocausts as the battle of
> the Somme or the German attack on Verdun, except as originating in the
> brains of military dotards.... The World War was the first war in history to
> be thoroughly mechanized, on a fully modern, presumably "efficient" basis.
> It was also the first war in all history to produce no great generals, no great
> leaders, and perhaps not a single piece of first-class strategy. In other words,
> the triumph of the machine! (The Spyglass, 193)

For the rest of his life, Davidson would associate mechanization with the incipient corruption of modern civilization.

The war leaves Davidson's persona disillusioned and traumatized. He has nightmares about ghastly images of carnage, and he feels isolated, alone, and alienated. Davidson reflects his persona's alienation by distancing him from the poetic narrative and fracturing the form into brief speeches of disembodied voices, obviously drawing from *The Waste Land*. As an alternative to modernist alienation, he searches for concrete values in the traditions of his forefathers. He imagines the pagan warriors, the devout puritans, the natural scientists, and the bloodthirsty Vikings of the past who worshiped manly gods, and he reconsiders his relationship with the Judeo-Christian god. He finds religion less than satisfactory, and he finds the materialism of his generation contemptible, so he returns to the land that spawned the tall men for immutable, tangible values. In the poem's ultimate stanza, he says, "Remember the rifles / Talking men's talk into the Tennessee darkness / And the long-haired hunters watching the Tennessee hills / In the land of big rivers for something" (117). His "something" carries tremendous import. It means, in one sense, the hunter's quarry, and, in another sense, the poet's answers to the contradictions of the modern world. Davidson spent much of his career searching for something that he feared was vanishing.

Davidson could not conceive of the South as a modern space consistent with the urban, industrial spaces he encountered in the North and Europe during the war. He saw modernity and its attendant aspects of urbanization and industrialization as destructive and dehumanizing, partly because he associated them directly with the war. He had serious problems with the shift from sectionalism to nationalism, and his sense of traditional southern identity was especially strong and defensive. The irony is that Davidson wrote self-consciously modernist literature about his discontent with modernity, and the same is largely true of Percy and Green. For white, male southern writers who served in the war, the crisis of the conflict was not limited to combat. Reconfiguring their nationalist identity led them to make other major ideological shifts: Percy lapsed into conservative traditionalism, Green became a liberal antimodernist, and Davidson committed to reactionary agrarianism. Their personal responses differed, but they were responses to the same stimulus and were part of a much broader radiation of distal modernism.

These three writers moved through a specific sequence of ideological positions as a result of the war. Before the war, they identified ideologically as southerners aligned with the lost cause. When the war started, they shifted expeditiously to a naïve version of American patriotism, affiliating themselves with the United States and enlisting in the war effort. During the war, their ideological identifications became more complicated as they absorbed the experiences of interregional contact, proximal modernity, and combat. After the war, they produced texts that reflected their more complicated ideological perspectives in which they associated the war with modernity, critiqued the inevitability of modernity in the South, and attempted to integrate their war experience with their conception of the South. Their work incorporated the same issues of mechanization and nationalism that preoccupied European modernists into a southern con-text, far removed from the actual sites of combat and industrialization.[44] In *Grounded Globalism*, James Peacock offers a model of how that process of nationalist reintegration works as it moves from oppositional regional identity to a sense of a regional identity within a global context. For these white southern writers, the crisis of World War I, the first global modern war, led to a more critical awareness of sectionalism within a much broader social context, the nervous apprehension of the white southern writer in the modern world.

3

THE ARMY OF THE DISILLUSIONED

Black Southerners, World War I, and Civil Rights

When Wilbur Little, a African American soldier, returned to Blakely, Georgia, from service in World War I, a group of white men met him at the train station and forced him to strip off his uniform. A few days later, he defied their warning not to wear the uniform again in public, and a mob lynched him (Dray, 248). His lynching and the lynching of fifteen other African American veterans returning from the war sent the message to all African American soldiers returning from the war that their sacrifices for the cause of liberty in Europe would not lead to racial equality in America.

The war signaled the beginning of a new period in the struggle for black citizenship. By the end of the war, most white southerners realized that their peculiar nationalist duality made them simultaneously southern and American. But for black southerners, the war brought into conflict three competing identity markers—race, region, and nation—that operated in a complex, oppositional relationship. A black person born in the South was legally a citizen of the United States and a resident of the South, but blackness had the effect of negating a black person's claims to citizenship making that person both not American and not southern. Black southerners had a precarious claim to nationality of any sort, at least until the war began. Michelle Stephens comments in *Black Empire* that "blackness, as much as any other racialized consciousness during this period, was an imaginary burdened by the national" (5). By wearing the uniform of the US Army, black southerners who served in the military made a claim to citizenship, even if white southerners refused to recognize that claim.

The fragmentation of American nationalism along ethnic lines during the war aggravated the nation's racial division. Regardless of their national origin, white Americans could reasonably expect full rights of American citizenship, but black Americans could not. The war, meanwhile, raised the possibility of a black identity that transcended nationality, which Paul Gilroy describes in *The Black Atlantic* as a counterculture of modernity. Jennifer James agues in *A Freedom Bought with Blood* that black ambitions for citizenship were aroused every time America went to war, but unlike the Civil War and America's wars of imperialism in Mexico and Cuba, World War I pitted white ethnic groups against each other, so racial concerns were not at the forefront of the conflict. In this era of fragmentary American nationalism, race united white Americans from North to South into a hegemony that subordinated black Americans, denying their claim to American national identity.[1]

According to the 1910 census, more than 90 percent of black Americans lived in the South, where they lived as second-class citizens subject to white supremacy, but World War I had a massive impact on America's racial demographics. During the war, nearly one million southern blacks moved to major industrial centers in the North and the West. This enormous demographic shift, the early phase of the Great Migration, altered the traditional nature of agricultural labor in the South and resulted in new economic opportunities in manufacturing and services for blacks who moved outside the region. But the Great Migration also transplanted southern racial attitudes and practices to the North and the West, thus establishing a transregional racial hierarchy. Also, thousands of black soldiers served in the military during the war, an experience that, in spite of efforts by the War Department and most southern whites, gave African Americans a sense of empowerment. African American soldiers who served in France experienced comparative racial equality overseas, but they were subjected to segregation when they returned to America. After the war, black intellectuals and artists congregated in northern cities, where they openly criticized the treatment of African Americans in the South.

These changes led to a new, more confrontational period in the movement for civil rights—the New Negro movement—and a new form of black modernist literary production—the Harlem Renaissance. George Hutchinson explains in *The Harlem Renaissance in Black and White* that the war and nationalism directly contributed to the emergence of African American modernism:

> [T]he African American modernists provided the most probing questions about and the most challenging articulations of American cultural nationalism we have prior to Ellison, beginning with W. E. B. Du Bois's *The Souls of Black Folk*. Their repeated references to "unknown soldiers" who turned

out to be black, to "brotherhood" of black and white recognized only in the face of death on European battlefields, to the betrayal of kin by white men with "mulatto" sons, and to lynching not only as a crime but as a peculiarly American crime, all reflect the extent to which the Harlem Renaissance (and not just in its canonical texts) was caught up in a struggle over the meaning and possession of "America." (15)

Hutchinson is correct that the war led to a change in African American writers' perspectives, but he overlooks the mechanism that activated this change.[2] During the war, an enormous number of African Americans from the South were exposed to proximal sites of modernity in the shipyards of California, the factories of Detroit, the streets of New York, and the military encampments of France. For many of these African Americans, contact with modernity brought them a greater relative degree of equality than they experienced in the South, in spite of rampant discrimination in factory jobs, housing markets, and the military. The war, moreover, demonstrated that freedom and liberty were causes worth fighting for. After the war, black writers adopted a more confrontational tone toward the distal South, and this confrontational position is the fundamental characteristic of postwar African American modernism.[3]

African American writers portrayed the sacrifice of black soldiers in combat and the persecution of black veterans in the South to make a literary case for civil rights. The modernist trope of the black veteran performs several important functions. It expresses the disillusionment of postwar blackness, where the imaginary boundaries of region and nation were leveled to reveal a globalized racial inequality that normalized southern segregation on a transatlantic scale. It represents the localized efforts of black people to disrupt racial inequality through both individual and collective means. It signifies black writers' cultural campaign of racial resistance, using literary representations of disillusioned, dehumanized soldiers to make a case for civil rights. Novels about black southerners in World War I juxtapose the experience of soldiers in the proximal zones of modernity, where progressive social values create relatively egalitarian social structures, with the distal South, where segregation demeans black veterans. This chapter will explain the sociopolitical issues facing African Americans during World War I and then describe how three African American novelists—Victor Daly, Walter White, and Claude McKay—represented black soldiers in Europe and in the South. For them, writing was combat.

WE RETURN FIGHTING

To paraphrase W. E. B. Du Bois, the problem of America's involvement in World War I was, in many ways, the problem of the color line. As the war in Europe escalated in 1915, America's entrance into the war became apparent. While nationalist patriotic rhetoric intensified in America, a key transfer of social power took place within the African American community. Booker T. Washington, whose philosophy of accommodationism normalized American race relations at the turn of the century, died, making way for a number of more militant voices in the discourse on civil rights. Marcus Garvey, leader of the United Negro Improvement Association; Robert Abbott, editor of the Chicago *Defender*; and James Weldon Johnson, editor of the New York *Age*, were key figures in the discussion, but Du Bois, editor of the NAACP-sponsored magazine the *Crisis* and a frequent antagonist of Washington's ideology, emerged as the most visible spokesman for African Americans. The generational shift in power also marked a geographic shift in locus of power, from Tuskegee in the rural South to New York in the urban North. Du Bois regarded the coming war as a moment of opportunity for blacks to achieve social equality, and in 1917 he wrote an editorial for the *Crisis*, "Awake America," encouraging blacks to support America's entry into the war on the condition that civil rights be granted, including the end of lynching, the abolition of Jim Crow laws, the end of racial disfranchisement, and an integrated military (379).

To the War Department, however, this was a difficult position. While black southerners were important to the war effort, concessions that would alienate white southerners would be politically impossible. The prospect of blacks in the military inherently agitated many racists in the South, including many at the highest levels of government. Senator James Vardaman of Mississippi, for example, declaimed: "Universal military service means that millions of negroes will be armed. I know of no greater menace to the South than this."[4] Moreover, for many white southerners, the idea of black soldiers killing white people, even Germans, roused anxieties of a massive racial revolution. In fact, as Theodore Kornweibel explains in *"Investigate Everything": Federal Efforts to Compel Black Loyalty during World War I*, many whites feared that blacks would use the war as an opportunity to sabotage the country in collusion with German spies, which prompted the government to begin monitoring various black organizations, including the NAACP.[5] Most of Du Bois's demands, including an integrated military, would not be met.

But white policy makers also realized that the success of the war effort depended on black labor. The war in Europe staunched the flow of new immigrants into the Northeast, depleting the labor market at the same time that able-bodied young men were registering for the draft. Industrialists, seeking the nearest source of cheap labor, sent recruiting agents into the South, promising employment and good wages in northern cities. The lure proved strong, and waves of black southerners joined the Great Migration to the North.[6] The army also sought to tap this source of essential labor. Jennifer Keene explains in *Doughboys, the Great War, and the Remaking of America* that the War Department faced a difficult dilemma in maintaining the color line. Black labor could relieve many white soldiers for combat duty, but the presence of blacks in some camps led white soldiers to rebel, and Keene documents instances in Arkansas, South Carolina, New Jersey, and France of white soldiers intimidating black soldiers (83–104). To mitigate these types of incidents, army officials determined that blacks should be drafted into the army in equal proportion to whites but that they should not be trained for combat. A memo by Colonel E. D. Anderson, the recruiting officer responsible for black draftees, stated that the vast majority of black draftees were unfit for combat duty. He argued that putting a large number of black soldiers in combat would weaken the front line and give the Germans an advantage, so he recommended that the bulk of black draftees be assigned to labor battalions. Since laborers required virtually no training, he reasoned, black soldiers could be usefully occupied immediately, and white recruits could be freed to concentrate on their training. In his opinion, labor battalions, while an obvious benefit to the American war effort, would also paternalistically benefit the black soldiers: "This will be the first time in their lives that 9 out of 10 negroes ever had any discipline, instruction, or medical treatment, or lived in sanitary conditions and they should improve greatly."[7] Anderson's position became official War Department policy on the color line in the US military, which would, the government expected, have no impact on advancing civil rights. Instead, military service for blacks would be an extension of the color line in the South.

In spite of federal opposition, Du Bois and the NAACP used military service to wage an ideological campaign for civil rights, the first front of the battle for equality in World War I. In answer to the question "why should a Negro fight?," James Weldon Johnson wrote: "America is the American Negro's country. . . . Many of the rights and privileges of citizenship are still denied to him, but the plain course before him is to continue to perform all the duties of citizenship while he continually presses his demands for all the rights and privileges" (633). In an optimistic moment, Du Bois argued in "The African Roots of War" that black labor, in the form of colonial holdings in Africa, caused the war, and he predicted that war would eventually lead to the elimination of the global color line (642–51). Joel Spingarn, meanwhile, worked in the US War Department to find opportunities for blacks to contribute to the American war effort other than in labor battalions. He initially requested that a certain number of college-educated black men be trained in integrated officer training schools to command integrated combat units. His superiors at the War Department offered a meek compromise, the creation of one segregated officer training camp—Fort Des Moines in Iowa—and made him personally responsible for recruiting a sufficient number of qualified candidates. Spingarn appealed to Du Bois to support the segregated camp even though it fell far short of the latter's personal goals for the war. After much consideration, Du Bois agreed to support Spingarn's plan, because he believed that success on the battlefield could lead to advances in civil rights. David Levering Lewis explains that "Du Bois envisaged black officers fighting and dying across Flanders fields, led by Des Moines officers, as the high price of full citizenship in America—civil rights through carnage" (*W. E. B. Du Bois*, 530).

Du Bois printed a brief editorial, "Close Ranks," in the July 1918 issue of the *Crisis* that stated his position on the war and that symbolically conceded the issue of civil rights during wartime. He wrote:

> We of the colored race have no ordinary interest in the outcome [of the war]. That which the German power represents today spells death to the aspirations of Negroes and all darker races for equality, freedom and democracy. Let us not hesitate. Let us, while this war lasts, forget our special grievances and close our ranks shoulder to shoulder with our own white fellow citizens and the allied nations that are fighting for democracy. We make no ordinary sacrifice, but we make it gladly and willingly with our eyes lifted to the hills. (697)

Although Du Bois's statement appears to advocate expedient accommodationism, he implies that black soldiers in the US Army would be advancing their own cause by fighting for democracy. Events following the publication of this editorial, however, suggested that blacks could expect little return for their support of the war effort. The officer candidates at Fort Des Moines, many of the best and brightest young black men in the United States, suffered humiliating insults from their white training officers. Arthur Barbeau and

Florette Henri document in *The Unknown Soldiers: Black American Troops in World War I* that senior members of the War Department conspired to undermine the role of black officers. Barbeau and Henri cite official memos that stipulate that numbers of black officers should be severely limited, that black officers should be decommissioned for any minor infractions, and that no black officers should reach or exceed the rank of major. The prospects for military service as a means to social equality appeared bleak.

Blacks in uniform, meanwhile, inflamed racial violence in several communities where black soldiers were stationed. During the summer of 1917, the number of lynchings in the South spiked; a bloody riot erupted in East Saint Louis, Illinois, as black laborers moved into the area to work in the war industry; and a riot involving black soldiers occurred in Houston, Texas.[8] The soldiers stationed in Houston were in one of only two black army units in existence before the war started. The black soldiers were subjected to humiliating racial discrimination in Houston, which, coupled with the other blatant violence toward blacks taking place in the South and their disgraceful banishment to border patrol rather than combat, made them especially disgruntled. On August 23, 1917, violence erupted when a black soldier attempted to prevent a white policeman from beating a black woman. The soldier was beaten and arrested. Police also beat a black noncommissioned officer when he came to retrieve the soldier. Later that evening, a group of armed soldiers clashed with policemen and white citizens. Two soldiers and seventeen white men, including five policemen, were killed. A battalion of white soldiers was dispatched to intercede, and the entire black regiment was charged with mutiny. Twenty-nine soldiers were sentenced to death and executed, and many more were sentenced to life in prison.[9] As a result of the Houston riot, any remaining official support for blacks in combat waned, and plans for the black officer training school were almost canceled.

The Houston riot had virtually no impact on plans for a black draft, however. As Colonel Anderson's report "The Disposal of Colored Drafted Men" makes clear, these soldiers were never intended for combat. Riché Richardson trenchantly observes that "the report's construal of black southern soldiers as expendable and undesirable combatants also makes resonant the meaning of disposal as a throwing away or getting rid of waste" (85). Of the nearly 370,000 black American soldiers who served in World War I, only about 40,000 were trained for combat; the balance were disposed into labor battalions, where they worked in what Arthur Barbeau and Florette Henri call the "military equivalent of chain gangs" (90). According to official documents, the army's Services of Supply (SOS) was designed to mimic the normal experience of a black laborer in the South. Colonel Anderson writes:

> It is recommended that the question of race prejudice be not considered at all in the assigning of labor battalions to camps. These camps are mainly situated in the southern states. The negroes come mainly from the southern states. The saving of transportation to assemble the drafted negroes in camps nearest their homes and organize them into labor battalions and put them to work [*sic*]. Each southern state [has] negroes in blue overalls working throughout the state with a pick and shovel. When these colored men are drafted they are put in blue overalls (fatigue clothes) and continue to do work with a pick and shovel in the same state where they were previously working. If it is assumed that trouble will occur between whites and colored, that encourages it to occur, but if negroes are sent where they are needed and the possibility of trouble ignored there is not much probability of trouble occurring.[10]

Officially, the War Department intended for the US Army to be as segregated as the US South, thereby denying black soldiers the opportunity to earn civil rights by participating in combat.[11] To reinforce the essentially southern nature of black military service, most labor battalions were led by white southerners. In "An Essay toward the History of the Black Man in the Great War," Du Bois characterizes the officers assigned to labor battalions as "southern men of a harsh, narrow type," and he says that soldiers are "worked often like slaves" (700–701).[12]

The slippage between racial agency and national identity is apparent in the distinction between the two units of black soldiers that served in combat. Although most black draftees were assigned to labor battalions, a small number joined preexisting black National Guard units, which received training for combat. The Ninety-Third Division, called Harlem's Hell Fighters, consisted mostly of National Guard troops from New York,[13] plus a small number of National Guardsmen from Chicago and some black draftees. The War Department attached the division to an integrated unit of French Senegalese soldiers, and it distinguished itself for bravery, serving 191 days under fire with no soldiers captured. Many members of the division won decorations for valor, including the Croix de Guerre, France's highest commendation. The Ninety-Second Division, nicknamed the Buffaloes, on the other hand, served with the American Expeditionary Force and received few commendations. Composed mostly of black draftees, the unit received little training. Initially, most of the unit's officers were black graduates of the training school at Fort Des Moines, but over time they were replaced with white officers.[14] The Ninety-Second was one of the last divisions deployed to Europe, and it was placed under command of General Robert Bullard of the Second Army, who demeaned the unit consistently. He declared black officers unfit for duty and limited their service to intermittent patrols, although the unit did see some significant action in the final days of the war.

Du Bois took a clear message from the experience of black soldiers in France. After the war, he challenged the notion that racial solidarity during wartime would lead to civil rights in peacetime, opening a new, more confrontational front in the battle for equality.[15] Cataloging the grievances of black Americans, he noted the ills of the racial status quo—lynching, ignorance, exploitation, and segregation—and he exhorted the returning soldiers to continue their fight:

> This is the country to which we Soldiers of Democracy return. This is the fatherland for which we fought! But it is *our* fatherland. . . . we are cowards or jackasses if now that that war is over, we do not marshal every ounce of our brain and brawn to fight a sterner, longer, more unbending battle against the forces of hell in our own land.
>
> We *return.*
>
> We *return from fighting.*
>
> We *return fighting.*
>
> Make way for Democracy! We saved it in France, and by the Great Jehovah, we will save it in the United States of America, or know the reason why. ("Returning Soldiers," 380–81)

His martial rhetoric reflects a new widespread militancy emerging among blacks following the war, a sense of practical yet impatient optimism that blacks would soon enjoy the rights they had defended with their sweat and blood.[16] But the democratic ideals that black soldiers imported from France were soon met with the realities of southern racial discrimination. In fact, as C. Vann Woodward writes in *The Strange Career of Jim Crow*, "in the postwar era there were new indications that the Southern Way was spreading as the American Way in race relations" (115). As a result of southern black populations spreading into northern industrial centers, racial tensions after the war actually became more inflamed than they had been before the war. And many southern whites openly worried that blacks who had served in France might have brought home radical ideas about racial equality.[17]

They did. Du Bois explains that black soldiers who served in France, regardless of their duty, "saw the vision—they saw a nation of splendid people threatened and torn by a ruthless enemy; they saw a democracy which simply could not understand color prejudice" ("An Essay toward the History," 701). In this sense, the promise of civil rights through carnage may have been realized. Although the army deliberately attempted to southernize the experience of black draftees and thus maintain the color line, France itself suggested the practical possibility of racial equality on a transnational level. In *The Practice of Diaspora*, Brent Hayes Edwards describes "the culture of black internationalism" that emerged during the war as black Americans, most of whom came from the South, interacted with French people, colonial African soldiers, and other people from around the world, which radically destabilized their provincial world view (3). After the war, black soldiers brought a swagger marked with masculinity and cosmopolitanism back to the United States, and they challenged the color line.

Racial tensions erupted in the summer of 1919. Returning white soldiers and an upswing in European immigration crowded black workers out of northern factories, raising unemployment levels among blacks in spite of postwar prosperity. But southern blacks continued to move seeking opportunity. During what became known as the Red Summer, twenty-five race riots occurred, including major events in Longview, Texas, and Chicago, Illinois, that left many people—black and white—dead. More than seventy blacks were lynched that summer, including several black men in uniform.[18] But racial violence against blacks after the war often met with a new response—retaliation. The war in France demonstrated to black Americans that nationalism itself was a cause worthy of fighting for, and many blacks saw French race relations as the model America should emulate to reverse the creeping southernization of American race relations.

Nell Irvin Painter argues that "the senseless carnage of the First World War dealt white supremacy a tremendous blow," making way for the emergence of black cultural forms such as jazz as markers of mainstream American culture, as opposed to a racially subordinated subculture (132). At the critical juncture between increasing black social militancy and growing black cultural currency emerged a new, more confrontational generation of black writers, the New Negro movement. Mark Whalan argues in *The Great War and the Culture of the New Negro* that the connection between the war and African American culture has been overlooked, and he traces a pattern of masculine, cosmopolitan literary discourse that defines African American modernism. The connection between the war and black modernism is important, and it underscores Houston Baker's definition of black modernism as "black public-sphere mobility and fullness of United States black citizenship" (*Modernism and the Harlem Renaissance*, 83).

Postwar black modernists asserted their racial identity by creating a new, distinctly American form of cultural production that blended traditional folkways rooted in the US South with new intellectual currents emanating from Europe and the North to create a transregional, transnational, distal cultural form. George Hutchinson notes that, in most postwar literature about the experience of African Americans in the war, "the purpose is to firm up black people's resolve and vitality in the war's aftermath, and often to foretell the end of white supremacy" ("Aftermath," 189). For blacks, World War I, especially the exposure to social equality in France, was absolutely crucial to advancing the cause of civil rights. Blacks in uniform made tangible the rightful claim to full citizenship in America. For black writers, the war disrupted the racial status quo, revealing the hypocrisy between segregation and citizenship. The image of the South became a signifier for black separatism and a metaphor for segregation in black southern modernism, and the trope of the black southern veteran became a symbol of black dispossession within the United States. The black veteran tangibly proved his right to full citizenship as an American, but in the South, his traditional home, the black veteran was exploited, marginalized, and brutalized. When aestheticized by a black artist, the brutalization of the black soldier became an act of cultural resistance in the name of social equality.[19]

Not Only War Is Hell

Victor R. Daly portrays the brutalization of a black southern soldier in the novel *Not Only War: A Story of Two Great Conflicts*. The two conflicts to which the title refers are the war in France and the experience of being black in the South. The story features an interracial doubled pair of protagonists from South Carolina who romance the same woman and who serve in the same regiment in France, and the parallels between the white southern soldier and the black southern soldier make the tensions across the color line painfully, and sometimes tediously, apparent. The characters essentialize their respective racial identities so that they become near minstrel-like caricatures of blackness and whiteness, but the characterization serves a crucial purpose in this novel—to use literature to make the case for black citizenship. Curiously, considering the book's overtly racial theme, Daly does not depict the primary white character, Robert Lee Casper, as a direct antagonist; instead, Daly suggests that the real conflict in the story, other than the war, stems not from individuals but from deeply ingrained social values, which he optimistically suggests the war may serve to change.

The first half of the novel takes place in the South and most of the characters come from the South, but at the time Daly wrote the novel he claims to have never been to the South. Born in New York City, he embodied the northern black bourgeoisie. When the war began, he was a student at Cornell University, and he enlisted in the army and trained at the black officers' training camp at Fort Des Moines. He served with the Ninety-Third Division in France, where he saw combat and won the Croix de Guerre. He returned to Cornell after the war, graduated in 1922, published *Not Only War* in 1932, and worked as managing editor of Carter Woodson's *Journal of Negro History* until 1934, when he joined the US Department of Labor, where he worked until his retirement in 1966. Although a few other novels fictionalize the experience of black soldiers, his is the only novel written by an African American veteran, making his book unique and extremely valuable as a representation of the war and the struggle for citizenship.

Daly's choice to set the novel in the South is important. He writes in the book's epigraph:

> William Tecumseh Sherman branded War for all time when he called it Hell. There is yet another gaping, abysmal Hell into which some of us are actually born or unconsciously sucked. The Hell that Sherman knew was a physical one—of rapine, destruction and death. This other, is a purgatory for the mind, for the spirit, for the soul of men. Not only War is Hell. (3)

He juxtaposes the Civil War with World War I and connects war itself with racism. For black Americans, the objective of World War I, the realization of social equality, is the same as the objective of Civil War, so the linkage of these wars demonstrates the continuity of racial resistance since the end of slavery. J. Lee Greene comments that Daly "foregrounds racism as the ideological nexus between the American Civil War and World War I," but that nexus is as much geographical as ideological (136). Daly indicates that the South is an essential locus for the experience of blackness in America. Since most black Americans have direct personal or familial connections with the South and since blacks in the South experience social marginalization in the most overt way, the South itself acts as a complex antagonist in the novel. One could speculate that Daly's personal agenda in this novel is to humanize blacks and to press the case for social equality, and as an educated northern black man himself, he may realize that the most effective means for making that case is to address the experience of most black Americans in the South rather than a small segment of blacks in the North.

Daly portrays the conflict in *Not Only War* as both racial and regional. He characterizes Robert Lee Casper, the white antagonist, as kind but bound by southern tradition. His ancestors fought in the American Revolution, built a prosperous plantation, fought in the Civil War, rebuilt the plantation during Reconstruction, and successfully managed the politics of the New South. He is, as Daly says, "a true southerner" (8). When America enters the war in Europe, he enlists immediately, largely out of allegiance to the typical southern ideology. Daly summarizes this ideology astutely: "[Bob Casper] was faithful to his creed. He believed in the Baptist Church, the supremacy of the white race and the righteousness of the Democratic Party" (8). Casper embodies white male southern ideology, and Daly is careful to connect Casper's racism with his regionalism.

Daly doubles Casper with Montgomery Jason, an ambitious, intelligent young black southerner. A student at an unnamed black college in the South, Jason has devoted his intellectual development to the advancement of his race, and Daly depicts him as naïvely optimistic about citizenship. When his roommate calls World War I a "white man's war," he replies, "I think that if we roll up our sleeves and plunge into this thing, the Government will reward the race for its loyalty" (12). He voices virtually the same position that Du Bois articulates in "Close Ranks," but where Du Bois makes a bargain based on national security, Jason is in "a willful state of unknowing, a self-imposed blindness," according to Jennifer James (181). Daly subtly criticizes Du Bois's position on closing ranks because, after all, the idea of earning civil rights through carnage seems absurd. The sacrifice of innumerable black bodies to a foreign enemy could not even remotely serve to change domestic ideology. But a more tractable idea rests beneath this naïveté. By serving in the army, black southerners gain an incontrovertible identity as soldiers in a nationalist cause, a tangible validation of their American identity.

Casper and Jason come from the same area of South Carolina, but because of the strictures of racial segregation in the South, they have not met. They are connected, however, through a romantic triangle with Miriam Pinckney. Beautiful, with skin "like burnished gold" (15), and orphaned, Pinckney's character invokes the tragic mulatta trope. Her uncle, a tailor, arranges for her education, first at a convent school in North Carolina and then at Oberlin College in Ohio, where she studies music. She learns that racism has a unique regional basis. At the school in North Carolina, she develops a close relationship with a young white teacher from New England that affects her perception of racism and regionalism:

> Miriam's friendship with Frieda Bentley, her teacher, had made an indelible impression on the young southern girl. It had cured her of the awe and fear of white people which she had brought to school with her from her home in South Carolina. Furthermore, she soon learned that all white people were not the ogres and beasts that she had been taught to believe; and finally, it had effectively destroyed the inferiority complex which she had attached to herself and her own people. (23)

Contact with northerners destabilizes the color line for Miriam, but she follows its tenets when she returns to the South, mostly.

Daly uses Pinckney's character to signify the color line in the South. She engages in relationships with Jason and Casper simultaneously. While Casper makes no overt sexual demands of her, she understands the typical nature of a relationship such as theirs. "Southern white men," she thinks, "could only seek friendship with comely colored girls for one purpose—a social equality that existed after dark" (26). They develop a romantic relationship, which, though brief, appears to become physical. On one occasion, Jason discovers Casper and Pinckney in a parked car at night on a dirt road. He draws the logical conclusion, and he blames her for being foolish and himself for being gullible. Daly uses their relationship to illustrate the double standard for interracial relationships. As Joel Williamson explains in *The Crucible of Race*, white men who desired black women generated the myth that "Negro women were especially lusty creatures, perhaps precisely because white men needed to think of them in that way" (307). From the antebellum period on, sexual relationships between white men and black women were commonplace, but the myth of black female sexuality generated a corollary perception, the myth of the black beast rapist.[20] White southerners projected hypersexual characteristics on black men and women, and to a great extent the elaborate customs and mores of the color line were designed to prevent the possibility of sexual contact between white women and black men, primarily by demeaning and infantilizing black men. Thus, black men in uniform posed a significant threat to southern racial practice.

Jason enlists and is assigned to the Ninety-Third Division, which is training in Spartanburg, South Carolina, and Casper is attached to the unit as an

officer. After a few weeks in Spartanburg, the Ninety-Third deploys hastily, but Daly omits the actual reason for their rapid deployment, a series of
events that illustrates the practical effects of the color line in the South. In
October 1917, Noble Sissle, an officer in the 369th Regiment of the Ninety-
Third Division, entered a hotel lobby to purchase a newspaper.[21] A white
civilian patron of the hotel demanded that he remove his hat. When he did
not comply quickly enough, the white man knocked his hat off his head,
which caused a scuffle between white civilians and black soldiers. A black
officer stopped the fight before it escalated further, but later that evening a
group of armed black soldiers marched on the town, threatening to incite
a riot such as the one in Houston a few months earlier. The division commander managed to restore order before violence erupted, but the situation
prompted the War Department to defuse tension by sending the division
overseas. The War Department sent special assistant to the secretary of
war Emmett Scott, former personal secretary to Booker T. Washington, to
Spartanburg to ease racial tension in the camp. After the war, he described
the event in his *Official History of the American Negro in the World War* as
primarily a conflict of geography. "Spartanburg is a small southern city," he
says, "which closely follows what are usually regarded as southern traditions
and prejudices in the treatment of the Negro. Some of its citizens rather felt
that something was needed to let the jaunty Negro soldiers from New York
'know their place'" (79). According to Scott, the prospect of southern blacks
learning new ideas about the color line from outside influences threatened
southern whites.

Daly juxtaposes the distal South with proximal Europe when Jason and
Casper deploy to France, where they serve in different regiments of the
Ninety-Third Division under French command near the Argonne Forest.
Daly abbreviates the experience of combat in the book, with the exception
of a short scene that portrays Jason acting heroically and earning a promotion to sergeant. Instead, he focuses on relations between the black soldiers
and the white French civilians. Jason, who speaks some French, is assigned
as the billeting officer for his unit. Strict protocols governed the quarter-
ing of black soldiers, but a lieutenant, noting an excess of suitable quarters,
authorizes Jason and the other black noncommissioned officers to sleep in
the home of an elderly French woman in the town of Laval. The reception
Jason receives when he arrives at his billet, however, reminds him of home.
The old woman recoils at his appearance and declares that her home is only
available to officers. When the woman's granddaughter asks who is at the
door, the woman replies, "Un noir. . . . Un Americain" (50). Her comment

makes Jason dishearteningly aware of his fragmented nationalism. "The world over," he thinks, "a nigger first—an American afterwards" (50). Here, Daly suggests that race and nationalism are consistently in tension even within a transnational context that skews the ordinary dynamics of identity.

His experience of prejudice in France, however, proves to be brief when the woman's granddaughter, Blanche Aubertin, welcomes him into the home. Her presence, however, unnerves Jason, who has been thoroughly conditioned by the taboo on white women. He deliberately avoids the home during waking hours for several days until she finally engages him in conversation. She asks him to explain the South:

> Montie Jason was the first Negro, as well as the first American, that Blanche Aubertin had ever spoken to in her life. Now that he had lost some of his reticence, there were certain questions she was burning to ask him. Montie had a great deal of difficulty in making her understand that South Carolina was just as much a part of the continental United States, as Normandy was a part of France. Then she wanted to know why he was light brown in color, and had soft, wavy, black hair, while the other sergeants were all black, with funny, crinkly hair. Montie was amused at this; but he realized that the amusement was not due to the question itself, but to his own inability to answer it. She was so naïve. Then she wanted to know why all the officers were white men. (54)

The sequence of revelation in this paragraph suggests much about black identity and the color line. Since she has no previous experience with Americans, she has no understanding of the color line, but he teaches her first about how geographic region defines his identity, then about how race defines his identity, and then about how the customs of the color line are enforced. Jason's relationship with Blanche functions as a synecdoche for the African American soldiers' experience in France, a nation without race divisions that black soldiers saw as a "promised land."[22]

Inevitably, a confrontation takes place between Jason and Casper over Aubertin that inverts the romantic triangle between the two involving Miriam Pinckney. This conflict illustrates both the function of the black beast rapist myth as a means of enforcing the color line and the challenge of maintaining the color line in France. Upon finding Jason in Aubertin's home, Casper immediately concludes that he has raped her. When Jason, insulted by the insinuation, responds with asperity, Casper becomes incensed: "[H]e felt like striking the insolent nigger" (59). This moment, ironically, marks the first actual meeting between the men, and both find their roles dictated by their racial and regional identities. Casper's accusations enrage Jason, who realizes that his identity as a soldier has been replaced with his identity as a black southerner. "'I see,' [Jason] said at length, slowly and deliberately, between his teeth, 'you carry your dirty southern prejudice everywhere you go'" (59). Casper responds with a statement of paternalistic entitlement: "Listen to this nigger! I had those chevrons put on your sleeve, and I'll be damned if I don't have them ripped off again!" (59).

Casper acts as a signifier for a set of racist attitudes and southern social practices. While most Americans, at least in Daly's depiction, regarded the color line as a southern institution, during World War I the War Department made efforts to establish the color line as official policy among the Allies. While in Europe after the armistice gathering information on black soldiers, W. E. B. Du Bois discovered a document produced by the American Expeditionary Force to inform French military and civilian officials about how to treat black soldiers. The document, titled "Secret Information Concerning Black American Troops," articulates the "position occupied by Negroes in the United States," explaining the problem of black national indeterminacy:

> [Americans] are afraid that contact with the French will inspire in black Americans aspirations which to them appear intolerable.... Although a citizen of the United States, the black man is regarded by the white American as an inferior being with whom relations of business or service only are possible.... The vices of the Negro are a constant menace to the American who has to repress them sternly. For instance, the black American troops in France have, by themselves, given rise to as many complaints of attempted rape as all the rest of the army. (Du Bois, "Documents of the War," 17)

To mitigate the possibility of egalitarian ideas arising as a result of contact with French social equality, the document includes a number of guidelines for relations between French people and black Americans.[23] French soldiers, for example, should not eat with or shake hands with black soldiers, and French soldiers should take pains not to praise black soldiers in the presence of white soldiers. Finally, French citizens are admonished that "Americans become greatly incensed at any public expression of intimacy between white women and black men" (Du Bois, "Documents of the War," 17). Daly remarked in an article in the *Messenger* that thousands of black soldiers had married white women in France, and he "doubts if French honor suffered in any way for it."[24] The French were not immune to racism, but they were unfamiliar with the practice of the color line, and the disruption of traditional southern social mores in France challenged the color line.

If Casper caught Jason with a white woman in South Carolina, he could have had Jason lynched. Instead, he has Jason tried by court-martial. He receives a relatively light sentence (demotion to private), but the experience leaves him completely disillusioned about the place of black soldiers in the war. He hears the phrases used to legitimate this war in his head, but he realizes that they do not apply to him: "make the world safe for democracy—war to end war—self determination for oppressed people. But they don't mean black people. Oh no, black people don't count. They only count the dead" (61). Jason's comprehension of the black soldier's actual role in the war foreshadows the experience black soldiers will face upon returning to the United States. He essentially states that the acquisition of civil rights through carnage is a myth, meaning that black soldiers have been deliberately deceived into fighting for a national ideal they cannot attain, thus underscoring his own naïveté.

Yet Daly's fictionalization of the black soldier does not yet devolve into cynicism. While Jason recognizes that social equality is, at least for now, a myth, he maintains enough idealism to believe in common humanity. A German offensive begins soon after the court-martial, which forces the entire division to the front to repel the attack. Although stripped of rank, Jason continues to lead his troops into battle. As he charges a heavily fortified machine-gun emplacement, he takes cover in a trench littered with American corpses. From beneath the bodies, he hears Casper weakly groaning. This moment forces Jason to the ultimate test of his humanity. He waivers briefly as he considers the racist's fate: kill him, leave him, or help him. In a melodramatic climax, he tends to Casper's wound, but the irony of the situation preoccupies his thoughts. "This same man had preferred charges against him," he thinks, "that had caused him to be court-martialed and reduced to the ranks. And only because he, Montie, was a Negro—and Casper was a southern white man" (68). The desperation of the situation allows both men to overcome their regional and racial essentialism; Casper even avers enigmatically that since he had Jason charged, "war isn't the only hell that [he has] been through lately" (69). If Daly's novel has an outward social agenda, it crystallizes at this moment in the text as both men share a racial conversion experience. However, their mutual brotherhood and the message of social equality are only momentary. After a burst of machine-gun fire, the two men fall together, "two bodies slumped as one" (70). The book's final line underscores Daly's message: "They found them the next morning, face downward, their arms about each other, side by side" (70).[25]

The novel's ending suggests that social equality is possible only in the denationalized space of no man's land, and even then only actualized among the dead. As Mark Whalan observes in *The Great War and the Culture of the New Negro*, no man's land, the violated, disputed, uninhabitable space between the trenches, appeared as a common trope in works by several African American writers, and the song "All of No Man's Land Is Ours" was a popular jazz tune during the war (Whalan, 69–81). No man's land in the black soldiers' imaginary was the only space of social equality, which boded ill for the prospects of citizenship. In effect, "*Not Only War* is a powerful critique of American democracy and its failings during the war," as Chad Williams contends in *Torchbearers of Democracy*. Jason's naïve optimism and his personal commitment to racial equality prove to be fatal, suggesting that fighting for civil rights through carnage leads only to carnage.

Black soldiers who survived the war, whether they had served in the Service of Supply or in combat, found when they returned to the United States that their fight for citizenship had only just begun. While in one sense black soldiers did make their case for civil rights through military service, Jason's humiliation and his court-martial indicate that the argument has, except in isolated cases, been moot. The War Department deliberately segregated the ranks and intentionally maintained a state of race relations that mimicked race relations in the South, transporting the distal region into the proximal zone. Black veterans who returned to the South after the war expecting to find social equality or even respect were disappointed. In fact, they faced even greater animosity from white antagonists, who intended to deliver the message that any social equality they experienced in France would not be found in the South. Daly dedicated *Not Only War* to "the Army of the Disillusioned"—black veterans. But the point of the novel is not merely to dwell on disillusionment. It is to use that disillusionment as a means of resistance.

The Lynching of Dr. Kenneth Harper

Walter White's novel *The Fire in the Flint* uses disillusionment and postwar violence to make the case for civil rights for African Americans. Born in Atlanta in the 1890s, White had personal memories of the Atlanta riot of 1906, which led him to pursue his life's work in civil rights, eventually earning the nickname "Mr. NAACP." During World War I, he used his ability to pass for white—he had light skin, blond hair, and blue eyes—and his knowledge of southern racial customs to investigate lynchings and race riots for the NAACP. In *The Fire in the Flint*, he portrays the experience of Dr. Kenneth Harper, a black southerner who studies medicine in the North, serves as an officer in the US Army in France, and returns to his hometown in Georgia to open a segregated clinic, expecting a prosperous career as an accommodationist professional. He finds himself drawn into the nascent postwar movement for civil rights, and because he presents a threat to the white racial hegemony, he is lynched. White invokes the trope of the black veteran to illustrate the arbitrary, violent, emasculating, dehumanizing nature of race relations in the South after the war.

Although White did not serve in the army during the war, he did attempt to enlist. In his autobiography, *A Man Called White*, he recounts that he took a required physical examination to qualify for the officers' training camp at Fort Des Moines, but he and two other light-skinned recruits were summarily flunked, while a frail, dark-skinned applicant was accepted. Later, he learned why light-skinned applicants were denied. "Wild rumors," he says, "born of guilty consciences no doubt, were sweeping the South that the 'Huns' were industriously at work among Southern Negroes to spread unrest. These German agents and spies, so the tales ran, were capitalizing on Negro bitterness against lynching and race prejudice" (*A Man Called White*, 36). Because he was exempt from the draft, he went to work for the NAACP investigating lynchings in the South and writing scathing exposés to cultivate support for antilynching legislation.[26]

The Fire in the Flint is one of the most vivid descriptions of racism in the early twentieth-century South from the perspective of a black southerner, a testament to White's unquestioned expertise in the nuances of racial stratification in the modern South. He uses Dr. Harper as a medium through which to examine the postwar fluctuation in racial dynamics in the region. The book takes place in a generic southern town, Central City, Georgia, and the plot centers on Dr. Harper's urge for racial accommodation, not equality.[27] His mantra, following his father and Booker T. Washington, is that "[a]ny Negro can get along without trouble in the South if he only attends to his own business" (17). But his story reveals two obvious problems with this attitude. First, as southern blacks moved into northern cities during and after the war, southern race relations were increasingly becoming the norm for American race relations, a condition that, as White says, "greatly accentuated the race problem as a national, instead of merely a Southern, tragedy" (*A Man Called White*, 72). In other words, World War I made the color line a national, rather than a regional, problem. Second, increasing tensions between whites and blacks in the postwar South made it inherently impossible for a black man, especially a black intellectual, to mind his own business. Because of his education and his military experience, Dr. Harper poses an inherent threat to southern white supremacy.

Dr. Harper's exposure to relative equality and proximal modernity in the North and in France makes him incompatible with accommodationism in the South. Before the war, he attends Atlanta University and then studies medicine in New York, but that exposure does not necessarily make him a subversive agent. Central City, in fact, already has a black doctor who had studied in the North a generation earlier who manages to navigate the contradictory avenues of accommodationism. Dr. Harper, however, has the additional element of military service in France, which complicates his place in the community. After residency, he trains at the segregated officers' training camp at Fort Des Moines, receives a commission as a first lieutenant in the Medical Corps, and deploys to France with the Ninety-Second Division. He serves as a combat surgeon near the front line, where he learns enough of man's inhumanity toward man to come to abhor violence, and then he studies for six months at the Sorbonne. When racial violence erupts in Central City, he sees national racial integration based on his experience in France as an ideal objective:

> Maybe in time the race problem would be solved just like that . . . when some great event would wipe away the artificial lines . . . as in France. . . . He thought of the terrible nights and days in the Argonne. . . . He remembered the night he had seen a wounded black soldier and a wounded white Southern one, drink from the same canteen. . . . They didn't think about color at those times. . . . Wouldn't the South be a happy place if this vile prejudice didn't exist? (226)

Dr. Harper's idealization of equality calls upon precisely the same imagery as Daly's depiction of social equality in no man's land. White suggests that perhaps, in both cases, the key to civil rights is transcending place and nation as components of racial identity. Perhaps if there were no South, then there would be no racism. Considering that Dr. Harper deliberately chooses to return to Georgia and actively embraces his identity as a southerner, White offers the most radical position on cosmopolitanism in African American World War I literature.

The South is home for Dr. Harper and the legions of soldiers he metaphorically represents, but it also the place where blacks been have been
systematically emasculated and violated. Riché Richardson argues in *Black
Masculinity and the U.S. South* that black men in the South have been forced
into a set of binary masculine roles, either the effeminate Uncle Tom or the
aggressive black beast. Asserting masculinity was inherently oppositional
in this situation, and she sees black writers as offering many subversive
forms of male identity. Adriane Lentz-Smith explains in *Freedom Struggles*
that World War I changed conceptions of black masculinity; in promising
that "war would make men of them," the war ingrained the notion of black
manhood outside the ordinary binary (6). But the war did not destabilize
white supremacy, so assertions of masculinity after the war were met with
extreme violence. The South, in *The Fire in the Flint*, is the place where black
men are violently emasculated.

Central City is White's microcosm of the racist, distal South. After the
war, it shows signs of racial tension, especially among returning black soldiers. During the frenzied patriotism of wartime, white and black southerners had been mutually interested in military preparations, but for different
reasons. Black southerners had a suppressed agenda for supporting the war,
which made their readjustment to racial subordination after the war difficult. White explains the cognitive dissonance returning black soldiers felt
as the result of a suppressed ideology:

> Many [black southerners] entered the army, not so much because they were
> fired with the desire to fight for an abstract thing like world democracy, but,
> because they were a race oppressed, they entertained very definite beliefs
> that service in France would mean a more decent regime in America, when
> the war was over, for themselves and all others who were classed as Negroes.
> Many of them, consciously or subconsciously, had a spirit which might have
> been expressed like this: "Yes, we'll fight for democracy in France, but when
> that's over with we're going to expect and we're going to get some of that
> same democracy for ourselves right here in America." It was because of this
> spirit and determination that they submitted to the rigid army discipline
> to which was often added all the contumely that race prejudice could heap
> upon them. (43–44)

While most black soldiers intended to return fighting as Du Bois's editorial recommended, Dr. Harper sublimates his racial ideology beneath his
intellectual abstraction. Rather than ponder the struggle for racial equality

during the war, he prefers to occupy his mind with works of literature. Because of his accommodationism and abstraction, he takes on an effete gender identity, as Russ Castronovo argues, aligning himself with the Uncle Tom version of black masculinity.[28]

That attitude changes, however, once he experiences southern racism again. He meets a white doctor leaving a black patient, and the paternalistic doctor warns him not to spread any "No'then ideas 'bout social equality" because racial tensions have already escalated since "these niggers who went over to France and ran around with them French women have been causin' a lot of trouble 'round here, kickin' up a rumpus, and talkin' 'bout votin' and ridin' in the same car with white folks" (53). The white doctor's bigotry exemplifies white southern animosity toward notions of social equality, and it also reveals that white southern identity is embedded in a matrix of regional and racial attitudes. As Grace Elizabeth Hale explains in *Making Whiteness*, white southerners defined themselves in opposition to white northerners and southern blacks, so the junction of those two oppositional identities—black southerners converging with white northerners—caused white southerners great anxiety. Animosity toward blacks blurred with animosity toward northerners and, even worse, foreigners, which combined with generalized anxiety about the pace of disruptive social change taking place in the region: violence toward blacks was the inevitable outcome.

Racial violence forces Dr. Harper to become involved in the struggle for equality in spite of warnings to mind his place. He realizes the flaw in his father's mantra because he cannot mind his own business in the South. After witnessing the cruelties and absurdities of the color line—including treating white men for syphilis contracted from black prostitutes, treating black patients ignored by white physicians, and treating a dying black man murdered by a white man—he finds himself compelled to act on behalf of blacks in his community, abandoning the accommodationist self-interest that initially dominated his attitude toward the black community. He becomes involved with an organization of black farmers, the National Negro Farmer's Co-operative and Protective League, which he hopes will lead to civil rights for its members:

Though his interest was in the Negro tillers of the soil, success in their case would inevitably react favorably on the white—just as oppression and exploitation of the Negro had done more harm to white people in the South than to Negroes. Kenneth felt the warm glow of the crusader in a righteous cause. Already he saw a new day in the South with white and colored people free from oppression and hatred and prejudice—prosperous and contented because of that prosperity. He could see a lifting of the clouds of ignorance which hung over all of the South, an awakening of the best in all the people of the South. (146)

He believes that racial equality would benefit whites as much as blacks and uplift the entire region, but he realizes that the whites do not share his optimism.

After World War I, several grassroots organizations, such as the Brotherhood of Sleeping Car Porters, agitated for labor equality and civil rights.[29] White bases his description of the National Negro Farmer's Co-operative and Protective League on his experience covering the Progressive Farmers and Household Union of America, a group of black sharecroppers in Phillips County, Arkansas, who attempted to incorporate in 1919.[30] In an effort to intimidate the organization, a group of white farm owners and police officers fired on a meeting the Progressive Farmers held in a church. The sharecroppers shot back, a response that apparently surprised the white mob. Within hours, a riot erupted; many panicked whites fled, mobs randomly attacked and murdered blacks, soldiers just returned from Europe were mobilized to quell the violence, and the governor personally oversaw the restoration of order and the execution of justice.[31] Dozens of blacks were killed during the riot, and seventy-nine more were tried by a summary tribunal sanctioned by the governor, which sentenced a dozen to death and the remainder to harsh prison sentences. White visited Phillips County to investigate the riot on behalf of the NAACP. Using his usual technique of passing as a white journalist, he interviewed the governor, who blamed the violence on northern agitators, and met with several prominent members of the local white community.[32] White himself came close to being lynched during this sojourn. Only a timely warning prevented him from walking into a gruesome death.[33]

The plan behind the Co-operative League in the book calls for black sharecroppers, who have long been economically exploited by white land owners, to pool their meager resources to purchase farm supplies at a fair price and to provide legal representation to enforce fair contracts. But the organization's overt labor objectives implied subversive—in the opinion of white supremacists—civil rights objectives. Dr. Harper becomes the spokesman for the group, and he exhorts black people to fight for social equality. "You husbands and sons and brothers," he says to the crowd, "three years ago you were called on to fight for liberty and justice and democracy! Are you getting it?," to which the crowd responds, "No!" (179). Echoing the rhetoric of the labor movement and the civil rights movement, he tells the crowd that only collective, nonviolent action will secure the rights that have been denied them, and he warns them that continued passive resistance will produce no results. The war acts as a key signifier for citizenship in his speech. He realizes that the speech will make him a target for intimidation by the Ku Klux Klan and that the men and women who join his organization will also be taking a serious risk.

Violence first affects his family when a group of white Klan thugs abduct and rape his younger sister, Mamie. His younger brother, Bob, a Harvard-bound law student, seeks vengeance. He confronts the white thugs, shoots two of them dead, and flees. Bob, always more militant than his brother, may be a more accurate personification of the New Negro—the ethos expressed in Claude McKay's poem "If We Must Die"—than his more assimilationist brother. After the shooting, a lynching party, originally intended for Dr. Harper, convenes to track and eventually torture and kill Bob. But Bob, personifying McKay's poem, refuses to die like a hog. Calculating the number of bullets he has left and reserving one for himself, he faces the murderous, cowardly pack and shoots as many of them as he can before killing himself. His suicide is an act of radical masculinity because he refuses to allow white supremacists the chance to emasculate him through spectacle violence.

His sister's rape and his brother's murder drive Dr. Harper into an unmitigated rage. He recalls the shibboleths of democracy that he idealized, and he realizes the absurdity of American racism and the arbitrariness of the color line:

> "Superior race"! "Preservers of civilization"! "Superior" indeed! They called Africans inferior! They, with smirking hypocrisy, reviled the Turks! They went to war against the "Huns" because of Belgium! None of these had ever done a thing so bestial as these "preservers of civilization" in Georgia! Civilization! Hell! The damned hypocrites! The liars! The fiends! "White civilization"! Paugh! Black and brown and yellow hands had built it! The white fed like carrion on the rotting flesh of the darker peoples! And called their toil their own! And burned those on whose bodies their vile civilization was built! (271)

White juxtaposes the vicious violent attacks with the vacuous abstractions of white supremacy to reveal the utter futility of accommodationism. When Dr. Harper first returned to Central City, he had intended to observe the tenets of the color line, and when he organizes the Co-Operative and Protective League he intended to advocate for economic and social justice, but only after his brother's death does he actually understand the full cost of racial equality. Now, he sees that equality means transcending the white supremacists' ruthlessness, which suggests, in White's depiction, that violence will beget violence.

Dr. Harper, however, does not initiate the violence, although his first impulse is to follow Bob's example and kill every white person in sight. As he eventually begins to regain his composure, he receives a call that forces him to displace his contempt for white people. For the previous few days he had been treating Mary Ewing, the daughter of a white storekeeper, for uterine hemorrhage. Hers had been a difficult case, and the white physicians in the community actually deferred to his superior training.[34] Under his care, Mary made progress, but on the evening of his return to Central City her mother calls, telling him that she has had a turn for the worse and begging him to attend to her. At first he refuses and curses the entire white race. When his anger subsides, he realizes a sense of common humanity—true racial equality—and, ignoring the danger, he goes to treat Mary. White himself describes the climactic scenario as "melodramatic," which may be an understatement, but it serves an effective purpose, challenging the taboos of race relations and gender construction in the postwar South (*A Man Called White*, 67). In addition to forcing him to recognize a white person as an equal, the scenario places him in a home with two white women without the supervision of a white man, which forces him to cross the color line. Even though he and the Ewings manage to find a momentary sense of equality in a moment of crisis, similar to the camaraderie between Jason and Casper in no man's land, their situation does nothing to change the culture of racism.[35]

The book concludes predictably. Klan thugs watching Dr. Harper achieve their pretext for lynching when they see him enter the Ewings' house. They assume that he has come for sexual purposes, shifting his gender identity from effeminate Uncle Tom to black beast, which they attribute to his exposure to French women. "I allus said these niggers who went to France an' ran with those damn French women'd try some of that same stuff when they came back!," says one of the thugs. "Ol' Vardaman was right! Ought never t' have let niggers in th' army anyhow!" (286). This statement encapsulates the ideology of the color line, reflecting both the most common justification for lynching and the most pernicious reason for preventing black soldiers from serving in the army. The thugs ambush him as he leaves the house, and, although unarmed, he fights back until overpowered. Rather than describe the macabre details of the lynching, White concludes the novel with a terse press release that affirms the norms of white supremacy by dehumanizing Dr. Harper. The release names him as "Doc Harper," reducing his profession and his education to a casual nickname, and charges him with criminal assault on the wife of a prominent white citizen. Moreover, the release suggests that he was a coward, saying that he "became frightened before accomplishing his purpose," and that he was guilty, saying that he confessed (300). The press release says that he was "put to death by a mob which numbered five thousand. He was burned at the stake" (300). In the case of the lynching of Dr. Kenneth Harper, white supremacists act as a collective entity to prevent the development of racial equality through a violent, ritualistic spectacle of black degradation.

This ritualization, Trudier Harris argues in *Exorcising Blackness: Historical and Literary Lynching and Burning Rituals*, is essential to preserving the culture of racism. Any subversive action, real or imagined, on the part of black people constitutes an act of evil, defined as a transgression against the white social hegemony. "In order to exorcise the evil and restore the topsy-turvy world to its rightful position," Harris writes, "the violator must be punished. . . . Symbolic punishment becomes communal because the entire society has been threatened; thus the entire society must act to put down the violator of the taboo" (12). A lynching is not a mere punishment; it is a ritual designed to convey a message that white people control southern society by dominating black people.[36] The rope and faggot, as extensions of socially constructed whiteness, control and define blackness.

But White's depiction of a lynching undercuts the ritualization of the lynching spectacle. Amy Wood argues in *Lynching and Spectacle* that lynchings, which celebrated racist, rural values, were antimodern events, so one might hypothesize that eliding the lynching is a modernist aesthetic characteristic of the novel. Russ Castronovo, however, suggests that aesthetic concerns were not immediately important to White because they raise "the troubling implication that art in the context of lynching is somehow responsible for violence" (1455). His portrayal of lynching rituals undercuts the rationale for preserving and maintaining white supremacy by focusing attention on the lynchers, not on the lynching victim. As a military veteran, a skilled doctor, a reluctant but cooperative race leader, a sensitive son and brother, and a charming love interest, Dr. Harper plays an idealized multiplex role in the text, but his idealization has a clear purpose. Chad Williams concludes that "White's black veteran is a militant yet tragic figure, symbolic of both the postwar determination of black people to fight for democracy and the virulence of white supremacy in dashing those hopes" (341). Dr. Harper, who once fought to preserve democracy, has been denied the most fundamental right granted to American citizens, the right to life, much less liberty and the pursuit of happiness. His brutal murder exposes for the literary audience the absurdity and arbitrariness of life on the wrong side of the color line. The book's ending makes the case that white southerners are the beastly savages.[37] *The Fire in the Flint* promotes the cause of social equality, using literary carnage to agitate for civil rights.

"RACES AND NATIONS ARE SKUNKS"

The war allowed hundreds of thousands of black Americans to serve in France, where, civil rights leaders hoped, they would experience social equality, which would eventually lead to full citizenship after the war. The army deliberately attempted to normalize the color line in Europe and to southernize race relations in the military, but the notion of an international community of black people sustained the movement for social equality. Paul Gilroy's theory of the black Atlantic, a "desire to transcend both the structures of the nation state and the constraints of ethnicity and national particularity," reflects this sense of international unity (19). The optimism that race leaders felt coming out of the war, however, eventually turned to disappointment, because the war did not lead to anything more than the false promise of citizenship. The black Atlantic would more accurately be termed the Atlantic South, the realization that black people in America, Europe, the Afro-Caribbean, and colonial Africa shared a common sense of discrimination, exploitation, dispossession, and violation. "As black intellectuals became increasingly aware that the principle of national self-determination did not apply to them," Michelle Stephens explains, "the underlying imperialism of the League of Nations became more and more apparent. . . . Black radicals in Harlem who had taken up the banner of self-determination used internationalism and revolution to modify and transform black nationalist ideologies" ("Black Transnationalism," 598).

Claude McKay was one of the leading black radicals in Harlem. Born in Jamaica in 1889, McKay moved to the United States just before the war started. From his vantage point as a foreigner living among black southerners who had recently migrated to the North, he could observe the alienation and dispossession of his fellow blacks. From 1915 to 1919, he worked as a Pullman porter traveling across the country, and he "began to face the highly personal yet broadly representative problems of black identity and alienation during World War I" (Cooper, 82). For McKay, like many other black intellectuals, the war was a watershed moment that shaped "his ideological worldview and specific ideas of race, nation, diaspora, and modernity" (C. Williams, 337). His writings illustrate his preoccupation with nationality and identity, and while he occasionally idealized Jamaica, his books reveal his sense of dispossession and his search for home. For example, he titled his first novel *Home to Harlem*, and he titled his autobiography *A Long Way from Home*, but the text of both these works suggests that home both for his characters and for himself is an illusion.

His sense of disaffection sent him searching through a series of ideological systems that seemed to offer racial brotherhood, including the African Blood Brotherhood and the Communist Party, although his "primary allegiance" was not to any ideology but to "black liberation" (J. James, 213). In 1922, he attended the Fourth Congress of the Communist International in the Soviet Union, and while in Russia, he wrote a short analysis of racism in America at Leon Trotsky's request to be used as a training manual for communist agitators attempting to spark proletarian revolution in the United States. The book, *The Negroes in America*, explains the history of racism since the end of the Civil War. The text juxtaposes socialist rhetoric with amateur sociological analysis, creating a curious capsule of post–World War I black radical ideology. McKay locates black identity primarily in the US South, where he says that blacks have been blamed and punished by white southerners for their defeat in the Civil War. He describes the South's post-Reconstruction white hegemony as vindictive, coercive, and cruel, and he describes black southerners as trapped between the arbitrary violence of the Ku Klux Klan and the stultifying accommodationism of Booker T. Washington.

While in the Soviet Union, he also wrote three brief vignettes, gathered in the volume *Trial by Lynching: Stories about Negro Life in North America*, that describe for communist agitators the most common occurrences of violence along the color line, the issues most likely to stir the passion for racial rebellion. The first two stories dramatize the most frequent kinds of incidents, the lynching of a black man for presumed sexual violence and the sexual victimization of a black woman. The third story, "The Soldier's Return," complicates the typical sexual dynamic of the lynching story with overt references to black military service and the idea of the New Negro. In the story, Frederick Taylor, an octoroon soldier capable of passing for white, returns to the ominously named town of Great Neck, Georgia. When he and the black soldiers return, the mayor addresses them from his porch, telling them "that the war was over, and so now they must take off their uniforms and return to the work which they had done before the war" (38). Trouble erupts a few days later when Taylor, still in his uniform, encounters "the half-witted daughter of the postmaster," who runs screaming from him completely unprovoked (39). When Taylor gets to town, he is arrested, accused of attacking the girl, and held in jail. A mob gathers with "torches, lanterns, a rope, and a can of kerosene" (39). The crowd drags Taylor from his cell and beats him as onlookers cry, "lynch him!" At the last moment the mayor manages to quiet the crowd sufficiently to explain that he witnessed the incident and that Taylor had done nothing wrong, which disperses the crowd and aborts the lynching.

But rather than release Taylor, the sheriff tells him that he is to blame. "Pauline was frightened by seeing you wearing [your] soldier's uniform," he says. "You know that in our town we don't like it when niggers wear soldier's uniforms" (40). The mayor, who has just saved Taylor's life, interrupts to explain precisely the white community's position on social equality:

> [I]n our town there's plenty of work, thank God, and work clothes don't cost much. My brother has splendid work clothes in his store. But for some reason, you don't like to do anything and, moreover, you drive a buggy. One would think you were really some white gentleman. It seems to me, Frederick, that it's still necessary to place you under arrest and try you for vagrancy. We will take the uniform of a soldier of the U.S. off you and give you an outfit which is more appropriate for you. In any case, we have to set an example. Niggers never learn prudence by themselves until we show them, good and proper, their place. There is still plenty of work for niggers in Great Neck. We won't put up with even one of them loafing without work and putting on airs, even if he was in France, and they treated him there just like a white man. You'll have to work in a chain gang for a few months, Frederick. (40–41)

McKay represents the South for an international audience as the place where black men are exploited for their labor and subject to arbitrary lethal violence at the mere possibility of expressing masculinity, regardless of their military service. Crucially, however, McKay's story subverts the aborted lynching by exposing the arbitrary construction of the color line.

McKay's novel *Home to Harlem* depicts another southern soldier disillusioned by the war who challenges the notion of black citizenship. Mark

Whalan notes that McKay, unlike many black authors, does not glorify "heroic, patriotic, educated, and bourgeois officers who lead the race both in battle and in the wider political struggle for black civil rights" (147). He has a different agenda, to expose the effects of the war on the international black underclass. The picaresque story focuses on Jake Brown, an army deserter who returns to Harlem, but Harlem, in spite of the title, is not his home. In fact, as the novel makes clear, he has no actual home because he has been radically dispossessed. Jake, like the majority of black people in Harlem during and after World War I, actually comes from the South—Petersburg, Virginia. He moves to Harlem just before the war to find work in the shipyards, and then moves to France, England, Harlem (again), Pennsylvania, and Chicago. Even though the novel ostensibly concerns home and Harlem, Jake has no enduring sense of attachment to any place because he has been consistently socially and economically displaced everywhere. So he roams from place to place looking for work. Everywhere he lives is essentially the South.

Unlike Montgomery Jason and Dr. Kenneth Harper, Jake does not enlist for patriotic ideals or for racial advancement. He enlists for adventure:

> In the winter he sailed for Brest with a happy chocolate company. Jake had his own dreams of going over the top. But his company was held at Brest. Jake toted lumber—boards, planks, posts, rafters—for the hundreds of huts that were built around the walls of Brest and along the coast between Brest and Saint-Pierre, to house the United States soldiers.
>
> Jake was disappointed. He had enlisted to fight. For what else had he been sticking a bayonet into the guts of a stuffed man and aiming bullets straight into a bull's-eye? Toting planks and getting into rows with his white comrades at the Bal Musette were not adventure. (4)

Also unlike Montgomery Jason and Dr. Harper, Jake's experience is typical of the vast majority of black soldiers who worked in the Services of Supply. He labors for the army just as he had for any other employer in the South or in the North. Disillusioned with military service, he asks, "Why did I ever enlist and come over here? Why did I want to mix mahself up in a white folks' war? It ain't ever was any of black folks' affair" (7–8). He deserts and works on the docks in London's East End, and then he ships aboard a freighter bound for New York as a coal stoker, working in the dirtiest, most inhumane position in the shipping industry.

McKay uses Jake as a signifier for the complexity of black national identity. The issue was complicated because the vast majority of African

American men in the early twentieth century had a rural frame of reference, so national distinctiveness was not an immediately relevant concern for them until the war began. Adriane Lentz-Smith explains that black soldiers had to first conceptualize a sense of their American identity, then a sense of themselves as national subjects within an international context, and then, possibly, a sense of a transnational racial identity (6). Without question, this was a complicated, disorienting process, and its abruptness likely made it disillusioning. The result, McKay remarks, is the realization of "the real hollowness of nationhood [and] patriotism" (Cooper, 49). Theories of black cosmopolitanism—such as Négritude, Black Atlanticism, and Pan-Africanism—articulate visions of a racial identity based on a diasporic past that manifests in a common, transnational consciousness. World War I was a critical moment in the history of black cosmopolitanism, but the realization of international blackness did not prove to be liberating. Instead, as Jake's story illustrates, it marked the emergence of the Atlantic South, the modern, transnational exploitation of black people in a postplantation economy.

The book's title, *Home to Harlem*, suggests the importance of a black cosmopolitan metropolis for the possibility of racial self-definition, but Harlem itself proved to be problematic in the black imagination. As J. Lee Greene explains, "novels that incorporate World War I as a theme or trope typically follow the genre's conventional depiction of Harlem as a debilitating social and psychological space. This picture contradicts the idyllic image of Harlem (and the North generally) that prevailed in southern black society" (149). Because most of the blacks in Harlem come from the South, they maintained a regional southern identity that complicated the development of a national identity and that undercut the cohesiveness of Harlem as a community.[38] Rather than being a cosmopolitan black metropolis, Harlem is a marginal space, "a home for black fugitives, a fugitive nation or colony existing in the shadows," as Michelle Stephens describes it (*Black Empire*, 146). Harlem—the black maroon colony in the midst of a white metropolis—was a product of the color line, a bounded space of blackness and a mediated site of modernity, which complicates the notion of Harlem as home for Jake. In this case, home is not where he belongs but where he is allowed to be.

The international color line cuts across racial agency, national identity, and interracial sexuality, and McKay demonstrates that black masculine sexuality is inherently constricted. Although Jake voices an urge only for black women, he makes a number of comments that suggest that he had relations with white women in Europe. At one point he says that women are alike regardless of their race or nation—"Sometimes they turn mah stomach, the womens. The same in France, the same in England, the same in Harlem" (34)—and he claims to have no interest in mulatto women after having white women because "they's so doggone much alike" (36). He sounds a similarly jaded chord later when he says, "It's the same ole life everywhere . . . in white man's town or nigger town. Same bloody-sweet life across the pond. I done lived through the same blood-battling foh womens ovah theah in London. Between white and white and between black and white. Done seen it in the froggies' country, too" (285). In Jake's experience, racial and sexual tension is ubiquitous, and even countries that seem relatively open to interracial relations actually have a set of prohibitions in place to discourage the behavior. Consequently, Jake feels most secure with black women, but he finds numerous dangers in his relationships with black women, too, which eventually force him to leave Harlem again.

Jake takes a job on the Pennsylvania Railroad, which draws upon McKay's experience as a porter. Every place the train stops, Jake and the other black servants on the train find a virtually identical set of segregated, filthy accommodations and the same types of vicious amusements: nightclubs, gambling parlors, and prostitutes. Although he feels at ease in this bottom stratum of society, he realizes that he has no freedom to ascend above this level. Every place he goes, he can expect the same existence: he experiences it in the South, he experiences it in Harlem, he experiences it in Europe, and he experiences it in the North. McKay implies that blackness yields a set of predetermined living conditions encapsulated by poverty, vice, and labor exploitation. The life that Jake and thousands of other black men who left the South sought to escape is the only life available to him. The experience of racism in the South is just one component of a vast transnational black identity that segregates black from white.

McKay extends this vast diasporic black identity in the character of Ray, a Haitian intellectual who works with Jake on the railroad. Meeting Ray changes Jake's worldview, which remains implausibly provincial even after years of travel. He thinks of himself as "an American Negro," and he looks down on "foreign niggers," whom he imagines as uncivilized: "Africans" were "bush niggers" and "West Indians were monkey chasers" (134). Ray realizes that his nationality complicates his racial identity, and his relationship with Jake and other workers on the train leads him to reconsider the relationship between race and nationality:

These men claimed kinship with him. They were black like him. Man and nature had put them in the same race. He ought to love them and feel them (if they felt anything). He ought to if he had a shred of social morality in him. They were all chain-ganged together and he was counted as one link. Yet he loathed every soul in that great barrack-room, except Jake. Race . . . why should he have and love a race? (153)

McKay voices through Jake and Ray the complex process of creating a black international identity that moves dizzyingly through the stages of localism, nationalism, and transnationalism only to result in disillusionment.

Blackness is thus a form of global exile. Ray's and Jake's displacement has roots in the nexus of nationality, race, and sex, which McKay dramatizes in a sexual misunderstanding. When his former army friend and drinking buddy Zeddy Plummer, jealous over Jake's relationship with an estranged girlfriend, threatens to report him to the authorities as a deserter, Jake has a moment of realization:

Yet here he was caught in the thing that he despised so thoroughly. . . . Brest, London, and his America. Their vivid brutality tortured his imagination. Oh, he was infinitely disgusted with himself to think that he had just been moved to the same savage emotions as the vile, vicious, villainous white men who, like hyenas and rattlers, had fought, murdered, and clawed the entrails out of black men over the common, commercial flesh of women. (328)

Jake sees that the construction of the color line has a specifically sexual function designed to prevent his access to the bodies of white women. He also sees that this cartography of race and sex functions in the same way regardless of his place—Virginia, New York, Brest, London, or Pittsburgh. His black body determines his social place regardless of where he is on either side of the Atlantic South.

Faced with jail for desertion, Jake feels the effects of radical disposses-sion, which lead him to finally reject the possibility of equality or citizen-ship in the United States. He has an argument with his girlfriend about leaving, and he tells her exactly why he deserted from the army. "I didn't run away because I was scared a them Germans," he says. "But I beat it away from Brest because they wouldn't give us a chance at them, but kept us working in that rainy, sloppy, Gawd-forsaken burg working like wops. They didn't seem to want us niggers foh no soldiers" (331). The prospect of intern-ment as a deserter prompts Jake to consider disavowing his nationality and returning to Europe, but his girlfriend argues against it. She counterintui-tively invokes the language of nationalism to make her point: "What you wanta go knocking around them foreign countries again like some swallow come and swallow go from year to year and nevah settling down nous to git lost in" (332). But, as the novel makes clear, Jake, and the race he represents, has no country.

Home to Harlem, which Michelle Stephens calls the "black modernist narrative" of a "globalized black community," undercuts the idea of both Harlem and home (*Black Empire*, 131). Ray articulates the problem. "Races and nations were things like skunks," he thinks, "whose smells poisoned the air of life." He explains the lure of nationality:

> Civilized mankind reposed its faith and futures in their ancient, silted chan-
> nels. Great races and big nations! There must be something mighty inspirit-
> ing in being the citizen of a great strong nation. To be the white citizen of a
> nation that can say bold, challenging things like a strong man. Something
> very different from the keen ecstatic joy a man feels in the romance of being
> black. Something the black man could never feel nor quite understand.
>
> Ray felt that as he was conscious of being black and impotent, so, cor-
> respondingly, each marine down in Hayti must be conscious of being white
> and powerful. What a unique feeling of confidence about life the typi-
> cal white youth of his age must have! Knowing that his skin-color was a
> passport to glory, making him one with the ten thousands like himself. All
> perfect Occidentals and investors in their grand business called civilization.
> That grand business in whose pits sweated and snored all the black and
> brown hybrids and mongrels, simple earth-loving animals, without aspira-
> tions toward national unity and racial arrogance. (154–55)

Ray makes an especially apt diagnosis concerning nationalism. More than simply a marker of identity, nationalism is a hegemonic force. In any impe-rialistic or racial power dynamic, the stronger entity will assert nationalism as a means of excluding and defining the subaltern entity. So the condition of exploitation and violation that defined blackness in the South essentially extended to any white-occupied space, including the North, Europe, colo-nial Africa, the Caribbean, and South America. For black people in the early twentieth century, the whole world was essentially the South.

McKay picks up Jake's story again in the novel *Banjo: A Story without a Plot*. Ray and Jake appear among a group of displaced blacks from around the world in the port of Marseille, where the disillusioned cast of characters work, drink, and loaf aimlessly in a manner that rivals the Lost Generation angst of Hemingway and Fitzgerald. As the book's subtitle warns, it has no significant plot, but what makes it interesting is its subversive sense of nationalism. The issue had obviously been important to McKay in *Home to Harlem*, as he had both Jake and Ray comment on it extensively, but the issue is intentionally sublimated in *Banjo*. Michelle Stephens calls the characters in *Banjo* "denationalized," and Brent Hayes Edwards describes the book's primary theme as "vagabond internationalism" (198). Many of the characters in the book have their papers stamped "nationality doubtful," which is a signifier of their radical alienation and dispossession (McKay, *Banjo*, 312). At the end of the book, Ray voices his doubt that "the Negro could ever find a decent place" in white-dominated civilization, so he commits himself to wandering (324). His doubt could be interpreted as a sign of loss, specifically losing the hope of social equality.

For African Americans, exposure to proximal sites of modernity had complicated consequences. African American involvement in the war began with the notion that military service would lead to equality, but that idea effectively vanished and was replaced with the realization of a transnational experience of racial oppression. African Americans left the South in large numbers to find equality and opportunity in the North and in France. Compared to segregation, exploitation, and brutalization in South, they found more freedom in proximal sites of modernity, but the interregional contact during the war also spread segregation as a social practice beyond the South. The same pathways that radiated modernity into the region allowed regressive southern social practices to influence proximal sites of modernity, which indicates that radiation works in both directions. Blacks who returned to the distal South after the war found that the war had done little to change the culture of white supremacy, but fighting a war for freedom, liberty, and democracy in Europe emboldened many African Americans to confront white supremacy. Works of literature that exposed the region's hypocrisy, valorized the African American soldier, and depicted a tone of racial opposition were a crucial component of black modernist representations of the South.

4

DOMESTIC DISRUPTION

WORLD WAR I, MODERNITY,
AND SOUTHERN WOMEN'S FICTION

World War I rewrote the fiction of southern womanhood. Rooted in the same invented past as plantation fiction and the lost cause, southern women's roles in the early twentieth-century South were constricted, limited to domestic and maternal duties and segmented along race and class lines. The war disrupted gender roles, blurred racial and class divisions, and allowed women across the country an unprecedented degree of personal agency. As a result of women's growing political and economic power, the United States ratified the Nineteenth Amendment to the Constitution, granting women the right to vote after the war. The amendment itself demonstrates that the struggle for gender equality attained tangible success during World War I, but the movement for women's suffrage realized far more success in the Northeast than in the South, where gender roles continued to follow a strictly codified Victorian model well into the twentieth century. Gender roles tended to be more rigid for southern women than for northern women, but even in the South, World War I disrupted the family's domestic space, allowing southern women a slightly greater degree of personal agency, and this agency led southern women writers to portray their roles critically.

In their introduction to *The Female Imagination and the Modernist Aesthetic*, Sandra Gilbert and Susan Gubar explain that social changes taking place in proximal zones yielded a new form of women's writing. They explain that "dissonance between male and female responses to crucial socio-historical events like the suffrage movement, World War I, and the entrance of women into the labor market [led to the evolution of] two entirely different versions of the world, visions so different we felt we had to speak not only of male and female modernisms, but of masculinist and feminist modernisms" (2). Farther from the sites of modernity, in the distal South, the war's impact was more subdued. The fighting took place an ocean away, and relatively few southern women left the South during the war, but modernity came to them in the form of thousands of men from across the country who trained in the South, in the form of national changes in women's rights that resonated in the South, and in the form of temporarily increased social and economic opportunities. Black and white southern women's representations of the war are the clearest illustration of how modernism radiates into distal zones through networks of contact. Southern women's modernism tends to focus on disruptions within the domestic structure, using the home and gender roles as a metaphor for global events.

Most studies of modernist southern writers focus on male writers, either the white male southern writers associated with the Southern Renaissance or the black male southern writers associated with the Harlem Renaissance. Susan V. Donaldson and Anne Goodwyn Jones observe, in their introduction to *Haunted Bodies: Gender and Southern Texts*, that studies of the Southern Renaissance have notoriously marginalized women writers: Louis D. Rubin Jr. and Robert Jacob's *Southern Renascence* mentions only Katherine Anne Porter and Ellen Glasgow, Richard King's *A Southern Renaissance* mentions only Lillian Smith, Daniel J. Singal's *The War Within* mentions only Ellen Glasgow, Michael O'Brien's *The Idea of the American South* mentions no women writers, and none of these works mention any African American women writers. This persistent oversight diminishes the impact of women writers on postwar southern literature, but southern women writers were an important component of southern modernism.

Southern women's depictions of the war's impact on the South reveal an interesting phenomenon. Often during a war, women's social agency expands temporarily as men vacate positions of responsibility, leaving a political and economic role for women to fill, and in the South these dynamics occurred both during the Civil War and during World War I. Nina Baym argues in "The Myth of the Myth of Southern Womanhood" that "at least some southern women writers at the end of the [nineteenth] century and after turned against the postbellum southern myth and attempted to expose it as a myth in order to move the South and its women beyond its restrictions" (184). This tension between gender determinism and feminism increased after World War I, and works by black and white southern women writers set during the war often portray women characters as alternately challenging the patriarchal order and defending it as they attempt to negotiate the disruptions of modernity. In "Gender and the Great War," Anne Goodwyn Jones notes that William Faulkner and Katherine Anne Porter offer competing portrayals of women after the war. Faulkner's Narcissa Benbow Sartoris and Belle Mitchell Benbow in *Flags in the Dust* are self-absorbed and immoral, but Porter's Miranda in "Pale Horse, Pale Rider" takes on a traditionally masculine occupation during the war as a newspaper reporter. She relinquishes her job at the end of the war, which leads Jones to conclude that "wars shake up traditional structures, but only temporarily" (146). This temporary shake-up, however, is sufficient to expose the hypocrisy of southern patriarchy and the capacities of southern women's agency to expand. Southern women's modernism depicts this inherent instability in southern gender relations. This chapter explains how the war disrupted established gender roles in the South, analyzes how African American women writers wavered between Victorian propriety and impulses toward social transgression, traces the expansion and contraction of women's agency in novels by Ellen Glasgow and Elizabeth Madox Roberts, and describes the new southern women trope that emerged after the war in novels by Frances Newman and Zelda Fitzgerald. Southern gender roles are a social fiction, and modernist southern women's fiction rewrites the gender roles.

WORLD WAR I AND THE NEW SOUTHERN WOMAN

Well into the twentieth century, gender roles in the South involved the public and legal marginalization of women. Through the nineteenth century, women were not allowed to vote or own property, and their bodies were legally the property of their fathers until their marriage, at which time they became the property of their husbands. The southern household followed a paternalistic, patriarchal model with authority invested in the dominant male figure, to whom all female, filial, and labor relations were subject.[1] Yet even as southern society categorically marginalized women's roles, it paradoxically celebrated and vaunted the virtue of southern women, primarily the virtues that reinforced and masked female subordination. Thomas Nelson Page's encomium to white southern womanhood, for example, sets the tone: "Her life was one long act of devotion—devotion to God, devotion to her husband, devotion to her children, devotion to her servants, to the poor, to humanity."[2] The praise of virtues such as devotion, humility, charity, commitment, sacrifice, loyalty, and chastity inscribed an image of the southern woman as the angel in the house, an image that became a cultural icon and a social problem.

In *The Southern Lady*, Anne Firor Scott notes that the reality of southern women's lives rarely matched the symbol of southern womanhood. In some cases, in spite of severe social limitations, individual women achieved a significant degree of agency, usually either by using or by sacrificing their social status. One example was Jesse Daniel Ames, a white southern woman who crusaded against lynching, but cases such as hers were exceptional (Hall, *Revolt against Chivalry*). In many other cases, southern women themselves enforced and encoded gender roles. Scott quotes from numerous diaries and documents that represent southern women struggling to attain, not defy, the ideal of southern womanhood. In the same vein, Anne Goodwyn Jones argues in *Tomorrow Is Another Day*: "[T]he image wearing Dixie's Diadem is not a human being; it is a marble statue, beautiful and silent, eternally inspiring and eternally still. Rather than a person, [she] is a personification, effective only as she works in the imaginations of others. Efforts to join person and personification, to make self into symbol, must fail because the idea of southern womanhood specifically denies the self" (4).

World War I complicated both the selfhood and the symbolism of the southern woman. The exigencies of wartime and the sudden loss of labor in the exclusively male workplace allowed women temporary entrance into the labor force.[3] Susan Zeiger comments that "[t]he war heightened and thus made visible the underlying contradiction between prevailing definitions of womanhood on the one hand and women's increasing participation in the waged labor force on the other" (173). Women also served auxiliary roles in each branch of the armed forces, marking the first large-scale enlistment of women in the American military.[4] Women played traditional roles of mother, lover, and supporter in the war effort, but they also played traditionally unfeminine roles of worker, provider, and leader. Peter Filene documents in *Him/Her/Self: Gender Identities in Modern America* that the change in social roles had an impact on sexuality, creating tension between mothers of the True Woman generation who valued absolute chastity until marriage and their daughters of the New Woman generation who valued sexual liberation. In many respects, the issue of sex, the underpinning for gender construction, became the central, if frequently unstated, issue in modernist southern women's fiction, and changes in sexual relations led to a change in gender ideology after World War I. "This revolution in gender ideology, a revolution that was by no means confined to the South," Anne Goodwyn Jones explains, "took on special intensity there, where rigid gender boundaries had always been part of a network of racial and class boundaries as well. To shake the pedestal, or even more disturbing, to refuse the phallus, was to put the entire structure of Southern thinking at risk" ("The Work of Gender," 43). Margaret Higonnet and Patrice Higonnet argue in "The Double Helix" that, while gender roles changed temporarily during the war, the underlying ideological structure remained intact, leading to a regression in social advancements after the war. This dynamic played out for southern women, and the peculiar ideological structures in the South made the process especially complicated.

Before World War I in the patriarchal South, southern women were both subject to and enforcers of strict social codes. In *New Women of the New South*, Marjorie Spruill Wheeler describes white southern women at the turn of the century as "hostages" to the lost cause. She explains that "the commitment to preserving the traditional role of southern womanhood was not just an isolated, idiosyncratic whim of nostalgic southerners; it was part of an intense, conscious, semi-religious drive to protect the South against the 'ravages' of Northern culture during a period of massive and often unwanted political, social, and economic change" (5). To the extent that gender became intertwined with regional identity, southern woman-hood became a cultural bulwark preventing both the erosion of traditional southern values and progress toward gender equality. Wheeler's charac-terization of southern women as hostages, however, may not be entirely accurate, as women were often complicit in maintaining the cult of the lost cause. The emergence of the United Daughters of the Confederacy in the 1890s, which would by the 1920s be the largest and wealthiest women's organization in the United States, suggests that southern women freely propagated the image, if not the reality, of southern womanhood (Cox). White southern female identity, thus, became incorporated in a racist, mas-culinist social hierarchy, leaving southern women in the ironic position of enforcing their own subordination. The penalty for feminist ideas or acts of feminine agency in the South at the beginning of the twentieth century continued to be social exclusion, the same penalty the Grimké sisters faced when they spoke out against slavery in the 1830s.

The South, then, was an unlikely and unwelcoming place for any politi-cal agenda promoting gender equality. White southern women did partici-pate in the suffrage movement, but, as Elna C. Green explains in *Southern Strategies: Southern Women and the Woman Suffrage Question*, they did so in less visible ways than their northern counterparts. By 1913, every southern state had an active chapter of the National American Woman Suffrage Association, an organization affiliated with the Women's Christian Temperance Union, which agitated for women's right to vote. As the

United States moved toward war, the suffrage movement gained strength in the Northeast, but an antisuffrage movement, led by the female Anti-Ratification League and other organizations, emerged in the South. The antisuffragists argued that biblical edict placed the woman in the home and that women's involvement in political activity, whether by voting or by running for office, would result in the moral decline of southern society, the ascendancy of Yankee domination, and the end of white supremacy. At the same time, African Americans in the South were effectively disenfranchised through Jim Crow laws, so the suffrage movement excluded African American women. Southern men, avatars of patriarchy and paternalism, were disinclined to support the suffrage movement, and many prominent southern businessmen and politicians encouraged and funded the antisuffrage movement. When the time came for the ratification of the Nineteenth Amendment, most southern states voted against it. The South clearly was not a promising landscape for women's liberation.[5]

Yet the New Woman did inhabit the South, although in a primarily private rather than public incarnation.[6] Slowly at first, white southern women began to register to vote and then to cast ballots, but the most evident tensions in southern gender roles developed within the home and between two generations of southern women. The generation coming of age during the war took greater advantage of social and political freedoms than their mothers' generation, who came of age under the lost cause. In the South, the New Woman, who personified the sexual and personal liberation of the Jazz Age, intersected with the Southern Belle, who personified the virtue and repression of southern culture. The New Woman complicated the representation of southern womanhood, and southern women writers after World War I employed the figure of the belle as an indicator of changing women's roles. Female characters in postwar southern literature lose the veneer of virtue, so the fiction of southern womanhood becomes more complicated, which is an important characteristic of southern women's modernism.

The deromanticization of southern femininity signifies both social and artistic progress. The simplistic construction of the angel in the house gave way to complex, problematic depictions of female characters in literary texts that reflected the sophistication and anxiety of modernity. In *No Man's Land*, Sandra Gilbert and Susan Gubar note that World War I exacerbated gender tension, or "radical sexchanges":

> All of the metamorphoses of sexuality and sex roles—the gender trans-
> formation connected with the decline of faith in a white male supremacist

empire, with the rise of the New Woman, with the development of an ideology of free love, with the revolt against the discontents fueled by a widespread cultural "feminization" of women, and with the emergence of lesbian
literary communities—seem to have been in a crisis that set the "whispering
ambitions" of embattled men and women against each other. (258–59)

Gilbert and Gubar trace these metamorphoses through a number of works
primarily by writers in proximal sites of modernity that portray changing
gender roles during the war. Works such as Siegfried Sassoon's poem "For the
Glory of Women" and Virginia Woolf's novel *Mrs. Dalloway* overtly address
the social and artistic changes taking place in the context of the war.[7]

Postwar modernist texts by most transatlantic women writers represent
the war as a domestic crisis.[8] Every aspect of domestic life was disrupted,
and women on the home front participated in the cultural sense of trauma
almost as intensely as the men in the trenches. The domestic and military
fronts were forced into conflict in a way that radically destabilized women's
roles, and the loss of loved ones coupled with the loss of identity. Rebecca
West's *The Return of the Soldier*, Edith Wharton's *A Son at the Front*, Willa
Cather's *One of Ours*, and Virginia Woolf's *Mrs. Dalloway* use the experience of loss to depict the war as a period of social fragmentation and individual alienation. Aesthetically, these texts represent a shifting range from
Victorian-era linear narrative to modernist experimental narrative. The
fragmented, nonlinear structure and internal narration of *Mrs. Dalloway*
signals the convergence of postwar modernity and women's modernism.
Rita Felski explains in *The Gender of Modernity* that the literary and artistic
movement of modernism is based on the social and historical movement of
modernity, and she argues that the woman's place within both these movements is problematic. To the extent that women are excluded, the movements are masculinist, and to the extent that women are involved, the
movements are feminist. She emphasizes the point that gendered responses
are based on the unique variables of each form of social change.

Southern women's modernism combines aspects of proximal modernity
with the distinctive, distal attributes of southern womanhood: the angel in
the house, white supremacy, Confederate veneration, suffragism and anti-
suffragism, the New Woman, and World War I. Aesthetically, the literature
tends to be less experimental than the work of European and northern
American women writers, but the social issues, particularly the sense of
identity instability, are consistent with modernism. Nina Baym suggests
that the destabilization may have been even more significant for southern

women "because society in the South was represented as arrested at an earlier stage of historical development than the North, and to the extent that
the southern male was thought to be defending his way of life precisely for
its agrarian basis, the woman's ideology is actually more revolutionary there
than in the North" (189). Southern women's modernism involves the complex interrelation of gender identity, southern identity, and racial identity.
Anne Goodwyn Jones describes the challenge facing southern women writers in the face of modernity:

> The South's confrontation with modernity, and with modernism, evoked
> conflict and resistance as much as it did emulation and imitation. "Modern"
> (and "modernism") seemed to many to mean precisely what was not
> southern, what was even antisouthern. Could an identifiable South survive
> such radical change? If not, did southerners need to retreat into the past? As
> for gender, could there be a modern southern woman, or was the very idea
> an oxymoron? For others, modernity (and modernism) seemed not only
> incompatible with, but in some senses to have emerged from, the South:
> the Civil War had shaken some southern hearts and minds as profoundly
> as World War I was to shatter European confidence a half-century later.
> ("Women Writers," 276)

Modern southern women writers negotiated this complicated terrain by
challenging the definitions of both "modern" and "southern" and by representing a global crisis as a domestic crisis.[9]

To the extent that the war destabilized southern womanhood, it altered
southern women's identity, but after the war the South continued to be a
dominantly masculinist—and racist—society.[10] So the social changes for
southern women, while disruptive, were not extreme. The changes in literary representations of southern womanhood were more progressive, but
social categories—race, age, class, and place—affected artistic experimentation. Social changes taking place during the war had the greatest impact
on young, upper-middle-class white women, especially those who had contact with proximal sites of modernity. The writing of women in this group,
including Frances Newman and Zelda Fitzgerald, shows signs of antitradi-
tional literary experimentation indicative of modernism. Change affected
older middle-class white women living in the South, but these women, such
as Ellen Glasgow and Elizabeth Madox Roberts, had a greater personal
investment in traditional southern identity, and their writing shows fewer
signs of experimentation even while criticizing southern cultural norms.

Black women writers from the South, most of whom migrated out of the South, are more complicated. Their social concerns typically, and understandably, address issues of racial identity more than issues of regional identity, and their aesthetic sensibilities typically show fewer signs of modernist experimentation. So in an equation of social change and rhetorical change that bears out Felski's theory of gender and modernity, the war's impact on the representation of southern womanhood reflects the war's social impact on the southern woman writer.

I SIT AND SEW: BLACK SOUTHERN WOMEN AND WORLD WAR I

Ann Shockley argues that black southern women faced even more restrictive gender conventions than white southern women. She quotes Alice Dunbar-Nelson by way of example, who comments that black husbands and fathers enforced "the white male's attitude of woman's place built on the rock of southern chivalry" (Shockley, 128). Gender roles for black women in the South—at least for middle-class black women and, thus, for the women most likely to have opportunities to write—were based both on traditional southern womanhood and on segregation. Gender roles in the black domestic space, in fact, valorized whiteness. Just as advertisements for hair straighteners and skin-bleaching products in early twentieth-century African American periodicals indicate an obsession with imitating the white body, the drive to imitate the white household, even to the degree of employing black domestic servants, indicates an obsession with the white lifestyle. But the white middle-class version of the American dream was a reality for a relatively small segment of African Americans, especially African Americans in the South. There, because of institutionalized economic disparity, black women often found themselves in a double bind. In *Afro-American Women of the South and the Advancement of the Race*, Cynthia Neverdon-Morton explains that black men, as Dunbar-Nelson's quotation suggests, believed that the woman's place was in the home, but many black women were forced to work outside the home to supplement the family's income, often working a full day as a servant to a white household before returning, exhausted, to their own neglected households to perform domestic labor for their own families (3).

Traditionalism and patriarchy were strong in the black southern community, so opportunities for black women to write creatively were rare, and African American women writers tended to prefer traditional writing conventions. During the World War I era, black women's writing demonstrated a Victorian sensibility predicated, at least in part, on reinforcing traditional patriarchal gender roles. Just as young white women living outside the South were more likely to use experimental forms, however, representations of World War I by younger black women writers were more likely to share modernist characteristics than the work of older writers. Race complicated the interplay between modernity and modernism because the previous generation of African American women had invested themselves heavily in the uplift movement, intending to demonstrate that black families could emulate Victorian ideals. Many African American women were not entirely receptive to the disruptions of modernity, and their depictions of World War I illustrate the tension between impulses for Victorian propriety and for citizenship through confrontation.

Black women's involvement with the suffrage movement, for example, was complicated. In *African American Women in the Struggle for the Vote*, Rosalyn Terborg-Penn explains that black women faced many more obstacles during the movement than their white counterparts: they faced both racism and sexism simultaneously, some factions of the white suffrage movement excluded black membership, fewer black women had financial means to allow involvement, black male support for suffrage eroded by the beginning of the twentieth century, and black codes in the South effectively made black political involvement impossible. Nonetheless, some black women did campaign for the vote, including a few in the South. One of these was Maggie Shaw Fullilove, an educated woman and wife of a doctor in Yazoo City, Mississippi, who wrote a novel, *Who Was Responsible?*, that depicts a woman becoming involved in the temperance movement and the suffrage movement. As a woman of intellect and means, Fullilove was among those best positioned to advocate for black women's rights, but other than writing the novel and a few essays, she does not appear to have been involved in organizing or recruiting black women in the movement. The novel, moreover, does not have an explicit race theme, and the book's characters are not racially identified, so a reader could easily assume that the protagonist is white. And the protagonist's political involvement is a means to an end, the abolition of alcohol. The title's question refers to the death of the protagonist's husband, an alcoholic, and suggests that both the protagonist specifically and the social structure generally are responsible. After the protagonist's death, his wife joins the Women's Christian Temperance Union and campaigns for prohibition, later becoming involved in war preparedness and suffrage. Although a significant indication of black southern women's engagement with political affairs, even this representation of social change from the perspective of a black southern woman is embedded within a framework of traditional social values.

Black women's involvement with the war follows the same pattern as black women's involvement with the suffrage movement, but the war actually seemed to promise more immediate social advancement for the race than the suffrage movement, and many black female activists were willing to focus on racial progress at the expense of gender progress. Nikki Brown argues in *Private Politics and Public Voices* that "the World War had the effect of masculinizing gender relations within the African American middle class, reframing discussion from black participation to black male participation" (6). While some working-class white women found work in factories and munitions plants, working-class black women were mostly excluded. While some white women served in Europe as nurses and support staff with organizations such as the YMCA, black women were almost completely excluded. While a few white women actually served in the American military, black women were prohibited. Black women were active in the Red Cross and in various war preparedness movements, and black women, like white women, played a crucial role in motivating male participation in the war. But this role—the gold star mother, the devoted wife, the virtuous lover—was partly a function of jingoistic propaganda and partly a function of patriarchal family ordination. For black women, the war was an unpromising means for advances toward race and gender equality.

Although black women's public roles in the war effort were limited, a few women created important public roles for themselves. Addie W. Hunton and Kathryn M. Johnson were the first black women to serve with the YMCA supporting troops near the front line, and they describe their experiences in *Two Colored Women with the American Expeditionary Forces*. Their book records the experiences of black soldiers living among the French people, and a recurring theme in the book is the contrast between American racism and French equality. They observe the irony that "colored soldiers were greatly loved by the French people," yet they were consistently reviled, abused, and oppressed by their fellow Americans (85). During the war, Hunton and Johnson provided one of the few support centers available to thousands of black American soldiers. They provided an essential connection to home for these soldiers, spending much of their time reading and writing letters for illiterate soldiers and, acting as ersatz Victorian mothers, guarding their Christian and moral character. Echoing a theme in Victor Daly's novel about black soldiers in France, Hunton and Johnson reinforce the sexual separation between black American soldiers and white French women, appealing to Christian virtues, and they also show great concern for their own virtue, commenting frequently on lustful advances from the soldiers. They play two complicated roles—simultaneously advocating for the equal treatment of black men and reinforcing the image of devoted and dependent women. Their primary concern was to maintain a semblance of domestic norms in spite of the war's impact on black men. Their story illustrates the difficulty of black women's modernism after World War I: although they had personal contact with proximal modernity and relative equality in France, they were overdetermined by their racial and gender roles. But their story is an important indicator of the possibility of black women's modernism.

Alice Dunbar-Nelson was one of the most outspoken black female supporters of the war effort in the United States. She was also one of the most unconventional black female leaders of the period, and her involvement with the war effort is one example of her unconventionality.[11] Born into a Creole family, she attended college, married poet Paul Laurence Dunbar, married twice again after his death, had numerous affairs and lesbian relationships, and published works of poetry, fiction, and drama while maintaining an active career as a public speaker and journalist. Unlike the women involved with the uplift movement, she cared little for her public reputation. During the war she organized rallies for black enlistment, including a massive Flag Day event in 1918, and she had an affair with Emmett J. Scott, the special assistant to the secretary of war and former personal secretary to Booker T. Washington. After the war, she wrote a chapter titled "Negro Women and War Work" in *Scott's Official History of the American Negro in the World War*. Her account of black women in the war suggests that they were able to forget their special grievance against the white race, echoing the tone of W. E. B. Du Bois's call to close ranks for the duration of the war. She claims, for example, that "into [the] maelstrom of war activity the women of the Negro race hurled themselves joyously. The asked no odds, remembered no grudges, solicited no favors, pleaded for no privileges. They came by the thousands, hands opened wide to give of love and service and patriotism" (375).

The same jingoistic tone can be found in her play *Mine Eyes Have Seen*, originally published in the *Crisis* in 1918. The play depicts a dispossessed family of southern blacks who fled their home after their father's lynching to find work and safety in New York. There, like thousands of other black families, they are crowded into a tenement, and their illusions of security and prosperity are shattered. When the family's younger son, Chris, receives a draft notice, he initially refuses to accept his assignment, which, considering the family's situation, provokes a surprising response. His older brother, who has been maimed in an industrial accident, calls him a coward, and a chorus of tenement dwellers, overhearing the heated discussion, add their voices to the argument. This chorus constitutes a cross section of America's most destitute citizens: the widow of an Irish soldier, a Russian Jewish refugee, and an army mule driver on leave. They each in turn exhort Chris to do his duty, and then, as the chords of "Battle Hymn of the Republic" lilt into the room, his invalid brother makes a final passionate speech:

> It is not for us to visit retribution. Nor to wish hatred on others. Let us rather remember the good that has come to us. Love of humanity is above the small considerations of time or place or race or sect. Can't you be big enough to feel pity for the little crucified French children—for the ravished Polish girls, even as their mother must have felt sorrow, if they had known, for OUR burned and maimed little ones? Oh, Mothers of Europe, we be of one blood, you and I! (247–48)

Finally convinced, Chris agrees to do his duty, imploring his mother and his girlfriend not to fear for him. Claire Tylee observes that the play "assumes ... that citizenship is dependent on a masculine notion of self-worth based on strength and courage to do one's patriotic duty" ("Womanist Propaganda," 158). Dunbar-Nelson trades heavily on domesticity and traditional gender roles in the play, appealing primarily to senses of masculine duty and responsibility.

Dunbar-Nelson's best-known poem, "I Sit and Sew," underscores patriarchal gender roles, however. The poem's persona is a woman working in war relief, knitting and sewing for soldiers at the front—in effect, engaged in gender-appropriate wartime domestic tasks. But she longs to be involved in a more significant way:

> I sit and sew—my heart aches with desire—
> That pageant terrible, that fiercely pouring fire
> On wasted fields, and writhing grotesque things
> Once men. My soul in pity flings
> Appealing cries, yearning only to go
> There in that holocaust of hell, those fields of woe—
> But—I must sit and sew. (84)

The persona expresses a sense of frustration with her socially inscribed role, feeling inept and inadequate as she labors over her "useless task," yet she succumbs to the standards of the patriarchy. The fact that one of the most unconventional African American women of her generation reinforces the codes of patriarchy illustrates how profoundly powerful they were.

After the war, some African American women writers adopted a more confrontational attitude toward white supremacy, consistent with the work of postwar African American male writers. Mary Burill's play *Aftermath*, for example, portrays a returning soldier as armed and ready to meet violence with violence. John Thornton returns to South Carolina with a medal for courage he won in France. When he reaches the family cabin, he asks for his father, but rather than the joyous homecoming he expected, he finds that his father has been lynched during his absence and that his sister has shielded him from the news. John takes his army revolver and explains to his sister and grandmother the lessons he learned during the war:

> I've been helpin' the w'ite man git his freedom, I reckon I'd bettah try now to get my own! ... I'm sick o' these w'ite folks doin's—we're "fine trus'worthy feller citizuns" when they're handin' us out guns, an' Liberty Bonds, an' chuckin' us off to die; but we ain't a damn thing when it comes to handin' us the rights we done fought an' bled fu'! I'm sick o' this sort o' life—an' I'm goin' to put an end to it! ... This ain't no time fu' preachers or prayers! You mean to tell me I mus' let them w'ite devuls send me miles erway to suffer an' be shot up fu' the freedom of people I ain't nevah seen, while they're burnin' an' killin' my folks here at home! To Hell with 'em! (90–91)

Burrill's play projects a defiant racial attitude, the same tone found in Claude MacKay's poem "If We Must Die," but the play, much like *Mine Eyes Have Seen*, continues to portray women as passive. John's grandmother begs him to pray rather than fight, and his sister hugs him and warns him that he will be killed. This suggests a curious dichotomy in the relationship between gender and violence. Women in a traditionalist society may condone violence in the name of nationalism, such as the speaker in Johnson's poem who sacrifices her son to patriotic idealism, but black women should not or would not condone violence in the name of racial equality. Partly because of black women's social distance from the war, their attitudes, even in representations by black women writers, continued to reflect traditionalist notions about appropriate gender roles. Burrill's play, in spite of its overt militancy, places primary emphasis on maintaining and preserving the black domestic sphere.

Perhaps the best example of a modernist representation of the war by a black woman writer is Zora Neale Hurston's *Jonah's Gourd Vine*. In this novel, the war's actual impact on the southern family is minimal—it occupies about five pages of text—but it creates sense of disruption in a technique similar to John Dos Passos's newsreels in *U.S.A.*, a montage of decontextualized images and disembodied voices. To be more specific, the war spans five paragraphs of disjointed narrative, such as "Conscription, uniforms, bands, strutting drum-majors, and the mudsills of the earth arose and skipped like the mountains of Jerusalem on The Day. Lowly minds who knew not their State Capitals were talking glibly of France. Over there. No man's land" (148). Hurston captures the whirling cacophony of wartime for those removed from the war: the excited young men, the old men discussing Wilson, Roosevelt, and Du Bois, the anxious mothers, the braggadocio of the returning soldiers claiming white female conquests in France, and finally "the world gone money mad" (149). Hurston's depiction contrasts African American folk culture with the onrush of modernism, yielding a unique and prescient literary form.[12]

While Hurston evades the Victorian sentimentalism that characterizes the writing of many of her contemporaries, her portrayal of gender roles in the black southern community inscribes women's marginalization. The novel's protagonist, John Buddy Pearson, ministers to the largest black Baptist congregation in Florida while philandering notoriously. Within this masculinist social structure, women compete with each other for the role of Pearson's wife. The best wife, based on Hurston's text, is the one who most closely conforms to the image of the angel in the house. In this novel, Hurston, who would go on to challenge patriarchal gender roles in *Their Eyes Were Watching God*, seems to affirm and enforce the same virtues associated with traditional southern womanhood: loyalty, charity, chastity, and sacrifice. This circumstance, in context with the even more traditional portrayals of black women's roles by other black women writers and with the significant challenges complicating black women's involvement with the suffrage movement and war preparedness, indicates that World War I had a small but significant impact on black southern women's writing. Among black women writers from both the North and the South, the theme of racial uplift would continue to influence aesthetic development well into the 1930s. It is not surprising, therefore, that black northern writer Jesse

Redmon Fauset's novel *There Is Confusion*, which uses the war as a primary dramatic background, shows many of the same signs of literary sentimentalism as the work of black southern women writers. For black women, the boundaries of race increased the limitations of gender, putting them at a greater social distance from the domestic effects of the war.

Dispossessing the Angel in the House

After the war, as men returned to their homes and jobs, women's wartime social gains regressed. Many women lost the opportunity to work outside the home, but women had demonstrated a capacity for economic agency, which broke a persistent barrier, and even though the suffrage movement largely disbanded during the war, women received the right to vote after the war. In the South, the cycle of social progression and regression is particularly evident in the contrast between women's living conditions before the war and after. Ellen Glasgow's *Vein of Iron* and Elizabeth Madox Roberts's *He Sent Forth a Raven* both represent white southern women during this period, and their portrayals challenge the notion of the angel in the house. They depict southern women living within the rigidly patriarchal social structure acquiring personal agency during the war, including new social, economic, and sexual freedoms. At the same time, these texts suggest that the sociocultural system in the US South is actually a patriarchal veneer covering a matriarchal core, implying that women have greater authority within the patriarchal social order than they may first appear to have.

Ellen Glasgow may be the best example of the contradictory and complex social position that women occupied as modernity radiated into the region. She was raised in a prominent family from the Virginia Tidewater region within the confines of southern patriarchy. Her father managed Tredegar Iron Works, one of the largest factories in the South, and he played the role of patriarch by defining and dominating the lives of his family members. While he showed signs of devotion to his church and his company in public, he had affairs with several black servants and tyrannically brutalized his wife and children in private. Glasgow regarded him as "a consummate hypocrite" and "a fraud," and one could speculate that her attitude toward her father propelled her into behaviors out of keeping with the myth of southern womanhood (Goodman, 20–21). She rebelled against the patriarchy by becoming one of the most visible suffragists in Virginia. Beginning in 1909, she was involved with the National American Woman Suffrage Association, and she later wrote in her autobiography, "If women wanted a vote, I agreed they had a right to vote, for I regarded the franchise in our Republic more as a right than as a privilege; and I was willing to do anything, except burn with heroic blaze, for the watchword of liberty" (Glasgow, *The Woman Within*, 187).[13] During the war, the suffrage movement in Virginia, never as well organized as its northern counterparts, dispersed. Glasgow spent several years in England between her involvement with the suffrage movement and the beginning of the war, where she had contact with proximal sites of modernity, and she returned to Richmond in 1916. Upon her return, she began a relationship with Henry Anderson that resulted in an engagement. Before they were married, however, Henry received a commission to lead the Red Cross relief effort in the Balkans. While there, he had an affair with Queen Marie of Romania, gossip of which reached Glasgow. She and Henry never officially ended their engagement, but they were never married. In her later years, possibly because of her broken engagement, Glasgow became increasingly conservative about social matters, even becoming a supporter of the Southern Agrarians, and she reversed some of her earlier feminist ideals.[14]

Considering her perspective on gender in the South, her evolving portrayals of southern women's identity are both clearly connected to her personal experience and indicative of broader social trends. In *Virginia*, Glasgow personifies the ideal of southern womanhood in Virginia Pendleton, a woman taught to valorize her own subservience to men.[15] When her love interest abandons her, she is incapable of independent life. In *The Romance of a Plain Man*, which was published in 1909 while Glasgow was heavily involved with the suffrage movement, she dramatizes the suffrage movement in the South in the character of Mataoca Bland, a woman who defies her family's Victorian conventions and ultimately gives her life to the suffrage movement. *Barren Ground*, published fifteen years later, portrays Dorinda Oakley unlearning the lessons of gender subordination and fashioning herself into an independent and successful businesswoman. *Vein of Iron*, published in 1935, follows the Fincastle family of Virginia from the turn of the century to the Great Depression, and it provides the most comprehensive image of changing gender roles and the progression and regression that accompanied World War I.

Ada Fincastle, heroine of *Vein of Iron*, comes from a patriarchal southern family. The entire family depends upon the father, John, for economic support, and he makes all decisions concerning the family's welfare, but he is a problematic patriarch, not because he is domineering and hypocritical but because he is idealistic and ineffectual. He had once been a promising

Presbyterian minister renowned for his eloquence and brilliant mind, but the church excommunicated him because he wrote a philosophical treatise that defied established dogma. Glasgow contrasts Ada's ineffectual father with her resilient grandmother, the woman who embodies the "vein of iron" ethos. While Ada's father ruins his career and eventually his health with his descent into abstraction, her grandmother manages to keep the family together through her commitment to faith and fortitude. Although thoroughly and unquestioningly Calvinist, Ada's grandmother adapts to change, including the changes brought on by the war that seem to threaten the annihilation of southern society. Lucinda MacKethan argues that this novel "envisions a matriarchal design" because it represents men sharing responsibility with women and because it emphasizes community over individuality. She goes on to define a matriarchal design as "a structure of relationships based on sharing rather than competitiveness, on negotiation rather than self-assertion, and on integration rather than exclusion" ("Restoring Order," 90). In *Vein of Iron*, Ada frequently chooses not to assert herself, instead choosing to follow her grandmother's example and adapt to new conditions while maintaining the spirit of tradition. Her story reveals how matriarchy supports patriarchy.

Glasgow opens the novel in an insular community named Shut-In Valley, emphasizing the South's detachment from world events, but the war disrupts ordinary life for the Fincastle family. In her preface to the novel, Glasgow writes that the book is not about the war; rather, those events are part of the setting, "scarcely more than an incident in the larger drama of mortal conflict with fate" (xiii). Nonetheless, the war forces Ada into marriage, forces the family to leave the valley to move to a city, and forces Ada to work outside the home, all events that erode the family's traditional patriarchal structure. Ada's grandmother, who lived through the Civil War, says that "war isn't real to me if it leaves a window-pane in your house" (156). Her comment makes a contrast from the immediate forms of disruption that take place when the battlefield intersects with the domestic space, and the mediated disruptions that take place when the battlefield is far removed from the domestic space. Ada does not experience violence or trauma first-hand, but the war changes the circumstances of her daily life.

Ada's most direct connection to the war is her lover, Ralph, a second lieutenant in the army. The war complicates their relationship in ways that challenge the chaste version of southern femininity. Ralph is divorcing his first wife, which makes him unavailable according to social propriety, but when he secures a brief furlough before shipping to France, he and Ada spend it living in mock domesticity in an abandoned cabin. Although their affair runs counter to their religious values and social mores, they see it as their only opportunity to be together before Ralph's mobilization. The war leads Ada to assert her social and sexual independence, but she does so in a way that reinforces patriarchal gender roles. While in the cabin with Ralph, she plays the role of wife as much as lover, providing for his domestic needs as well as his sexual desires. Ada gets pregnant during their two-day affair in the cabin, and she is left alone, pregnant, and unmarried, while Ralph serves in France. She endures the disapproval of everyone in the community, including her grandmother, but she is not cast out as she might have been ordinarily, which suggests a special wartime dispensation or a general weakening of social mores. She and Ralph communicate only through letters, which function as their symbolic domestic space. "By the time you read this," she writes in the letter informing him of her pregnancy, "I shall be sitting up, perhaps walking about, and thankful anyway that the long waiting is over. Nothing in this world is so bad as waiting for it. That is why I couldn't bear war. But nothing else matters if only you will come back and we can all be happy together in the same place" (216–17). In this letter, she suggests that the performance of southern gender roles will constitute a return to normalcy after the war.

The war, however, makes normalcy elusive. After her grandmother dies, Ada takes on responsibility for her ailing father and moves the family into the city, where she is able to find work:

> After two months, she was astonished afresh whenever she remembered the abundance of work and the ease with which she had found a position in the autumn of nineteen hundred and eighteen. The prejudice against women as workers had not survived the economic urgency of a world conflict. There had been no eager preference, immediately after the Armistice, for returned soldiers. Women in industry would always be cheaper than men, and since the war was won, prosperity was more agreeable, if not more important, than patriotism. The first place she had sought in November was hers for the asking. (231)

By moving to the city and taking a job, Ada challenges the conventions of patriarchy, initially as a necessary expedient.[16] Women who earned their own incomes also gained a significant degree of independence from their male supporters, enabling them, at least hypothetically, to make their own decisions about how to use their incomes, how to spend their time, and how to use their bodies. Women in the workforce sowed the seeds of feminism in the South. Ada's feminism, however, is reluctant and expedient. When Ralph returns from the war, Ada leaves her job, they get married, and her life assumes many of the conventions of southern womanhood, which illustrates the pattern of progression and regression that typically follows wartime change.

In the novel, the end of the war ushers in a wave of modernization that changes the social structure. In relatively urban and modern Queenborough, a fictionalized version of Richmond, the streets are paved, the houses have electricity and indoor plumbing, and the postwar economic boom drives a wave of consumerism.[17] One of the fastest-growing segments of the economy and most obvious signs of modernization is the automobile industry, as motor cars become as common as carriages. Ralph takes a job selling cars when he returns, using the processes of modernity to replicate patriarchy. He tells Ada, "You must let me take care of the household. I'll have a salary of three thousand dollars besides a commission after I sell a number of cars. I'll be sure to sell cars. Everybody who has money is buying" (246). He manages to support the family well at his job, until he crashes a car while giving a woman a test ride, leaving him bedridden for several weeks. The incident raises suspicions that he and the woman were engaged in an affair, but the rumors are never substantiated, and Ada resigns herself to care for her husband during his convalescence. In this incident, modernity and patriarchy collide, and the effects revert to patriarchy.

Ada is a transitional figure between the Southern Belle and the New Woman.[18] The New Woman challenges the conventions of southern womanhood, and Ada encounters them at her job, where she observes that they are "all alike . . . all wore that stare of bright immaturity, all moved with flat bosoms, with narrow hips, with twisting ankles on French heels" (235). She deplores their behavior, their drinking, their jazz music, and their licentiousness, but they are the natural product of change in the South. Although Ada does not become a feminist, she realizes that these women will inevitably unravel the construct of southern feminine identity.[19] Then again, social change does not happen unilaterally, for southern men changed just as significantly during this period. Glasgow notes in her preface to *They Stooped to Folly* that "the years since the First World War are becoming the dark moon for a number of exalted illusions. It is at least open to question whether women would ever have rebelled against their confining attitude had they not observed a diminishing humility in the novels written by men. At all events, after the War, male disillusionment with virtue, which had

thickened like dust, invaded the whole flattened area of modern prose fiction" (*A Certain Measure*, 232). Perhaps male disillusionment with virtue,
which Glasgow sees in the work of many male writers, reflects the southern
patriarchy's waning interest in gyneolatry, a shift concurrent with the growing agency of southern women and consequent to the domestic changes
taking place in southern cities as a result of the war.

Elizabeth Madox Roberts's *He Sent Forth a Raven* demonstrates how
modernity radiates to an isolated farm family in rural Kentucky.[20] She
portrays the farm as a patriarchal regime dominated by the eccentric des-
pot Stoner Drake. In the novel's opening, Drake rails at God, vowing that
if his second wife dies "he would never set his foot on God's earth again"
(3). When his wife indeed dies, Drake keeps his vow, continuing to run his
farm and his family from within his home. Self-confined but "master of his
house," Drake uses a horn to give commands to his overseers, and he relies
on his daughter, Martha, and his granddaughter, Jocelle, for contact with the
outside world. Roberts's ludicrous depiction of Drake, including his pen-
chant for hollow prophecy and his bizarre cosmographic texts, casts him
as a caricature of patriarchy, an image that invites comparisons to Milton
dictating to his daughters. Drake imagines himself as an incarnation of
Noah, piloting his ark amid the flooding decay of the modern world, which
implies that Jocelle is the raven to which the title alludes, the one who leaves
never to return.

Roberts's isolated, patriarchal farm is a synecdoche for the rural South
just after the turn of the twentieth century. The emergence of automobiles
and the construction of highways, which made much of the rural South
accessible and, according to Barbara Ladd, effectively signified the emergence of modernity, make their farm, Wolflick, even more isolated, as
no one goes there except "those who had some urgent need to go there"
(*Resisting History*, 18, 25). When news of the war in Europe reaches the farm,
Drake interprets it as a millennial sign heralding the imminent apocalypse,
but most of the other inmates on the farm reach a more pragmatic conclusion: the war means a boost in the market for agricultural products. At first,
the increase in production is the only noticeable sign of a war taking place
across the ocean from Kentucky, but inevitably the war becomes more disruptive. Drake, who consistently looks for cosmic signs in terrestrial events,
asks Jocelle on several occasions to interpret the war for him by explaining
its significance. Each time, she answers him blankly, suggesting that the war
in itself has no meaning for her. In time, however, the war does come to
have a significant meaning for her, although it begins indirectly.

Jocelle's cousin Walter is the agent of disruption. A belligerent character, he sees the war as an opportunity to escape Wolflick. When America enters the war, he enlists in the marines and leaves the farm for basic training. He returns on a brief furlough before mobilization and upsets the farm's ordinary routine because he has become an outsider and a transgressor. Jocelle finds his presence ominous and disturbing, and her foreboding proves to be well founded when Walter rapes her. Roberts sublimates the rape, perhaps the most crucial action in the text, so that it is barely discernible. It never actually happens in the narrative: Walter and Jocelle walk to a creek and then she returns to the house "faintly delirious" and "trembl[ing] with exhaustion," hiding in her room while the rest of the family wishes Walter farewell (162). Walter brings the war, and the terrors of the outside world, to Wolflick. When he leaves, "Jocelle, falling asleep at last, contrived a picture of ease, in which the war had left her and had gone on to some farther battlefield," but when she awakens, she feels that "the war had rolled its waves forward to include herself" (163). Afterward, she feels herself to be three people, suggesting a Freudian psychic fragmentation: she sees the "person of yesterday," a manifestation of the ego, the girl who cared for her aunt and heeded her grandfather; she sees a "person with ordered thinking," a manifestation of the superego, the woman who will persevere through the chaos; and she sees a third person, a newfound id, who "arose from moment to moment, stepping through the confusion in strong rhythmic stride, asserting itself, unafraid and unashamed, saying nothing but biding her time" (163–64). This fragmentation suggests that for southern women on the home front the trauma of war is psychological, which invites comparisons to other modernist women's novels of the war, such as Rebecca West's *Return of the Soldier*. Jocelle's trauma, however, is more a product of southern gender dynamics than the war itself. The war acts as a catalyst that allows Walter to act out his misogynistic fantasies and forces Jocelle into a personal crisis. The patriarchal order that subordinates women renders Jocelle helpless, but the new image of herself that emerges, the one who bides her time, suggests that Jocelle has a will to independence and an urge to break free from the patriarchal order.

Confused, she searches for a different form of order. She attempts to replace the patriarchal order with a matriarchal order, so she tells her aunt Martha, Walter's mother, about the rape. She tells Martha that Walter "wiped his dirty filth" on her the day he left, but rather than being outraged, Martha calls Jocelle a "war bride, a holy woman" (173). Martha, who lost her only opportunity for a romantic relationship to her father's whim, affirms the patriarchy, revealing the matriarchal core beneath the masculine veneer. Jocelle finds greater sympathy in Logan Treer, a county extension agent with socialist beliefs. He tells her of the possibility of a fellowship of all people, a community with no class or gender divisions. She finds his ideas interesting, but the lingering image of the war and global discord makes it impossible for her to believe him. She fears that war, both the war in Europe and the psychological war in her home, will continue forever. She gets a small bit of resolution when word comes that Walter has been killed in battle, but she does not find the psychological relief she expected, and she fears for Logan, who has been drafted into the army. The war alters Jocelle's perception of reality, dividing peacetime from wartime. On the farm, she raises war chickens and war corn, and the farmers discuss the prices of war land; the events of the war become more immediate and real than the events on the farm itself. After Walter's death, Martha taunts Jocelle as a "war-bride, war-witch, war-widow" (212). Jocelle sees herself as outside the normal, patriarchal order, and she imagines that the end of the war may have the effect of instituting a new order closer to Logan's vision of collective fellowship.

When the war ends, Jocelle wonders "what would it be for war to cease? ... having been for so long a time pitched to the fervor of war" (215). Her inner conflict symbolically resolves because she realizes that she is in love with Logan Treer, which gives her a new sense of order in an equitable relationship. He returns from the war, they are married, and Drake expels them from the farm, a postlapsarian Eden by any stretch of the imagination. His expulsion is nominal because her marriage to Logan signifies a modernist form of egalitarian gender relations that displaces the tyrannical patriarchy. They move to a farm of their own and have a family, but a new type of change stemming from the war again threatens to destabilize their family. Postwar prosperity, the same economic tide that made Ada Fincastle's family temporarily prosperous in *Vein of Iron*, causes serious land inflation in rural Kentucky:

> A great disaster had begun to sweep the country. Farms were being bought and sold at prices far in excess of those which the returns from the crops would now justify. The war-madness had come into the fields. From farm to farm, there was now too much yield, too many stock animals, too many plowed fields.... The cataclysm that had centered at Wolflick seemed now to have spread outward into every surrounding mile, and Jocelle looked abroad over the country in Logan's look, seeing what he saw. (245)

What Logan sees is the ripening of conditions for a socialist revolution, although he never actually plays a role in agitating or organizing for such a revolution. The time for the traditional southern economy based on labor-intensive agricultural production clearly has passed, but what may be most significant about this passage is that it represents Jocelle as looking outward. The internal conflict that plagued her on her grandfather's farm seems to have dissipated. With the birth of her child, a girl, she achieves a sense of psychological integration, and she forgives her isolated, pitiful grandfather, who sits alone by the hearth at his farm, unable to set foot again on God's earth.

Roberts and Glasgow both depict southern women adapting to wartime change in the South by finding a degree of social and economic agency, and their works reflect social changes taking place as modernity radiates into the region. Their novels demonstrate that social changes for women often take place more out of necessity or crisis than out of a sense of progress, and these changes can be regressive. For southern women coping with the war, challenges to patriarchy were inherently destabilizing because their identities had been invested in maintaining patriarchy. Ada and Jocelle find themselves swept along in a wave of events that are beyond their control and that disrupt their lives. They find themselves outside patriarchy not because they want to be but because they have to be, which puts the very notion of feminine agency in doubt, so the social gains made by southern women during the war were, at best, problematic. But problematic social advancement is the defining characteristic of modernity for southern women. An earlier generation of southern women responded to the Civil War by reaffirming patriarchy, often literally inscribing it in stone in the form of monuments throughout the South. For this generation, to complicate the issue of gender signifies a feminist advance.

Glasgow and Roberts blazed a path of southern women's modernism that other writers would follow.[21] Katherine Anne Porter, for example, frequently depicts disruptions in southern domesticity, especially in her Miranda stories. The short novel "Pale Horse, Pale Rider" takes place during World War I as an influenza pandemic ravages Denver, nearly killing Miranda before taking her lover, a soldier.[22] The pandemic leaves Miranda outside the structures of patriarchy, independent but alone. The effects of modernity and disruption in domesticity are frequent themes in post–World War I southern women's writing. Stories by Eudora Welty, Lillian Smith, Flannery O'Connor, Carson McCullers, and others portray southern women chafing at traditional patriarchy, not defending it. Their characters seek not husbands and families but self-fulfillment and personal realization, whether in a relationship or not. The war temporarily expanded women's agency, and although it contracted after the war, it never returned to its original form.

THE NEW SOUTHERN WOMAN

Amid the expansion and contraction of social agency for women in the South, a new icon of femininity emerged, the New Southern Woman. At the turn of the century in the proximal sites of modernity, the New Woman image developed as a representation of relatively independent womanhood. A New Woman was likely to educated, free spirited and independent, and aware of her own sexuality; she was less likely to be interested in marriage.[23] As modernity developed in Europe, she became a recurring character in many literary works, including Ibsen's play *A Doll's House*; novels by women writers Olive Schreiner, Sarah Grand, and George Egerton; and Kate Chopin's novel *The Awakening*. After the war, the New Woman incorporated with another icon of femininity, the Southern Belle, in *The Hard-Boiled Virgin* by Frances Newman and *Save Me the Waltz* by Zelda Fitzgerald to produce the New Southern Woman.

The New Southern Woman illustrates the tension between the conventions of southern womanhood and modernity. The southern belle archetype emerged in the nineteenth century in the work of dozens of writers as an avatar of southern values. Invariably, she was young and beautiful, chaste and virtuous, and, as the object of masculine adoration, the justification for a culture of honor and for the segregation of the races. Her story arc usually begins with her initiation into romance, which is her reason for being, and culminates in her marriage. In *The Southern Belle in American Fiction*, Kathryn Seidel notes that "when the traditional southern mythos clashed with the forces set loose by World War I, the South's fantasies about itself no longer provided the sanctuary of values that had been sufficient for sixty years after," so the archetypal belle underwent a transformation (xiv). The belle, an object of femininity, combined with the New Woman, a symbol of feminine will and self-definition, to produce a complicated feminine figure who attempts to assert her own will while enveloped in the milieu of traditional southern womanhood.

Frances Newman was the embodiment of a New Southern Woman. The youngest and, by her own account, homeliest daughter of a prominent family in Atlanta, she grew up among the highest circles of southern society, which valorized the Southern Belle ideal that she did not fit. Her father was a Confederate war hero who later became a US district court judge, and her mother was a direct descendant of the founder of Knoxville, Tennessee. Although her parents deployed every resource at their disposal to marry her off, even sending her to finishing schools in Washington, DC, and New York City, where she could meet eligible men, she never married. She did, however, have several affairs, usually with much younger men, and she used the few lines of work available to women to make an independent career. She worked as a librarian, spending most of her career at Georgia Tech, and she wrote freelance articles and reviews for newspapers. Although raised on the ideal of southern womanhood, she lived much of her life just outside the usual parameters of accepted southern femininity, and she was perfectly positioned to satirize southern gender relations. Her primary interest, however, was not gender but literature.[24]

In her foreword to the reprinted edition of *The Hard-Boiled Virgin*, Anne Firor Scott describes the novel as a "pervasive and corrosive" feminist text (xvi). Although Newman did not imagine herself as a feminist, critics have appropriated her as a feminist writer. Reginald Abbott argues that Newman's works have been recovered primarily to serve as markers of early twentieth-century feminist ideology in the South, and Barbara Wade contends that *The Hard-Boiled Virgin* is about the inherent tension between southern womanhood and modernity. But the novel itself undercuts a feminist reading because the protagonist, Katharine Faraday, appears to affirm the values of southern womanhood, even without subscribing to them. While she does not marry, she does not assert herself as an independent entity, and although she loses her virginity, she does so without embracing her sexuality. In *Tomorrow Is Another Day*, Anne Goodwyn Jones explains that the novel reflects Newman's own social ambivalence because she simply did not care deeply about the usual social institutions that dominated southern women's lives, such as family, feminism, and the South itself. Jones addresses the issue more directly in her foreword to *Dead Lovers Are Faithful Lovers*, explaining that "like many southern feminists, Newman eschewed the label feminist because it connoted political advocacy. And like many southern women, she showed little interest in the political and social issues that gripped her milieu" (xxxii). To the extent that she was a feminist, Newman was a feminist in spite of herself. By virtue of being an independent, intellectual woman in the 1920s, she violated southern gender norms. Her primary objective, however, was to be a modern, provocative artist.

By the standards of Atlanta society, she succeeded in her attempt to provoke. *The Hard-Boiled Virgin* caused a major scandal in the city; one reviewer described it as "grounds for lynching," and it was banned in Boston (A. Scott, foreword to *The Hard-Boiled Lover*, xii). Consequently, it sold well. The quality that attracted attention to the book and that offended the prurient sensibilities in Atlanta, Boston, and most of the rest of the country was the book's oblique references to female sexuality. Although not nearly as explicit as the pulp novels that would dominate the literary marketplace in the 1930s and 1940s, by the standards of the 1920s any novel that merely suggested female sexual behavior caused outrage. Newman's novel, in other words, had the same impact on Atlanta that D. H. Lawrence's *Lady Chatterley's Lover* had on London and that James Joyce's *Ulysses* had on Dublin. Her impact may have been even greater, however, because she was both female and southern and, thus, expected to be completely ignorant of sexuality. She accurately assesses that "in Georgia no lady was supposed to know she was virgin until she had ceased to be one" (174). But her protagonist, Katharine Faraday, knows what a virgin is and knows that she is one. In several scenes in the novel she accidentally, almost chastely, discovers aspects of her sexuality. In the bath she discovers her vulva, for example, but she does not regard it as a source of pleasure:

> Between her flat chest and her thin legs, she noticed a line she had never noticed before—a delicate line which was slightly browner than the area she thought was her stomach, and which began just below the curious little dent her mammy called a navel. And she had a sudden revelation that when her first child—of whose advent she had so little doubt that she had already baptized her Violet, with Diana reserved for her little sister—came into the world, the part of herself which she thought was her stomach would burst along the delicate brown line, and that she would naturally shriek, and that her daughter would dart into the world like Pallas Athena darting from the brain of Zeus, and that a doctor would then give her ether and sew her up. (35–36)

Her clinical, metaphorical description is representative of the discussions of female sexuality in the text. Other than the fact that she recognizes that female sex organs exist, nothing about her book depicts actual sexual behavior, much less eroticism. This fact, coupled with the extreme reaction to the text, reveals that taboos on women's sexuality were still in force in the South even during the Jazz Age following World War I.

Her self-discovery takes place against the backdrop of the war. Katharine Faraday's relationships mostly involve soldiers, and she is in Europe when the war begins, so the text has an element of proximal contact, but the war never advances into the foreground with the exception of one passage in which she enjoys the company of a young German:

> Katharine Faraday was always able to enjoy saying that she had lost all confidence in her own intelligence on the day when a war followed the assassination she had enjoyed so much, and she was able to enjoy feeling that she was completely different from all the American women who enjoyed the war so much even after it ceased to be a merely European war. She thought that her reason was entirely responsible for her convictions, and when she enjoyed feeling broad-minded because she did not believe that all the little boys in Belgium had been deprived of their right hands or that all the women in Belgium had been found raving and naked and breastless and virtueless in abandoned German trenches, she knew that she was remembering the night when Lothar Falkenhayn had held her hand until morning without offering her the indignity of a kiss. (225)

This passage is fairly indicative of Katharine Faraday's perspective. She deliberately distinguishes herself from other women, those traditional southern women who enjoy the war, and she makes sexualized observations while chastely enjoying the company of young men. As a New Southern Woman, she thinks and acts independently, looking beyond the war propaganda, and she engages in romance without scheming toward marriage.

The distinction she makes between herself and other women is important because she recognizes that she represents a new form of femininity. Raised in the image of a Southern Belle, Katharine learned the differences in gender expectations for boys and girls. "She knew," for example, "that any boy is born to a more honourable social situation than any girl" and that a pretty girl has definite advantages over an ugly girl (30). She also realizes that her intelligence is a liability for a southern woman, not an asset. Her education at finishing school is a process of stupefaction, as her teachers feel that it is their "duty to southern womanhood" to leave "the brains of young ladies in a state of paralysis" (58). Considering that southern womanhood depended on women playing submissive and dependent roles, mental acuity, beyond the ability to make charming conversation and manage a household, would have been at best superfluous. Newman satirizes gender roles in the South, but her satire is tempered with a degree of sincerity. As an intelligent woman living in the South who has been socially demeaned for not following the ordinary course of southern womanhood, she realizes that these institutions have tangible meaning. Newman struggled to support herself and her dependents on the meager income available to her as an independent woman in the South, where, after postwar regression, few opportunities for employment for women were available.

In her anthology *The Short Story's Mutations*, Newman argues that the war had little impact on modernist literature. "Joyce is not so much a follower as a contemporary of Freud," she writes, "just as he is a contemporary and not a product of the war called the European War because no one has thought of a name for it." She allows that the war "undoubtedly inspired a great deal of poetry" because "men have a tendency to become rhythmical and primitive and hysterical in the vicinity of the cannon's mouth." But she does not believe that fiction has the same relationship to current events:

> [T]he years since nineteen seventeen have not been epoch-making years in American fiction because they are the years since the war ceased to be entirely European—no rational person could believe that Sherwood Anderson wrote Winesburg, Ohio because the Germans just signed a humiliating armistice and had given the French their revenge.... And no rational person could believe that James Branch Cabell wrote The Cream of the Jest because his country was declaring war on Germany. (304–5)

In retrospect, her statement is a fascinating illustration of how modernity radiates. Modernity developed in Europe before the war, and both Joyce and Freud were influenced by the profound effects of industrialization and urbanization on the human experience. American writers outside proximal sites in the United States, including Anderson and Cabell, continued to write works that represented rural experience, but they incorporated elements of modernist technique into their works. *Winesburg, Ohio*, *The Cream of the Jest*, and *The Hard-Boiled Virgin* are all individual examples of distal modernism, but Newman overlooks the broader impact of the war on the entire region.

Zelda Fitzgerald's novel *Save Me the Waltz* portrays a traditional Southern Belle developing into a New Southern Woman. F. Scott Fitzgerald edited the book severely, and it has been consistently dismissed by critics. In the foreword to the 1967 republication, for example, Harry T. Moore calls it a "literary curio" (vii). Many critics regard the book as a derivative of F. Scott Fitzgerald's work, particularly his novel *Tender Is the Night*, which is also based on their tumultuous marriage.[25] But this critical discourse has the effect of privileging the masculine perspective and marginalizing the transgressive feminine text.[26] While it may be true that *Tender Is the Night* is a more successful book both critically and commercially, *Save Me the Waltz* stands on its own as a feminist narrative of southern gender roles changing in the wake of World War I. In the same way that Frances Newman and Ellen Glasgow may not have imagined themselves as feminists, Zelda Fitzgerald likely did not see herself as a feminist, but she has become, and deserves to be, an icon of the modern southern woman. And even though Fitzgerald did not self-consciously identify herself as a southern writer, Lisa Nanney is correct that "*Save Me the Waltz* is a southern novel" (222).

The novel is based closely on Zelda's life, which is a template for the New Southern Woman. She was the beautiful and willful child of southern aristocrats: her father was a highly respected judge in Montgomery, Alabama, and her mother was a legendary beauty from Kentucky, once known as "the wild lily of the Cumberland" (Milford, 4). Zelda was the youngest of their children, and she had a precocious talent for attracting attention, especially from young men. In spite of her recklessness and coquetry, her childhood was highly conventional, and she quickly learned and mastered the roles of southern femininity. As Nancy Milford explains, she understood that southern women were expected to be submissive, that beauty and the appearance of purity had value, and that creative dissembling was a necessary survival skill. For a woman raised on the fiction of southern womanhood, the advent of the New Woman and the relative freedom of post–World War I American society seemed to offer space for personal realization, but the deeply ingrained values of southern womanhood proved, at least in Zelda's case, to impose debilitating limits on that freedom, illustrating the inherent tension of New Southern Womanhood.

In *Save Me the Waltz*, a young woman who identifies with the patriarchal system becomes disenchanted with it. The book opens with a description of Alabama's relationship with her father, who is described as "a living fortress" (3). The sense of security he provides protects his daughters, particularly his youngest, Alabama, from "the changing exigencies of their times," which has the effect of leaving the daughters "crippled" and clinging to their father (4). In this way, submissiveness is ingrained into the girls from an early age, and while their behavior has the appearance of recklessness, it is predicated upon masculine privilege. Judge Beggs's daughters have some degree of relative freedom for two reasons: because they are beautiful and thus embody the most valuable trait of southern womanhood, and because their father is an important man and they are an extension of him. His primary obligation to his daughters is to get them suitably married, while their mother models the self-sacrificing ideal of the angel in the house. "The wide and lawless generosity of their mother," Fitzgerald writes, "was nourished from many years of living faced with the irrefutable logic of the Judge's fine mind. An existence where feminine tolerance plays no role being insupportable to her motherly temperament, Millie Beggs, by the time she turned forty-five, had become an emotional anarchist" (11). The mother is subordinate to the father, and she offers emotional support to her daughters, but she clearly does not model independence. By the time Alabama becomes a young woman, she has internalized the lessons of southern womanhood: "She had a strong sense of her own insignificance; of her life's slipping by while June bugs covered the moist fruit in the fig trees with the motionless activity of clustering flies upon an open sore" (31). The juxtaposition of fruit, a metaphor for young femininity, with a wound indicates that while Alabama enacts southern womanhood, she suffers from the performance.

Young Alabama, whose name underscores her southernness, sees romance as her reason for being, so the trainloads of dashing young soldiers streaming into the training camp near her hometown seem exciting.[27] She finds the prospect of war thrilling: "All night long Alabama thought about the war. Things would disintegrate to new excitements. With adolescent Nietzscheanism, she already planned to escape on the world's reversals from the sense of suffocation that seemed to her to be eclipsing her family, her sisters, and her mother" (29). She finds a sense of significance in the attention of men who swarm the town "like benevolent locusts eating away at the blight of unmarried women that had overrun the South since its economic decline," but Fitzgerald's language hints at the grotesque decay beneath the romantic veneer (34). Alabama dances and flirts with the men, and she collects their insignia—trophies of her own conquests—in a glove box. She says proudly that "no other girl had more and even then she'd lost some" (35). In Alabama's case, the war throws the usual dynamics of southern womanhood, specifically the competition for male attention, into a fever pitch. For her, the war does not represent new economic or social opportunities; instead, it represents a new landscape for the performance of southern femininity. This pattern is in itself a function of patriarchy. If Alabama were a working-class woman, the war may have made necessary economic opportunities available, but she is a member of the social elite, so even in a marketplace teeming with new positions, she seeks only the occupation for which she has trained since birth, as a wife.

Alabama falls in love with perhaps the most dashing of the young men, an artist from New York named David Knight. After a brief courtship, they are engaged to be married. Their engagement proceeds according to clear masculinist guidelines for economic exchange. David asks Judge Beggs for permission to marry Alabama, a transaction that reveals the crux of patriarchy. Judge Beggs's primary concern is David's financial stability, not Alabama's wishes. David lies about his family money and future earning prospects, and the exchange, ominously, reminds him of a strange dream about "a troop of Confederate soldiers who wrapped their bleeding feet in Rebel banknotes to keep them off the snow. David, in his dream, had been there when they found that they did not feel sorry about using up the worthless money after they had lost the war" (39). The dream implies that he sees his engagement to Alabama as an economic conquest. His marriage to Alabama represents a new conquest of the feminized South by the masculine North, a common trope for post–Civil War symbolism that Nina Silber discusses in *The Romance of Reunion*. After their marriage, David asserts his dominance over Alabama; he even tells her, "you belong to me," reinforcing his possession, which in regionalized terms symbolizes the North dominating the South (45). When he begins to suspect that she is having an affair, he accuses her of "reversion to type," telling her, "you've gone Southern again" (85). He projects conceptions of southerners as lustful and licentious on his wife, extending the negative perception of the South in the mind of the North.

The book's most significant disruption occurs when David and Alabama leave the South after their wedding, and his charade of financial solvency comes to an end. They appear to embody the Jazz Age fantasy of creative dissipation in New York, but Alabama finds herself trapped within the bonds of femininity. She plays the same role to David that her mother played to her father, as a beautiful and emotionally unstable adornment, a projection of his own success. His success, though, is an illusion, which comes apart when her parents visit. Their disapproval leads her to articulate the paradox of feminism and southern womanhood: "[I]t's very difficult to be two simple people at once, one who wants to have a law to itself and the other who wants to keep all the nice old things and be loved and safe and protected" (56). As a product of southern womanhood, Alabama has been inculcated in a gender dynamic that enforces protection for women, and for her any difference is unsettling. David continues to restrict her agency, but he does not continue to provide her with protection, which leads her to a crisis of identity. She realizes that southern womanhood is no longer sufficient for her.

When they move to Europe, she takes on a new identity in a proximal site of modernity. She becomes a ballet dancer at a relatively advanced age, and she rejects, at least temporarily, the roles of wife and mother, the only viable roles available to her as a southern woman. In this crucial moment, the competing strands of southern womanhood and New Womanhood intertwine. By rejecting the subservient gender roles for an artistic outlet, Alabama asserts a feminist identity. When she develops an injury, however, and can no longer dance, her identity collapses, and she suffers a debilitating nervous breakdown.[28] This turn of events implies that the tension of this intermediate identity is difficult to maintain.

The tension becomes evident when Alabama returns to Montgomery to visit her father on his deathbed. Back in the South, she recognizes the role of patriarchy: "The old town where her father had worked away so much of his life spread before her protectively. It was good to be a stranger in a land where you felt aggressive and acquisitive, but when you began to weave your horizons into some kind of shelter it was good to know that the hands you loved had helped in the spinning—made you feel as if the threads would hold together better" (196). Her experience with modernity, however, has changed her attitude toward southern womanhood. "She saw her mother," a paragon of southern womanhood, "as she was, part of a masculine tradition. Millie did not seem to notice about her own life, that there would be nothing left when her husband died. He was the father of her children, who were girls, and who had left her for the families of other men" (201). Alabama sees herself as both inside and outside southern womanhood. Certain aspects of her relationship with David clearly show signs of patriarchy, but she has evolved from the woman who saw romance as her occupation to a woman who can imagine self-definition outside the roles of wife and mother.

Whether or not she achieves that form of definition is questionable. Save Me the Waltz comes to an abrupt end just after Judge Beggs's death. Alabama and David return to New York, where she attempts only to put her past behind her, swapping southern domesticity for northern domesticity. The novel's structure, spanning Alabama's relationship with her father from her birth to his death, suggests that masculinity defines Alabama's life, but her apparent intention to empty "this deep reservoir that was myself" implies that she is on the verge of creating a modern, feminist identity (212). Her story demonstrates that southern womanhood, like all other identities, is a rhetorical construction predicated on the values of a specific time and place. The South modernized during and after World War I, but the process was slow and recursive, which is reflected in the expansion and contraction of women's agency during and after the war.

Women who had direct contact with modernity were more likely to depict the significant differences between the distal South and proximal sites of modernity, such as the disjunction Alabama feels upon returning to Montgomery. Those examples, however, while signaling the impact of modernity on southern womanhood, should be considered in context with the vast majority of other southern women, whose living conditions evolved much more slowly, continuing to maintain most conventional aspects of southern womanhood long after the war. The literary representations of these changes, both radical and gradual, signal the radiation of literary modernism in the work of southern women writers. Modernism radiates at distinct rates depending upon a person's geographic and social distance from sites of modernity. Because of the double bind of race and gender, African American women writers were farthest removed from modernity, and their works tended to show relatively fewer signs of modernism, using mostly traditional textual forms and affirming patriarchal social structures. Ellen Glasgow and Elizabeth Madox Roberts illustrate the expansion and contraction of women's agency within the patriarchal structure during and after the war, and Frances Newman and Zelda Fitzgerald sketch out a new version of southern femininity that developed after the war. Collectively, these texts demonstrate that the war radiated modernity into the South beyond direct contact with proximal modernity.

5

MULES AND MACHINES

Modernity, World War I, and the Southern Economy

"He wanted to get in," Thomas Wolfe writes of Eugene Gant in *Look Homeward, Angel* (1929). "He wanted to be urbane and careless. He wanted to wear well-cut clothes. He wanted to be a gentleman. He wanted to go to war" (350). Although too young to enlist, Eugene finds a way to get involved in the war effort. During the summer of his sophomore year, he heeds the call of, not glory, but money:

> There were strange rumors of a land of El-dorado to the north, amid the war industry of the Virginia coast. Some of the students had been there, the year before: they brought back stories of princely wages. One could earn twelve dollars a day, with no experience. One could assume the duties of a carpenter, with only a hammer, a saw, and a square. No questions were asked.
>
> War is not death to young men; war is life. The earth had never worn raiment of such color as it did that year. The war seemed to unearth pockets of ore that had never been known in the nation: there was a vast unfolding and exposure of wealth and power. And somehow—this imperial wealth, this display of power in men and money, was blended into a lyrical music. In Eugene's mind, wealth and love and glory melted into a symphonic noise: the age of myth and miracle had come upon the world again. All things were possible. (424–25)

Eugene goes to Newport News, Virginia, a major naval shipping hub, where he finds an amalgamation of people looking to profit from the war—from southern boys fresh off the farm to urban, ethnic Yankees—all reveling in the opportunity for material gain. He takes a job as a checker supervising the loading of ships bound for Europe, and he learns that success in this wartime boomtown has much to do with luck and illusion. After a series of adventures during which he squanders most of his earnings on gambling and debauchery, Eugene leaves Virginia to return to school with only $130 and several amusing anecdotes to his credit.[1]

Eugene's brief experience amid the war industry in Virginia illustrates one of the most enduring forms of modernist radiation into the South, the emergence of mechanization. Economic development happened slowly in the South, and in 1916, more than fifty years after the abolition of slavery, the economy still depended upon the manual production of agricultural cash crops, primarily cotton and tobacco, in an elaborate system of tenant farming. An industrial complex developed that processed cotton into textile products, but the region lacked a significant manufacturing sector—with the exception of the steel mills in Birmingham, Alabama—and its transportation infrastructure lagged far behind that of the North. Most southern cities, such as Atlanta, Memphis, and Greenville (South Carolina), functioned as centers for warehousing and cotton trading, and most southern factories were textile mills that produced fabric from raw cotton. Charles Aiken explains in *The Cotton Plantation South since the Civil War* that a form of social inertia inhibited economic innovation in the region, but he notes that World War I was a pivotal moment for the cotton economy because the war destabilized the labor market and caused a spike in the commodities market, so the price of cotton rose and fell precipitously. Some southern farmers invested in mechanization to improve production and stabilize labor demands, but the southern economy continued to depend on cotton production for several decades.

The intervention of machines during World War I disrupted the southern economy in ways that resonated in modernist southern literature. Southern writers portrayed the region undergoing a difficult and protracted, although inevitable, transition. Any alterations to the traditionally agricultural society were met with equal parts of skepticism, detachment, and enthusiasm. Proximal modernity involved the development of technologies that disrupted human relationships, and machines that did the work of people altered labor relations, domestic relations, spatial relations, and spiritual relations. Writers and intellectuals in sites of proximal modernity began wrestling with these problems before the war, as in the case of Filippo Tommaso Marinetti's futurism, the paintings of Marcel Duchamp, and Henry Adams's reflections on the juxtaposition of the virgin and the dynamo.[2] Southern writers, however, in the distal area out of the shadow of the factory smokestack, did not begin to consider the consequences of modern technology on a large scale until after the war. The mechanized, industrial war made the South's economic lag obvious, so several writers began to imagine the consequences of mechanization on the region and to formulate responses to it.

In the decades between World War I and World War II, an animated conversation took place among several southern writers in fiction and nonfiction about the role of mechanization and industrialism in southern society and their potential to dehumanize labor and destabilize the social structure. The key economic issue in southern modernism is the imaginary possibility of modernity, because the southern economy did not actually diversify, industrialize, and urbanize on a large scale until after World War II. But after World War I, many southerners realized that the South was out of sync with modernity and that modernity would inevitably radiate into the distal South. This chapter describes the socioeconomic conflicts that developed as modernity radiated into the South and analyzes literary and intellectual responses to modernity in the wake of World War I from a cross section of thinkers who responded defensively to changes taking place in the South, including Ellen Glasgow, the Agrarians, W. J. Cash, and William Faulkner. Southern modernists portray mechanization as a force that disrupts the South's social order, and they tend to be wary of the effects of that instability, indicating their resistance to modernity.

Economic Development in the Cotton Kingdom

The war destabilized the already fragile southern economy, sending it through a dizzying cycle of boom and bust. In 1914, an infestation of boll weevils destroyed a large percentage of the region's cotton crop, but the commodity's relative scarcity drove cotton prices higher than they had ever been before, up to seventeen cents a pound.[3] Then, almost predictably, tragedy struck. The German U-boat campaign effectively closed international cotton markets. In the South, prices plummeted immediately to below eight cents a pound, and the southern economy faced utter destitution. American diplomats attempted to continue exports to both London and Berlin, two of the three largest overseas markets, but sentiment in the South ran staunchly pro-British, so many southerners preferred not to allow exports to Germany. As one southern minister asked his congregation: "Is cotton of so great a value that for it we will sacrifice our manhood, our independence, and our moral poise? I am profoundly convinced that the price of cotton is a fundamental moral question, and by it God is testing the souls of our people."[4]

The following year, President Woodrow Wilson authorized a plan of military preparedness that led to the construction of factories in the South for the production of war implements, and when war was declared, the South profited immensely. Nearly a million southerners, many of them displaced farm workers, joined the army, which drove up labor costs. Naval yards appeared in Virginia, South Carolina, and Florida. The need for raw materials created a greater demand for products produced in the South such as lumber, iron, oil, steel, tobacco, textiles, and cotton. Southern cotton went into everything from uniforms to bandages to explosives. The demand was so great that "the years 1917–1919 were the best cotton has ever seen. The average price for those years was twenty-seven cents, and the thirty-five cent cotton of 1919 was the most valuable crop ever produced" (Tindall, 60). For a tantalizingly brief period of time, southern cotton farmers realized a substantial profit on their crop, and at the same time new factories were built across the South that employed thousands of workers at inflated wages. Many southerners were able to purchase the modern conveniences that had become common in the North such as indoor plumbing, telephones, automobiles, and mechanical farm implements. After the war, with the demobilization of the army, the cessation of wartime industry, the decreased demand for cotton, and the advance of the boll weevil, the southern economy largely returned to its prewar stasis. Between the end of the war and the beginning of the Great Depression, cotton prices fluctuated, but they never approached the profitability of wartime. Ironically, the memory of wartime prosperity drove many southern farmers to ignore calls for diversification and to continue to plant cotton.[5]

After the war, a number of regional planning commissions began work on schemes to electrify, urbanize, commercialize, and industrialize the South, which, by the time of the New Deal, resulted in major federal programs such as the Rural Electrification Act and the Tennessee Valley Authority.[6] As Dewey Grantham explains in *Southern Progressivism: The Reconciliation of Progress and Tradition*, World War I presented an opportunity for economic development and social reform in the South:

> The war generated strong currents of change in the South, loosening some
> of the regional restraints on experimentation and innovation. It intensified
> the process of nationalization, expanding the role of the federal govern-
> ment, spreading the effect of national regulations and standards, and bring-
> ing southerners more fully into the arena of national affairs. It resulted in an
> extraordinary mobilization of resources—private as well as public—some of

which were used for social purposes. These developments helped create new
avenues of efficiency, public service, social control, and social justice. Social
reform was thereby encouraged, although it was frequently constrained, in
the South as elsewhere, by an attitude of intolerance and coercive confor-
mity. (408–9)

But the changes southern progressives sought in regional economic development and social justice came slowly, largely because of southern farmers'
stubborn dependence on cotton.

Most of the changes in the southern economy that took place during the
war were temporary. In 1920, the South was still rural and agricultural, and
the lag between southern development and northern development grew.
The aggravating factor was southern farmers' commitment to planting
cash crops to the absolute exclusion of everything else, even food for subsistence. Repeated appeals for agricultural diversification from agricultural
economists and political leaders went unheeded, so the acreage planted in
cotton actually increased from year to year. The greater production of cotton in the South drove market prices down, requiring farmers to produce
more cotton to yield a profit from their crops. Replanting nutrient-deplet-
ing cotton repeatedly in the same fields exhausted the soil quickly, causing
farmers to spend greater percentages of their profit on fertilizer. The cycle
of diminishing returns forced increasing numbers of farmers every year
into bankruptcy. Black farmers, poor white farmers, and bankrupt farmers
formed a vast underclass of sharecroppers who existed in a perpetual system of planting, picking, and poverty. Because of a low tax base and poorly
developed infrastructure, the region lagged behind the nation in education,
health care, highway construction, infant mortality, and most other markers
of development.

Although the South did not develop as rapidly as the North, the southern market was a crucial part of northern economic development because
banks, retailers, and manufacturers based in northern cities depended on
sales to southerners, and southern cotton producers depended on northern banks for financing and northern retailers for textile sales. T. J. Jackson
Lears notes that this arrangement retarded southern development. "Cotton
farmers faced the monopoly power of local merchants as well as distant
banks and railroads," he writes. "Caught in the coils of the crop-lien system,
most southern farmers were forced to neglect subsistence crops, devoting
every square foot of ground to the marketable crop of cotton and using what
they grew as collateral for usurious loans" (*Rebirth*, 135). The South fully

participated in the global process of modern economic development, producing a crucial market commodity, but the effects of producing that commodity reinforced the conditions of traditional agriculture in the region. This is one of the most profound ironies of modernity. To a great extent, the cotton produced in the South was responsible for the economic development that drove industrialization and urbanization, but actually producing the cotton mired the South in intractable agriculturalism and ruralism.

The South's economic marginalization was both a symptom and a cause of what Richard Godden describes as "ideological resistance to modernization" (*Fictions of Capital*, 141). It was a symptom because other areas of the country developed at a much more rapid pace, and it was a cause because southerners actively delayed their own development. The southern bourgeoisie—cotton planters, landowners, bankers, and businesspeople—maintained an elaborate economic infrastructure that perpetuated cotton dependence. Innovations such as crop diversification, major capital investment, and labor organization were deterred, and the ideology that maintained this state of developmental stasis permeated the culture of the period. Leigh Anne Duck argues in *The Nation's Region* that southern writers were keenly aware of their differentiation from the rest of the nation and that they instantiated a "dialogue between tradition and modernization" that concerned issues of capital development, especially as it concerned race and labor (3). Duck focuses specifically on segregation as a major point of contention, but during the war, machines displaced manual labor. For many southern modernists, technology signified the disruption of segregation, the radical destabilization of social stratification, and the obliteration of land as the central focus of everyday life. World War I was a crucial moment in this dynamic process because the economic expansion that took place during the war introduced technology to the region's means of production, but the extensive contraction that happened after the war deflated the labor market and rendered most technological investment moot.

The representation of technology in southern modernism contrasts tellingly with the mainstream of American modernism. In *Shifting Gears: Technology, Literature, Culture in Modernist America*, Cecelia Tichi describes the effect of "gear and girder technology" on aesthetic form (16). Images of machinery and engineered structures pervaded the work of many proximal modernist authors such as Edith Wharton, Ernest Hemingway, John Dos Passos, and Ezra Pound, among others. Technology takes on a symbolic quality in their texts, signifying the mastery of people over the environment and the elevation of scientific rationalism over religious faith.

Machines are not always celebrated, however, and the effects of dehumanization are sometimes evident, particularly in two important modernist films, Fritz Lang's *Metropolis* and Charlie Chaplin's *Modern Times*. But even the texts and films that critiqued modernity recognized its inevitability.[7] Southerners, however, challenged modernity in its most basic forms. Jack Temple Kirby, for example, recounts that TVA engineers in the 1930s found many rural communities where a cash nexus did not exist, where the elements of modern technology were absent, and where the conditions of everyday life were fundamentally unchanged from the previous century (120). Because the conditions of modernity were often absent from the rural, agricultural South, it stands to reason that the aesthetic of technology was also missing.

Southern modernism occupies a complicated space in that it has a clear apprehension of modernity, but the systems of modernity are distant from the conditions of everyday life. Faulkner's portrayal of Jason Compson in *The Sound and the Fury* (1929) reflects the nature of this duality. Rather than plant cotton, he speculates in the cotton commodities market, obsessing unhealthily over minute changes in the price of cotton set by buyers in the North, but his allergy to gasoline indicates that he is not comfortable with the new technology of the twentieth century. He metaphorically epitomizes the state of the southern economy between the end World War I and the beginning of the Great Depression: dependent on the agricultural past, uncomfortable with the mechanical future, and confused about the transitional present. The inherent tension in the text between technological modernity and aesthetic modernism underscores the South's social and economic alterity in the postwar United States.

Southerners resisted, and frequently continue to resist, development.[8] The vexing issue is to understand why southerners would resist modernity. The most evident explanation is the South's commitment to white supremacy. By the beginning of the twentieth century, white southerners had effectively reestablished their complete social and economic domination of the region. In the 1920s, as labor unions gained influence in northern cities, the second wave of the Ku Klux Klan gained influence in the South and the Midwest. The entire economic and ideological apparatus of the region depended upon maintaining white supremacy, and the possibility that modernity would challenge that system by possibly allowing blacks into the workplace was anathema. This is an entirely reasonable speculation, but southerners may have had another reason to fear modernity, World War I itself. The war was an evident outgrowth of modernity in Europe, and mass-produced technology in the form of tanks, airplanes, and machine guns contributed to the experience of horror. Southerners had invested an entire generation in recovering from the devastation of the Civil War, and those who served in France or who were otherwise engaged with the war saw the extent to which it devastated Europe, so they may had seen an advantage in returning to pastoralism as a means of perpetuating peace within the nation.

LABOR, MECHANIZATION, AND MODERNISM

In *Barren Ground*, Ellen Glasgow depicts the war's disruptive impact on a remote Virginia farm, seemingly far removed from the war itself. She claims that she wrote the book in response to the war, writing in her autobiography *The Woman Within* (1954): "[T]he war went on, life went on, death went on. . . . Beneath dead and dying illusions, *Barren Ground* was taking form and substance in my imagination" (241). The war plays only an indirect role in the text, however. None of the primary characters in the story join the military, and the novel's climax concerns romance, not combat. The novel draws upon some elements of sentimental fiction, the type of melodramatic writing often associated with nineteenth-century women authors such as E. D. E. N. Southworth and Augusta Jane Evans, but Glasgow subverts the traditional sentimental plot by incorporating social criticism into her text. While Dorinda Oakley's story in *Barren Ground* begins as a turbulent romance, it evolves into commentary on the development of southern agriculture. When the war disrupts the available labor supply, Dorinda invests in technology to modernize her production, which signals the inevitable encroachment of mechanization into the southern economy. *Barren Ground* is an unlikely modernist text.[9] The crucial modernist element of the novel is the effect of mechanization change on everyday life in an area otherwise far removed from urbanization and modernity. The intervention of agricultural mechanization on a farm where the methods of production had changed only slightly since America's colonization was a momentous change.

Glasgow indicates that most rural southerners in 1914 did not understand the war's significance on their own lives. "Nathan," Dorinda's husband, "was the only man at Pedlar's Mill who had taken the trouble to study the battles in France," and Dorinda and her neighbors find his concern for the war and his prophecy that the United States will eventually be drawn into the conflict dubious (417). As the war continues, more people take positions, and a wave of anti-German sentiment emerges. Dorinda comments that "that old German who has just moved into the Haney place" attended Nathan's funeral, and, likely referring to the German U-boat campaign, she asks, "I wonder what he thinks now of Germany?" (459). The typical southerner's tendency to view the war before America's involvement as a distant curiosity should be understandable. Few had a vested interest in the conflict except to the extent that it influenced commodities markets, and the region's willingness to side with the Allies speaks more to the proportion of southerners with Anglo, rather than Germanic, ancestors.

Dorinda imagines that the war is an economic struggle between agriculture and industry. She recognizes that the war will be "fought and won with the help of farmers," and she sees her role as an essential provider of food and resources, so "when she saw victory in terms of crops, not battles, could she feel she was a part of it" (460). As a producer, she cannot fathom the willful waste of so many resources and young lives in the attempt to defeat what amounts to her as an abstraction. She describes the Germans as "less a mortal enemy than an evil spirit at large," which contrasts with her obsession with the concrete, tangible elements of her life. Even when she dreams, she sees the rotation of crops progressing through her mind: "Potatoes. Corn. Wheat. Cowpeas. Clover. Alfalfa. And back again" (460). She translates the conditions of modern combat into a repetitive agrarian cycle, forcing the fundamentals of agricultural southern culture onto the disruption of wartime. In this way, she offers a model for how the distal South encountered a war across the ocean.

Through consistent hard work, single-minded focus, self-sacrifice, and tenacity, Dorinda transforms her family's dilapidated farm into a successful operation by combining agriculture with mechanization.[10] The impact is most evident after the war:

With the return of peace, she had hoped that the daily life on the farm would slip back into orderly grooves; but before the end of the first year she discovered that the demoralization of peace was more difficult to combat than the madness of war.... Even at Pedlar's Mill there were ripples of the general disintegration. What was left now, she demanded moodily, of that hysterical war rapture, except an aversion from work and the high cost of everything? The excessive wages paid for unskilled labor were ruinous to the farmer; for the field-hands who had earned six dollars a day from the Government were not satisfied to drive a plough for the small sum that had enabled her to reclaim the abandoned meadows at Five Oaks. One by one, she watched the fields of the tenant farmers drop back into broomsedge and sassafras. She was using two tractor-ploughs on the farm; but the roads were impassable again because none of the negroes could be persuaded to work on them. (463)

Dorinda's apprehension signals the war's direct impact on southern farms, where inflation and a competitive labor market has made manual farming inefficient. While most farmers and laborers enjoyed the brief period of prosperity, Dorinda sees it as a challenge because it disrupts the labor force, which leads her to invest in mechanical devices to offset the lost labor. As Nicholas Peter Sargen explains in his economic analysis of the spread of agricultural mechanization, *"Tractorization,"* Dorinda purchases a prototypical tractor long before they would become common enough to displace manual laborers, and her two tractor ploughs presage the modernization of the southern economy.[11]

The labor shortage leads Dorinda to invest more heavily in mechanical devices, even though she recognizes the dehumanizing effects of mechanization:

Machinery could not work alone, and even tractor-ploughs were obliged to be guided. She had installed an electric plant, and whenever it was possible, she had replaced hand labour by electricity. In the beginning she had dreaded the cost, but it was not long before she realized that the mysterious agency had been her safest investment. The separator in the dairy was run by electricity. With the touch of a button the skimmed milk was carried by pipes to the calf-yard or the hog-pen. Pumping, washing, churning, cooling the air in summer and warming it in winter, all these back-breaking tasks were entrusted to the invisible power which possessed the energy of human labour without the nerves that too often impeded it, and made it so uncertain a force. (468)

While the farm cannot be entirely automated, Dorinda prefers the costly initial investment of electric and mechanical devices to the uncertainty and recalcitrance of human laborers. Pursuing this policy makes her farm more profitable than the farms of her neighbors, but in time they too begin to implement machines to replace human labor, thus displacing a massive number of unskilled laborers who had once formed the backbone of the southern economy.

Sociologists studying the impact of mechanization on the southern economy before World War II saw the increased productivity that technology promised as a mixed blessing. On one hand, farms such as Dorinda's that invested in mechanical devices after World War I were able to produce more efficiently and cost effectively, so they were able to remain profitable even during the Great Depression. But on the other hand, large-scale farmers who invested in mechanization displaced thousands of families who had worked on shares or as tenants, which intensified the unemployment and poverty of the Great Depression, especially in the South. By the 1930s, some sociologists feared that the negative demographic impact of mechanization would be long term. C. Horace Hamilton, for example, wrote in 1939 that "even though technological unemployment brought about by the introduction of one machine may disappear in time, we would still be faced with problems of a continuously changing technology and hence continuous problems in human maladjustment" (68). Hamilton's analysis reveals that some scholars viewed mechanization as both a problem and a solution, which may encapsulate the attitude of virtually every southerner impacted by the effects of labor-saving agricultural technology.

The new technology solves some of Dorinda's labor problems and reduces her farm's operational expenses, thus improving her profitability, but although post–World War I technology offered some useful devices to replace human labor, running a successful farm during that era still required an enormous amount of manual labor. As a woman, Dorinda has an unexpected advantage in maintaining relations with her laborers. While most of the farms in the area run by men use coercion and financial domination to control racially segregated laboring populations, Dorinda approaches workers with a less threatening demeanor. Using her maid Fluvanna as an intermediary, she makes arrangements with several African American families to provide labor at reasonable wages. The fact that Dorinda uses families—"the Moodys, the Greens, and the Plumtrees"—as the basic unit of labor, as opposed to making arrangements with individual workers, reflects one of the unique aspects of southern labor relations under the sharecropping system (469). While sharecroppers often changed farms after each harvest, extended families tended to remain in the same community. With the large-scale displacement of laborers brought on by the encroachment of mechanization, sociologist B. O. Williams hypothesized that "if mechanization should come to agriculture as it has to industry, and the corporate form of organization should prevail, this positive force of familism might be lost" (76). Williams's prognostication echoes the sentiments of the Southern Agrarians, which exposes an apparent difference of opinion between

Glasgow, who apparently favored agricultural mechanization, and the Agrarians, who opposed the displacement of farming families.

Five years after the war, Dorinda appears pleased with the results of her investment in mechanization. Her farm has prospered, her products bring in a substantial profit at the market, and she has gained a reputation for productivity among her fellow farmers, no mean feat for a woman in a male-dominated field.[12] She feels satisfied with her accomplishments, and "even [her most persistent problem] the labor question had been lessened, if not solved, by the application of electricity and gasoline" (476). Mechanization has clearly been beneficial to Dorinda's farm, but five years after the war the long-term effects of mechanization were just beginning to be felt by the laborers who would eventually be displaced. *Barren Ground* predicts a major paradigm shift in the southern economy that would primarily affect the lowest classes of southern workers. The economic shift necessarily had consequences for the culture of the American South. Even as the post–World War I economy evolved from manual agriculture to mechanized agriculture, southern artists and intellectuals simultaneously celebrated the region's progress and condemned the region's break with tradition.

After the publication of *Barren Ground*, Glasgow found herself some-what conflicted about the changes taking place in southern society as a consequence of agricultural mechanization. In "'Passion Transfigured': *Barren Ground* and the New Agriculture," William Conlogue notes that the Southern Agrarians objected to Glasgow's portrayal of the mechaniza-tion and industrialization of the southern farm as an ideologically benign aspect of economic evolution (30–31). Allen Tate, in particular, criticized her in 1929 as "one of the worst writers in the world" because he both detested her prose and disagreed with her politics.[13] Glasgow's later novels, specifically *The Sheltered Life* (1932) and *Vein of Iron* (1935), demonstrate a shift in her portrayal of the southern farm to emphasize the organic relationship between the human body and the soil and cease to advocate mechanization. In some respects, the change in Glasgow's artistic rep-resentation of the southern farm reflects the growing displacement and dehumanization of lower-class southern farmers. This change altered the Agrarians' general opinion of Glasgow's literary merit. Tate praised *The Sheltered Life*, and he invited Glasgow to contribute an essay to *Who Owns America?*, the ideological sequel to *I'll Take My Stand*. Glasgow's changing attitudes reflect the internal antagonism taking place within the South as southerners wrestled with the leading edge of modernity radiating into the region.

THE AGRARIANS, MODERNITY, AND ANTIMODERNISM

By the end of the 1920s, increasing agricultural mechanization, such as that portrayed in *Barren Ground*, displaced large numbers of laborers, black and white, sending droves of people to industrial centers in the North and growing urban areas in the South to seek work in factories. Progressive ideologies, such as Marxism and Darwinism, threatened to alter the dynamics of race, class, and gender relations in the region. Increasing awareness of class consciousness and widening class divisions within the South, coupled with more intense scrutiny and criticism of the South in the national media as a result of broader cultural exchanges between the South and the North, made some southern intellectuals more self-conscious about their southern identity and more prone to defend the region. All of these circumstances contributed to the publication of *I'll Take My Stand: The South and the Agrarian Tradition* (1930), a collection of essays by twelve self-proclaimed southerners, most of whom were in some way affiliated with Vanderbilt University and some of whom—most notably John Crowe Ransom, Donald Davidson, Allen Tate, and Robert Penn Warren—had been members of the Fugitive group, which between 1922 and 1925 published the *Fugitive*, the leading journal of modernist verse based in the South. This apparent contradiction, that many of the leaders of the Agrarian backlash that ostensibly sought to preserve southern traditions were also artistic innovators who embraced modernist techniques, challenged traditional forms, and overtly repudiated "Southern Literature,"[14] has confounded literary scholars and historians alike, leading to a long-running and occasionally querulous debate over how to interpret the Agrarian response to modernity.[15]

A number of conditions converged in the late 1920s to spark the Agrarian movement. The first concerns the Agrarians themselves, all of whom were intellectual, cosmopolitan—John Crowe Ransom, Donald Davidson, and Herman Clarence Nixon served in Europe during World War I—and self-consciously southern. While some of the Agrarians who had been involved in the *Fugitive* had embraced modernism, by the late 1920s many of them had come to identify with the southern past: John Crowe Ransom wrote a book that defended religious fundamentalism, Allen Tate wrote a biography of Stonewall Jackson, Donald Davidson wrote an epic poem celebrating his Tennessee ancestors, and Robert Penn Warren wrote a biography of John Brown that investigates the slave debate.[16] When the South came under attack from within and from without as a result of the Scopes Trial in Dayton, Tennessee, the response to the scrutiny at Vanderbilt was an increased emphasis on scientific research and the publication of Edwin Mims's paean to progress, *The Advancing South* (1926). Amid the apparent worship of economic advancement in the South, a state of intellectual panoply seemed to be at play in America with socialists, New Humanists, Distributionists, and other factions vying for influence.[17] Meanwhile, the Agrarians, all of whom hailed from the rural South, observed serious threats to their imaginary version of the southern way of life as mechanization displaced legions of farmers, forcing them to seek work in factories and reshaping demographics in the region. In response to all of these circumstances, Allen Tate, John Crowe Ransom, and Donald Davidson collaborated to recruit a group of like-minded southern intellectuals to contribute to a collection of essays that would, as Donald Davidson explained in a letter to a potential contributor, "center on the South as the best historical and contemporary example in American society of a section that has continuously guarded its local and provincial ways of life against a too rapid modernization."[18]

All of the contributors ascribed to an ideological statement of principles. Originally drafted by John Crowe Ransom and edited by each of the contributors, the statement outlines the Agrarian agenda. Clearly reactionary in tone, the Agrarians intended primarily to warn their fellow southerners of the evils of industrialism and modernity. In their statement, they claim that the collectivist nature of modern industrial society could lead to a communist state, which threatened the religious, social, and cultural values of the American South by glorifying science and technology at the expense of God and humanity. They also claim that the tedium of industrial work would diminish man's sense of vocation and his enjoyment of labor. They predict that industrialism could potentially damage the relationship between man and nature by adversely affecting religious and aesthetic experiences. They warn that industrialism creates a cult of consumerism that causes people to idolize inanimate objects, thus forsaking their relationship with nature, community, and spirituality. Against the industrial way of life, which they take to be the prevailing American way of life, they offer the traditional, pastoral southern way of life, "the culture of the soil," as an alternative to the age of the machine. Beyond making this assertion, however, they decline to make any specific suggestions for how to achieve this idyllic way of life.[19] This statement of principles can be read as a regressive response to Marinetti's futurist manifesto, outlining a conservative reaction to modernity, and comparing the two documents illustrates the range of responses to modernization between distal and proximal zones.

The changes taking place in the southern economy following World War I, specifically the advent of mechanical and electrical labor-saving devices such as the ones Dorinda uses in *Barren Ground*, trouble the Agrarians for two key reasons. First, they dispute that saving labor and increasing production, the intended purposes of mechanization, actually have a beneficial effect. The implication, in their opinion, of investing in labor-saving technology as an economic imperative is to strip labor of its dignity, to make the act of laboring "mercenary and servile," and to dehumanize the laborer (Twelve Southerners, xl). This phenomenon, they argue, leads inexorably to their second objection to mechanization, the collectivization of resources. They predict that increased mechanization will lead to "overproduction, unemployment, and a growing inequality in the distribution of wealth," which will require the creation of an "economic superorganization," leading to a socialist state (xli).[20] They argue that "the Communist menace [is] a menace indeed" and that the American economy, if it continues its "blind drift" toward industrialization, will become "the same economic system as that imposed by violence upon Russia in 1917" (xli). The Agrarians sought not merely to preserve the southern way of life from encroachment by northern influence but to prevent the collapse of the capitalist economic system in the West.[21] At one point, in fact, Allen Tate and Robert Penn Warren suggested that the title of their book should be changed to "Tracts against Communism"; and on another occasion John Crowe Ransom, as a representative of the Agrarians, debated V. F. Calverton, a Marxist critic, over the fate of the American economy.[22] The flaw in their argument is that by 1930 the majority of agricultural labor in the South came not from small farm owners but from sharecroppers, who were inherently exploited laborers, so the Agrarians were essentially pitting one form of dehumanization against another. Their version of southern agriculture is an invented form of pastoralism based on conservative fantasy, not economic reality.

Only one essay in the collection actually discusses the southern economy, and, curiously, that essay, Herman Clarence Nixon's "Whither the Southern Economy?," takes a moderate approach to southern industrialization. Nixon, a political scientist who eventually became a liberal proponent of the New Deal and split with the other Agrarians, concedes that opposing industrialism in the South is futile since "there is no point in a war with destiny or census returns" (176).[23] But he deplores "this spread of southern worship of industrial gods after the World War" (176). His essay describes the state of the southern agricultural economy since the end of

World War I and the impact of increasing industrialism and consumerism on the economy, and he notes that much of the industrial development that has occurred in the South serves the needs of agriculture, such as railroads that transport cotton, textile mills that transform cotton into cloth, and new machines to improve the harvesting of cotton. The centrality of cotton becomes a refrain for Nixon. He says that "cotton and the South distinguish each other," explaining that the region's economy, infrastructure, labor, and politics are all designed to serve the interests of cotton production (184). He warns that altering the South's traditional economy too rapidly may lead to unforeseen results. Displacing large populations of workers could cause a socialist revolution; the need for vast quantities of natural resources could lead to a war of acquisition, similar to Germany's invasion of Belgium and France; and the disruption of the world's most stable economy could destabilize the global economy, resulting in untold calamity. Nixon allows that industrial development in the South is unlikely to lead to such dire consequences, but he admonishes American policy makers to be aware of the changes taking place in the southern economy and the potential ramifications of those changes. He ultimately calls "for southerners to say affirmatively that the South must cultivate its provincial soul and not sell it for a mess of industrial pottage" (199).

The Agrarians' call for action caught the attention of other southern intellectuals, but with a few notable exceptions, specifically Cleanth Brooks and Richard M. Weaver, these intellectuals supported southern industrialization. William Terry Couch edited *Culture in the South* (1934), a collection of essays by southern intellectuals that examined numerous aspects of southern culture. Couch and his colleague Howard Mumford Jones speak directly to the Agrarians in their preface to the book, pointing out a fundamental flaw in their argument: "the serious error of interpreting southern life in terms of industrialism *vs.* agrarianism" (vii).[24] Couch, and many other southern intellectuals, did not see industry and agriculture as mutually exclusive endeavors, nor did they see industry as a clear and present threat to the southern way of life. On the contrary, many hoped that investment in industry might enhance life in the South by lessening the impact of poverty, ignorance, and insularity. For example, Clarence Poe, editor of the magazine *Progressive Farmer*, contributed an essay on farmers to Couch's collection. After describing—with credible statistics—the state of farming in the South and the realistic possibility of economic agricultural development in the region, Poe responds to the Agrarians by saying that "with 'Better Business' added to 'Better Farming,' no one need fear there will not also be

'Better Living' all over rural Dixie. The tendency as a whole, in my opinion, will favor the development, not of commercialized farming . . . but of small farmers of the general type described by the twelve young southerners who recently defended the South's agrarian tradition in that thought-provoking volume, *I'll Take My Stand*" (342). Poe's response overlooks the ideology that propelled the Agrarian movement, saying nothing about Marxism or dehumanization, but he clearly articulates the commonsense response of many southerners dependent on agriculture who wished for the realization of agricultural modernity in the South.

Poe's response points out a major fallacy in the Agrarian agenda. While the Agrarians purported to defend the tradition of small farmers rooted in the community and tending their own land, in reality only a small number of farmers in the South in the early twentieth century owned their own farms. Many farmers, instead, either leased fields from large landowners or worked on shares. Clarence Poe documents that in 1930, for example, tenant farmers tended 72 percent of cultivated land in Mississippi (326). At the end of each harvest cycle, tenants often moved in search of new accommodations, so they had little personal connection to the land.[25] They were, in fact, as dehumanized as the mules that pulled their plows. In the years immediately following the publication of *I'll Take My Stand*, many of the Agrarians extended their comments to address this criticism and to offer practical measures to safeguard the southern tradition. In "The Pillars of Agrarianism," Frank Lawrence Owsley, one of the original twelve southerners, describes a plan for redistributing land in the South whereby a government agency would purchase land and distribute, to capable farmers, plots of eighty acres "with sufficient stock to cultivate the farm," presumably including a mule (210). Owsley's plan would empower the government to prevent the sale and mortgage of distributed land, to establish guidelines determining the quantities and types of crops that may be produced on distributed land, and to restore "a modified feudal tenure where the state had a paramount interest in the land and could exact certain services and duties from those who possessed the land" (211). Many of the other Agrarians supported Owsley's plan, and Allen Tate hailed it as the most genuine description of Agrarian doctrine.[26] To a certain extent, the plan borrows from the Distributionists' agenda of widespread private landownership, but the intervention of a government agency draws more from the Agricultural Adjustment Act; neither safeguarded southern tradition.

The Agrarians' defense of rural agriculture against modernity is one of the clearest and most enduring examples of distal modernism. Because several of the Agrarians went on to become influential literary figures, their notion of southern pastoralism and their argument against mechanization became highly influential, and, as Michael Kreyling observes, they invented a version of southern literature that defined the South in opposition to the North. Virtually every writer and critic of the twentieth century has contended with their antimodernist ideas, which has further detached the perception of southern writing from modernism. But it is crucial to note that the Agrarians, at the time that they produced *I'll Take My Stand*, were responding to changing conditions in the region, not causing changes in the region. In truth, their ideas did not actually come into intellectual vogue until the Cold War, when, as Paul V. Murphy explains in *The Rebuke of History*, their vision of cultural nationalism and ideological self-sufficiency proved attractive to conservative intellectuals seeking to establish traditional paradigms of nationalist culture.

At the Fugitives' reunion in 1956, the youngest, most ambivalent, and least ideological contributor to *I'll Take My Stand*, Robert Penn Warren, offered the most accurate retrospective assessment of the Agrarians' project. He describes their sense that humans as individuals were losing their identity and fundamental place within society, and their fear that humans would become as interchangeable and irrelevant as spare parts. Tellingly, he uses the metaphor of the machine to illustrate his point: "[I]t's the machine of power in this so-called democratic state; the machines disintegrate individuals, so you have no individual sense of responsibility and no awareness that the individual has a past and a place."[27] His description resonates with many other modernist intellectuals' concerns about machines displacing humans in postwar society, and analogs to his position can be found in the work many distal modernists such as Virginia Woolf, T. S. Eliot, James Joyce, and Fritz Lang, among others. During the war, machines demonstrated their profound efficiency at taking human lives, and many modernist intellectuals worried that the era of technology would forever destabilize human relations.

THE NEW MECHANICAL ORDER

Between World War I and World War II, several writers interrogated the changing South in nonfiction books, including Clarence Cason's *90° in the Shade* (1935), W. J. Cash's *The Mind of the South* (1942), Virginius Dabney's *Liberalism in the South* (1932), Edwin Mims's *The Advancing South* (1926), and Ben Robertson's *Red Hills and Cotton* (1942). The proliferation of such works makes a case in itself for the extent of modernist radiation in the region, and the books make clear that modernity meant something different in the South than in sites of proximal modernity. "Industry," for example, in many parts of the nation meant manufacturing and Fordism, but in the distal South "industry" usually meant textile mills that employed poor whites living in company-owned mill villages. Likewise, the word "machine" in many parts of the nation referred to a device to save labor, but in the South it usually referred to a device, such as a tractor, that displaced manual laborers.

Edwin Mims, chair of the English Department at Vanderbilt University and the Agrarians' frequent antagonist, wrote with eager anticipation about the South's industrialization. He points to statistics in the *Manufacturer's Record* as proof of the region's development, and he notes, predicting the Agrarians' response, that some southerners would see the passing of "the old charm and leisure, the old picturesqueness and romance" in the region's industrialization (80). "Those who are aesthetic or academic," he intones, "fear that industrialism will lead inevitably to the standardization of these southern states until they are lost in the mediocrity and commonplaceness of contemporary American civilization" (80). Many southern writers, in fact, did share precisely this fear as they witnessed modernity radiate into the region. In *90° in the Shade*, Clarence Cason, for example, describes the South as "the machine's last frontier," a place trapped between manual agriculture and mechanical agriculture and struggling either to discover or to retain its identity as a region. He phrases the challenge southerners faced between World War I and World War II as follows: "Shall they return to the cultivation of cotton, tobacco, sugar cane, and rice under a system of agriculture largely manual, or shall they continue their efforts to carry these raw products farther along the economic progression by maintaining their faith in the machine?" (133).

Although some southerners found machines disruptive, they purchased them and dealt with the consequences. Ben Robertson recalls in *Red Hills and Cotton* that before World War I, southerners seemed to live self-sufficiently and to purchase very few things that they could not produce themselves, but after the war, his family "began to experiment with a tractor," and they bought an automobile (270). These new machines, in his perception, led to disastrous consequences. Within a few years, "machines were displacing labor on farms; machines were now making machines; they were displacing labor in factories," and this process had led inexorably to the "bursting of the industrial bubble," the Great Depression (272). Robertson, actually, praises the Depression because it forced southerners to revert to their traditional blend of cash crops and subsistence farming, which, in his opinion, enabled the region to be economically independent. The urge to defend ruralism against modernity was so great for some southerners that they preferred economic catastrophe to industrialization. This impulse depends upon a perception of the southern past as superior to the present or future. Far from being unusual, the impulse is actually typical in much of modern southern literature partly because antimodernism depends upon imaginative (re)constructions of the past.

But the antimodern impulse in the South also reflects reality as many southerners knew it. The most significant effect of industrialization across the region beyond agricultural mechanization was the emergence of textile mills, which proliferated with high demand during World War I. In the South, factories manipulated workers and their families, forcing women and children to work extremely long hours for low pay, and Virginius Dabney notes that "even in the most modern of these settlements there is usually an almost feudalistic relationship between the worker and the company" (320). The textile mill village was an extension of southern paternalism in which the mill owner forced his workers into utter dependency.[28] In fact, as Sinclair Lewis writes in *Cheap and Contented Labor*, many northern industrialists built textile mills in the South because unions were less common and labor was less expensive. Ben Robertson recalls the movement of white tenant farmers into the mills, and he, as a paternalistic landowner, explains why a southern traditionalist would see sharecropping as preferable to factory work. Sharecroppers were individuals accustomed to working for individuals, and "it was difficult to them to realize . . . that they were working for a corporation, complicated and technical and highly organized and involved" (280). The emergence of textile mills followed the patterns of traditional social structure, but work in a factory, monitored by a clock, under the direction of a corporation, surrounded by rows of machines disrupted the traditional patterns of labor. The mills, which processed raw southern cotton grown by sharecroppers into cloth produced by mill hands, were a characteristically southern encounter with modernity, one that was both traditional and disruptive, reflecting the paradox of southern modernism.

W. J. Cash diagnoses the South as schizophrenic in *The Mind of the South*. He sees the region vacillating between a set of values that yearns for a reified Progress and a set of values that defiantly clings to southern agrarianism. He uses the term "Progress," which seems to be a peculiar combination of modernization and consumerism, to describe his perception of modernity. Cash's analysis builds on the legacy of the lost cause, but he prevaricates between endorsing changes that will lead to a more urban, more industrial South and affirming traditions that maintain the South's agrarian uniqueness. He presents World War I as a crucial moment in the tension between these competing mind-sets. While New South boosters had advocated industrial development since the end of Reconstruction, their rhetorical construct did not become a realistic possibility until the infusion of capital investment in the region's resources and labor took place during wartime mobilization. After the war, in his view, the region faced the awkward challenge of acquiescing to modernity.[29]

Cash's analysis focuses on the Piedmont region of the Carolinas, the heart of the textile mill industry. He spent nearly his entire life in the area, and his personal experiences with racism, fundamentalism, and the exploitative economics of the textile mill town clearly inform his analysis of the South's dual obsession with modernity and tradition.[30] His father worked in the Gaffney Mills, and he grew up amid the South's most successful post-Reconstruction industrial development before World War I.[31] He describes the post–World War I South as reckless and wayward, naïvely buying into dreams of material success spread by duplicitous Yankees who sought to strip the region of its resources and exploit its workers. But southerners, he notes, were willing victims, easily seduced by the materialism of the postwar boom. "Into this [period of relative wealth] the South," he intones, "natively more extravagant than the rest of the country, more simple and less analytical, entered with the most complete abandon. If these years were years of increasing sickness for the all-important cotton-mill industry, they were nevertheless to be the heyday of the dream and program of Progress" (259). The dreams of enduring success, of course, were false, and soon inflated wages, inflated land prices, falling cotton prices, and increased international production returned the southern economy to its prewar conditions.

Writing on the verge of World War II, Cash could examine the sweep of the South's contentious engagement with modernity, and he was able to discern that mechanization, industrialization, and consumerism had obviously impacted the South. He attributes the disruption primarily to machines. Describing the consequences of modernization on everyday life in the South, he writes:

[T]he processes of commerce are essentially orderly and deliberate; they follow a fixed procedure and, beyond a certain limit, cannot be hurried or dislocated. As for industry, the machine, of course, is the very image of order, the embodiment of a fixed, rigidly conventionalized procedure through time, and the antithesis of the headlong impatience of a lynching mob. Is it unlikely

that all this had its effect of the mental pattern of men who dealt with it day
by day and fixed all their hopes on it, whether as worker or as master?
    ... [T]he machine is a jealous and exacting taskmaster. The plow-boy
may dream the whole day through as he walks behind his beast and still get
his field broken. The old-fashioned artisan, beset by a fancy or an emotion,
could dawdle for hours or days over his task with no other damage than a
slowing of its progress. But the modern high-speed machine demands from
its human helpers the most alert concentration on the task at hand, else in
short order the huge quantities of ruined material and the dislocation in
the schedule of deliveries have eaten up the master's profit and are hurrying
him to bankruptcy. (308)

Mechanization changed the organic rhythms of everyday life in the South,
accelerating production, impeding indolence, and threatening to eradicate
the agrarian fantasy.

Cash fears that the rise of a machine-based economy threatened to displace farmers as the crux of southern society, which led to tension between
the "new mechanical order," led by middle-class merchants and profession-
als, and the established agrarian order (271). But the shift in the southern
economy had the dual impact of lowering the social standing of both the
farmer and the laborer. Where the existing southern social order tended to
be rigid and paternalistic in a way that exalted the intangible value of the
land and the necessity of noblesse oblige, the new mechanical order valued
nothing as highly as the accumulation of wealth, he worries. Those who
acquired wealth, whether they exploited sharecroppers or textile workers,
dehumanized their fellow southerners. Cash, thus, diagnoses a top-down
erosion of the southern social structure: as the wealthiest and most powerful social class loses its paternalistic sense of benevolence toward and
responsibility for the lower classes, the lower classes lose what little standing in the community they had held. Farmers, especially, noticed a change
in their social station. Southerners of the new mechanical order, especially
the new commercial middle class, migrated to rapidly growing cities, and
they shunned the rural farmers, eventually making the title "farmer" synon-
ymous in the opinion of urbanized southerners with white trash, the lowest
echelon in southern social stratification.

In Cash's opinion, the radiation of modernity into the South forced
southerners to find a way to maintain regional identity. The broader cultural
exchange between northerners and southerners that occurred as a result of
the war promised to finally produce the period of prosperity that southern

demagogues had predicted since the end of Reconstruction, but the lingering residue of the lost cause and essential mistrust of Yankees made this
newfound "Progress" problematic. Cash uses the trope of the savage ideal
to explain this sense of conflict: "Another great group of Southern fears
and hates fixed itself on the line of what I have called the savage ideal—
the patriotic will to hold rigidly to the ancient pattern, to repudiate innovation and novelty in thought and behavior, whatever came from outside
and was felt as belonging to Yankeedom or alien parts" (319). Regardless
of the amount of economic development that took place in the region, the
South was still significantly less modern than the North. Other southerners sought ways to adapt to new ideas, new economic methods, and new
social developments while maintaining as much as possible of the southern
social system that the changes threatened to displace. And others, especially
intellectuals such as Cash, adopted a detached, analytical perspective on the
relationship between modernity and the South.

MACHINES IN THE DUST

Faulkner depicts the effects of modernization on the South in *Flags in the
Dust*. In the book, Bayard Sartoris, a World War I combat pilot, returns to
Jefferson, Mississippi, after the war and finds the town evolving from a typical southern farm community into what he characterizes as an avaricious
capitalist dystopia. Yankee investors moved into the town just before the
war, purchased huge tracts of land for timber, clear-cut it, left it to erode
until it was unfit for farming or habitation, and bought their wives in "New
York and New England" extravagant luxury goods such as "Stutz cars and
imported caviar and silk dresses and diamond watches" (400). Farmland
has been converted into "mile after mile of identical frame houses with
garage to match" until "the very air smelled of affluence and burning gasoline" (400). Faulkner mirrors the impact of mechanization on Jefferson with
the war's impact on Bayard. During the war, Bayard saw his twin brother,
John, shot down in France. Bayard's traumatic experience leaves him disillusioned and unable to reintegrate with the community at the same time
that mechanization signals the rural community's disintegration.[32]

The tension between modernity and ruralism in Jefferson, Mississippi,
becomes evident when Bayard buys a sports car. His aunt Jenny finds the
car extravagant, and she notes that Bayard's grandfather, president of the
local bank, would never finance such a purchase for a farmer because it
had no practical value (57). The car, unlike the tractors and milk separators

Dorinda purchased for her farm, does not save manual labor or increase production, so it represents a new type of machinery with fetish value. Faulkner, in a passage that accentuates the aesthetics of technology, describes it as "long and low and gray; the four-cylinder engine had sixteen valves and eight sparkplugs, and the people [who sold it] had guaranteed that it would do eighty miles an hour, although there was a strip of paper pasted to the windshield, to which he paid no attention whatever, asking him not to do so for the first five hundred miles" (81). Faulkner later juxtaposes the fetishized machinery with utilitarian machinery when Bayard persuades his grandfather to buy a tractor, a form of modernist machinery that actually had more significant consequences for the rural South.

Faulkner contrasts Bayard's car with his grandfather's carriage, a rural fetish. Old Bayard's extravagant carriage symbolizes his place within the community's stratified class system, and the time and labor required to maintain it demonstrate the paternalistic southern economy's social structure. Old Bayard maintains a family of black servants who spend their lives cooking, cleaning, serving, gardening, and tending the carriage and horses, an enormous investment of labor for transportation. Simon Strother, the patriarch of this family, resents the automobile, and he sees it as a threat to the rural community's system of labor. When Old Bayard rides to town in the car to prevent Young Bayard from driving recklessly, Simon complains that Old Bayard allows "a gent'mun's proper equipage" to go to "rack and ruin in de barn" (121). Simon makes a crucial connection between the social changes taking place and the war. He mumbles to himself, "wid all dese foreign wars and sich de young folks is growed away fum de correck behavior; dey don't know how ter conduck deyselfs in de gent'mun way," and he feels ashamed that Sartorises should ride "in de same kine o' rig trash rides in" (121). Simon understands that the carriage symbolizes a particular social structure, but he does not realize until he rides with Young Bayard that the car also represents power. When he reluctantly agrees to a short ride in the car, Bayard speeds along dirt roads, swerves recklessly to avoid a family in a mule-drawn wagon, and intentionally scares Simon nearly to death. Whereas the carriage symbolizes power because of the labor it requires, the car symbolizes power because of its destructive mechanical force. This is a crucial differentiation between the rigid social structure of the traditional South and the foreseeable disruption of mechanized modernity. Simon leaps from the car, signifying his rejection of modernity, but the damage has been done.

Bayard feels disconnected from the community because of his traumatic war experience. He focuses his anger and grief inward and uses the car and destructive behavior as a means of release. After recovering from broken ribs sustained during a car wreck, Bayard futilely attempts to reintegrate with the rural community:

> For a time the earth held him in a smoldering hiatus that might have been called contentment. He was up at sunrise, planting things in the ground and watching them grow and tending them; he cursed and harnessed niggers and mules into motion and kept them there, and put the grist mill into running shape and taught Caspey to drive the tractor, and came in at mealtimes and at night *smelling of machine oil* and of stables and of earth and went to bed with grateful muscles and with the sober rhythms of the earth in his body. (229, my emphasis)

Agricultural labor reconnects him with ruralism, but the smell of machine oil and the new tractor signify the radiation of modernity and mechanization into agricultural labor. The use of mules and manual labor will inevitably be replaced with tractors and machines.

Bayard inevitably returns to the pattern of self-destructive behavior. Haunted by his brother's death, he tries to explain the source of his trauma to his family, but his grandfather retreats into his deafness, and his Aunt Jenny dismisses it as typical Sartoris foolishness. Later, he forces his new wife to listen to the story, but she resists. After a violent nightmare, he grabs Narcissa by the arm and tells her that he saw German fighter planes ambush John.[33] When John's plane burst into flames, Bayard tells her, he "thumbed his nose at me like he always was doing and flipped his hand at the Hun and kicked his machine out of the way and jumped" (280). While he tells the story, Narcissa struggles with him, pulling her arm away and whispering desperately "please, please." To describe John's death, Bayard uses the word "machine" rather than the more specific term "airplane," implicitly blaming mechanization for his death. The violent way Bayard tells the story of John's death and Narcissa's inability to listen to the story demonstrates the direct relationship between wartime mechanization and modernist alienation. In *The New Death: American Modernism and World War I*, Pearl James argues that the story is difficult to tell and difficult to hear because it "defies traditional representation" (191). Because John died mechanically rather than naturally, the people in the rural community cannot understand what it means, and because John's body is not recovered, they cannot competently mourn his death.

Destructive machines dominate Bayard's memory, and he sees images of airplanes, machine guns, and tanks in his dreams. Many modernist novels about the war emphasize the machine's role in the conflict, and *Flags in the Dust* translates the motif into the rural landscape, where tractors brutally rip the earth open. Bayard's car, the mechanized fetish, is the literal and figurative vehicle for his self-destruction. Soon after his attempt to return to farming, he crashes the car into a bridge. Faulkner describes the crash scene as a juxtaposition of pastoralism and mangled machinery: "at the foot of the hill the road crossed the bridge and went on mounting again; beneath the bridge the creek rippled and flashed brownly among the willows, and beside the bridge and bottom up in the creek, a motor car lay" (230). Bayard survives the accident with a few broken ribs. He recovers and has the car repaired, but his aunt and grandfather refuse to allow him to drive alone, leading to disastrous results. A few weeks later, he crashes into a ravine, killing his grandfather. This moment in the text initiates several changes within the story: Bayard exiles himself from his family, his sense of alienation that began with the death of his brother grows deeper, and the Sartoris family begins to disintegrate. These changes, collectively, indicate the impact of mechanization on the South.

After his grandfather's death, Bayard exiles himself to the rural Macallum farm, where he attempts to reject mechanization, but he remains at the farm only a few weeks before sneaking away. On Christmas Eve, he takes shelter in a sharecropper's barn with his mules. Faulkner dilates on the mules' role in the pastoral southern economy and prophecies their inevitable extinction:

> Some Cincinnatus of the cotton fields should contemplate the lowly destiny,
> some Homer should sing the saga, of the mule and his place in the South.
> He it was, more than any other creature or thing, who, steadfast to the
> land when all else faltered before the hopeless juggernaut of circumstance,
> impervious to conditions that broke men's hearts because of his venom-
> ous and patient preoccupation with the immediate present, won the prone
> South from beneath the iron heel of Reconstruction and taught it pride
> again through humility and courage through adversity overcome; who
> accomplished the well-nigh impossible despite hopeless odds, by sheer and
> vindictive patience. (313–14)

The elegiac tone Faulkner uses to describe the mule's lot, the incongruous presence of "worn-out automobile tires," and the mule's inability to procreate signify that the mule will soon be supplanted, and eventually eliminated, as a source of power in the southern economy (315). The mule, in truth, embodies the rural southern economy: hybridized, stubborn, and virtually incapable of evolution.

Bayard leaves Jefferson, detaching himself permanently from the rural South. He embodies the radiation of modernity in the region, and modernity's impact on the region will be disruptive and enduring. As he leaves, in fact, the streets of Jefferson are paved for automobile traffic. In a highly symbolic scene that blends human labor with mechanical labor, a group of men, possibly a chain gang, use picks and shovels to prepare the roadbed, while "further up the street a huge misshapen machine like an antediluvian nightmare clattered and groaned. It dominated the scene with its noisy and measured fury, but against this as against a heroic frieze, the negroes labored on, their chanting and their motions more soporific than a measured tolling of far away bells" (403). The paving machine signifies the inevitable influx of machines and modernity into the South.[34] Cars will soon replace mule-drawn wagons, tractors will soon replace mule-drawn plows, and machines will replace manual labor. Although it happens much more slowly than in proximal sites of modernity, everyday life in the rural South eventually modernizes.

After wandering for months across Central and South America, Bayard finds himself in Chicago, where an army pilot and a "shabby man" who has designed a questionable experimental airplane convince him to test pilot the new plane (412). Perhaps in a final attempt to equal John's spectacular death, Bayard disregards obvious danger signs and flies the plane. Underscoring the machine's destructive power, Faulkner uses a restrained tone when describing Bayard's fatal flight. He details the aeronautic theory behind the new plane's design and explains how the plane responds to Bayard's controls.[35] He emphasizes the mechanical processes that destroy Bayard by using the word "machine" four times in one paragraph, including the ambiguous line that implies Bayard's death: "the machine swung its tail in a soaring arc, but this time the wings came off and he ducked his head automatically as one of them slapped violently past it and crashed into the tail, shearing it too away" (419). The machine's failure results in Bayard's death, and the broader implication is that mechanization is dangerous and dehumanizing, leading to alienation and eventually self-destruction.

Before World War I, the South's economy depended on manual agricultural labor to produce commodity crops, and it maintained a rigid social hierarchy to perpetuate labor relations. When mechanization radiated into the South during the war, it threatened to destabilize the social hierarchy by pushing laborers out of the fields and by changing the region's dominant means of production. Southern writers who identified with the existing social hierarchy recognized the implications of mechanization and modernity for the distal region, and their works quixotically defend the rural South from the vague specter of industrialization and progress. Collectively, their works yield a distinctive form of distal modernism that catalogs the responses of rural conservatives to massive social changes. The fundamental irony is that mechanization radiated into the South much more slowly than most southern writers indicated, so the region continued to be mostly rural and agricultural while proximal sites of modernity became more and more urban and industrial, so the difference in the conditions of everyday life between the distal South and the proximal North became more exaggerated in the years after World War I. But the war brought southerners into contact with modernity, and it changed their perception of the region and produced a unique form of modernist writing.

CONCLUSION

World War II and Southern Modernity

In Flannery O'Connor's *Wise Blood*, Hazel Motes returns from World War II to find the South changed. While in the army, he planned to return to Eastrod, Tennessee, after his discharge to become a preacher like his father and grandfather. His family, however, has abandoned their farm during his absence, leaving behind nothing but a chifforobe, so he leaves the rural South to go to a city where he "don't know nobody" and where he can "do some things" (5). Motes's return to the South inverts the story of Donald Mahon in Faulkner's *Soldiers' Pay*.[1] When Mahon returns to Charlestown after World War I, the community is virtually unchanged, but he is ravaged. When Motes returns to Eastrod after World War II, the rural community has virtually vanished because many of its residents have left their farms to find work in cities, with the government, or in the war industry. Two of the largest employers in East Tennessee by the end of World War II, in fact, were federal agencies that embodied modernity: the Tennessee Valley Authority and the Oak Ridge National Laboratory.

World War I brought southerners into contact with modernity at a distance, but World War II brought modernity to the South. The inherent tension between the South's rural, agricultural social structure and the urbanizing, industrializing processes of modernity generated a distinctive form of distal modernism in the work of southern writers after World War I. After World War II, however, the South itself began modernizing, becoming more urban and more industrial and leading many southerners to adopt mainstream American social practices. In 1940, 43 percent of southerners lived on farms and 65 percent were rural residents, but in 1950 only 15 percent of southerners lived on farms and 58 percent were rural residents (Hurt, 2). By the end of the following decade, the majority of southerners lived in urban areas. As the South became a proximal site of modernity, it became less distinctive as a region, southern identity became a less stable construction, and southern literature became more consistent with mainstream American literature.

World War II dramatically changed the South's social structures. Nearly sixteen million Americans served in World War II, and all but one of the army's major training centers were located in the South, creating an explosion of interregional contact. Many factories were also built in the South, such as the Bell Aircraft factory near Atlanta that produced B-29 bombers. It became one of the largest employers in Georgia and, under the name Lockheed Martin, continues to produce aircraft components.[2] The plant occupies hundreds of acres of former farmland, and the movement of workers into Cobb County initiated a massive suburban sprawl that extended the borders of metropolitan Atlanta. Similar processes of industrialization and suburbanization took place in Memphis, Charlotte, Houston, and many other urban centers across the South, especially in locations with proximity to a military base. As the region's economy changed, cotton production dwindled. As late as 1940, cotton continued to be the region's staple crop and cultural foundation, but by 1960 virtually no cotton was produced in South Carolina and relatively little was produced in Georgia or Alabama; California had become the largest cotton-producing state in the United States. The mechanical cotton picker, which went into mass production after World War II, replaced the labor of field hands, so thousands of sharecroppers were pushed off their farms and into cities. At the same time, the abundance of inexpensive, unskilled labor in the South lured more factories into the region, such as the International Harvester plant in Memphis that employed former sharecroppers to build mechanical cotton pickers. Within a few decades after World War II, manufacturing and finance challenged agriculture for economic primacy, and by 1960 "the South was an urban region: more than one-half of the region's population lived in towns or cities" (Goldfield, *Cotton Fields and Skyscrapers*, 143). After several decades of delay, southern urbanization happened rapidly. The Northeast had been mostly urban since 1920, but in the second half of the twentieth century southern cities outpaced northern cities in growth, and millions of northerners transplanted to the South, which was suddenly made more inhabitable by air conditioning, one of the marvels of modernity.

The increased contact between the regions placed significant pressure on the South to conform to mainstream American practices. "A time of intense nationalism," Morton Sosna observes, "the World War II period witnessed efforts within both popular and intellectual culture to define a certifiably 'American' identity and 'way of life.' The degree to which the South was seen deviating from this supposed 'American way of life' became an increasingly significant preoccupation during the war years and would continue into the postwar years" (Introduction to *Remaking Dixie*, xvi).[3] World War II changed the meaning of the adjective "southern"; it went from describing a distinct section of the United States to describing a divergence from the United States. During and after the war, southerners assimilated many mainstream American values, and America assimilated much of southern culture, especially popular culture. Faulkner's 1950 Nobel Prize address, which addressed the challenges of the Cold War, and his anointment as America's greatest writer are evidence of this assimilation.[4] Pete Daniel remarks that "the South would never return to its prewar customs. For better or worse, World War II reconfigured southern society" (20).

The defining characteristic of southern modernism was the disruptive apprehension of modernity in a society that had not yet modernized, and southern writers used World War I as a metaphor to describe the disruption taking place in southern culture. After World War II, however, the issue of southern modernization was moot, and a fascinating phenomenon occurred. Dozens of southern writers wrote about World War I, but, as Noel Polk observes, "it is a matter astonishingly to be noted how little so profound an event as World War II figures in the fiction and poetry of major southern writers of the middle of the century" (132). Several texts mention World War II, of course, but few are set during the war or focus on the war's effects on the region, which is a startling fact that begs for an explanation. The simplest and most likely explanation may be the consequences of modernity itself: after World War II, the South ceased to be what had been the South—a region of the United States defined by rural agriculture and race-based manual labor. In its place, a new region developed—the Sunbelt—that had historical roots in the South but that also had a less stable population and a more diversified economy. The obvious problem that appeared to distinguish the South from the rest of the United States after World War II was segregation, but the civil rights movement, which, as John Egerton argues in *Speak Now against the Day*, began in earnest after World War II, eventually ended legal segregation through a set of federal acts. At the same time, the underlying racism associated with southern white supremacy had become a nationalized ideology, which diminished the South's distinctiveness.[5] Southern literature since World War II reflects the shift in social structure, and it is often marked by attempts to demythologize the South, to parody the South, or to revise southern history.[6]

The South's postwar assimilation into American culture required negotiating two complicated issues, race and history. White southern identity had been rooted in the lost cause, a notion that extolled the South's cultural supremacy, and in white supremacy, the region's retrograde racial ideology. World War II destabilized southern culture, but the problems of race and history remained, so white southerners reinvented the region in a way that conformed to the American values of free enterprise and the profit motive while allowing space for racism and southern history.[7] Matthew Lassiter describes this version of the South as the "Sunbelt Synthesis," a literal reconstruction of the South into suburban communities that intentionally separated the races while driving economic development (11). The South's process of urbanization diverges from the North's in that southern cities suburbanized as soon as they urbanized, creating sprawling metropolises of linked communities that claim to offer small-town charm with big-city access. The phrase "small-town charm," however, is usually code for hastily constructed tract house subdivisions, often named for plantations, that economically exclude African Americans and poor whites.[8] This new iteration of the South confounds the rural and agricultural elements of southern tradition, and it has inspired many works of contemporary fiction, particularly by Walker Percy, Peter Taylor, and Richard Ford, that critique the rise of southern suburbia.

While millions of southerners left farms for the suburbs, millions more left the South altogether. James Gregory writes in *The Southern Diaspora* that "World War II initiated the greatest spatial reorganization of Americans in the nation's history, and southerners were at the heart of the process" (32). More than 1.5 million black southerners and 2.5 million white southerners left, many seeking jobs in the war industry in the Great Lakes region. In *The Dollmaker*, Harriette Arnow tells the tragic story of the Nevels family, who move from Kentucky to find work in Detroit. The war decimates their rural Kentucky community; most men leave to join the army or to find jobs, some are killed, and few ever return. Given the choice between buying their own farm—the agrarian ideal—and taking factory work in a war plant, the family heeds the siren call of Detroit, the epicenter of mechanical industrialization during World War II. But the city devastates the family. They live in a filthy, crowded tenement, their son vanishes, their daughter dies by falling under a train, and the husband commits murder. The book's harsh antimodern attitude signals that for many southerners the emergence of modernity meant the obliteration of the South. Regardless, millions of southerners left the South, and the pattern of outmigration did not subside until the 1980s, reshaping the nation's cultural landscape and making many southern social problems American problems.

World War II's impact on race relations in the South is complicated. The military was segregated in many of the ways that it had been during World

War I, so African Americans had few opportunities for combat roles; they served primarily in service capacities under the supervision of white southerners, and they were rarely commissioned as officers. Yet many historians argue that the civil rights movement that came to fruition in the 1950s and 1960s began during World War II, in part because A. Phillip Randolph and Walter White succeeded in pressuring President Roosevelt to sign Executive Order 8802, which officially integrated the war industry.[9] In 1944, two books were published that laid the intellectual foundation for the civil rights movement, Gunnar Myrdal's *An American Dilemma* and Rayford Logan's *What the Negro Wants*. After World War II, there were relatively few incidents of racial violence, whether lynchings or race riots, which signaled that some social progress had been made, and many African American veterans, including Medgar Evers and Amzie Moore, agitated for civil rights at tremendous personal risk. The most powerful literary portrayal of the African American experience in World War II is John Oliver Killens's *And Then We Heard the Thunder*, published in 1963 at the height of the civil rights movement. In the novel, a young man, Solly Saunders, who has moved from Georgia to Harlem enlists in the war to fight for democracy, a theme that echoes African American World War I literature, but witnessing the violent mistreatment of black soldiers leads him to disillusionment and radicalization, and the book ends with a race riot among American soldiers stationed in Australia, suggesting that the South's social problems have become the world's social problems.

World War II brought the fantasy of the South as a closed society to an end. Robert Penn Warren, whose comment that World War I broke the frozen South open appears at the beginning of this book, depicts World War II's impact on the South in the short story "The Circus in the Attic" (1947). The story's main character, Bolton Lovehart, is an abstracted historian manqué, heir to his family's dwindling fortune and its stifling reputation, who engages himself with carving circus figurines until World War II breaks out. The war arouses his enthusiasm, he obsesses over news reports, he sells his figurines to raise funds for the troops, he lives vicariously through his stepson's heroics, and he sells a portion of the family's land to a newly constructed "war plant" (52). When the war ends, Bolton returns to his figurines, but the community continues careening toward modernity. The streets are paved, the war plant becomes a plastics factory, and the community grows to "nearly twenty thousand people" (61). The story makes plain that the Agrarians' project to maintain the traditional South in the face of industrialization was a fantasy, of no greater use than whittling figurines while modernity advances inexorably onward.

John Egerton provocatively argues in *The Americanization of Dixie: The Southernization of America* that since the 1960s a set of homogenizing forces have made the regions less distinct and that this process has both positive and negative consequences. John Shelton Reed counters in *The Enduring South* that, in spite of homogenizing forces, southerners continue to define themselves in opposition to the national mainstream. The homogenizing forces that both these writers discuss are the processes of modernity: urbanization, industrialization, mass communication, popular culture, technology, and population movement. To the extent that the South is a traditional society, it is antithetical to modernization, so as modernity has overtaken the region, its distinctiveness has eroded. Martyn Bone asserts in *The Postsouthern Sense of Place in Contemporary Fiction* that late capitalism has made regional identity atavistic and that southern identity has been replaced with a transnational identity. Scott Romine responds in *The Real South* that the notion of authentic southern identity is inherently complicated and contingent on an array of unstable factors, all of which fluctuate in response to modernization. This discourse highlights the uneven development of southern culture. The South, which is—like all imagined communities—a dynamic social construction, has always been evolving, but the extended period of cotton production and race-based labor from the early nineteenth century to the mid-twentieth century established a durable southern identity that impeded modernization. World War I temporarily destabilized that cultural construction by exposing the South to modernity, but World War II largely dissolved it, leaving behind an atavistic, reactionary edifice built on an increasingly transnational, urban, and industrial region.

Perhaps the South now is an illusion, a vexing, anachronistic legacy that has no value in the modern globalized world. Perhaps the South is no longer exceptional or distinctive, and perhaps this is good for the United States. Perhaps modernity has obliterated regional differences to create one world. Faulkner raises this possibility in *Requiem for a Nun* where he describes the effects of post–World War II modernization on Yoknapatawpha County:

> the machine which displaced the man because the exodus of the man left no one to drive the mule, now that the machine was threatening to extinguish the mule . . . then Warsaw and Dunkerque displaced that tenth in his turn, and now the planter's not-yet-drafted son drove the tractor: and then Pearl Harbor and Tobruk and Utah Beach displaced that son, leaving the planter himself on the seat of the tractor, for a little while that is—or so he thought,

forgetting that victory or defeat both are bought at the same exorbitant price
of change and alteration; one nation, one world: young men who had never
been farther from Yoknapatawpha County than Memphis or New Orleans
(and that not often) now talked glibly of street intersection in Asiatic and
European capitals, returning no more to inherit the long monotonous
endless unending furrows of Mississippi cotton fields, living now (with
now a wife and next year a wife and child and the year after that a wife and
children) in automobile trailers or G.I. barracks outside liberal arts col-
leges, and the father or grandfather himself still driving the tractor across
the gradually diminishing fields between the long looping skeins of electric
lines bring electric power from the Appalachian mountains, and the subter-
rene steel veins bringing the natural gas from the Western plains, to the little
lost lonely farmhouses glittering and gleaming with automatic stoves and
washing machines and television antennae;

One nation: no longer anywhere, not even in Yoknapatawpha County,
one last irreconcilable fastness of stronghold from which to enter the
United States, because at last even the old sapless indomitable unvanquished
widow or maiden aunt had died and the deathless Lost Cause had become
a faded (though still select) social club or caste, or form of behavior when
you remembered to observe it on the occasions when young men from
Brooklyn, exchange students at Mississippi or Arkansas or Texas universi-
ties, vended tiny Confederate battle flags among the thronged Saturday
afternoon ramps of football stadia; one world. (211–12)

Faulkner's account of modernity in the South suggests that "one nation, one
world" will eventually absorb the region, homogenizing the nation's culture.
The tone in this passage could as easily be read as utopian as dystopian,
both a hope for a new future and a fear of cultural annihilation. This attitude, indeed, is emblematic of the South's modernization, simultaneously
promising and frustrating, constantly threatening to obliterate the region's
distinctiveness while constantly reinforcing the region's distinctiveness. In
this same book, Faulkner states that "[t]he past is never dead. It's not even
past" (80), and in a similar paradox, the modern South continues to be
southern.

NOTES

INTRODUCTION

1. In some works, the phrase "lost cause" appears with initial caps. I prefer not to capitalize the term because I worry that doing so reifies the term, thus reinforcing the ideology.

2. My thinking about modernity as a form of social disruption has been influenced in particular by Anthony Giddens's *The Consequences of Modernity* and Zygmunt Bauman's *Liquid Modernity*.

3. The transnational turn in modernist studies challenges the constriction of nationalist boundaries on literary aesthetics, but the focus seems to remain on common experiences of urbanization and industrialization on a global scale. See Rebecca Walkowitz, *Cosmopolitan Style*; Jessica Berman, *Modernism, Cosmopolitanism, and the Politics of Community*; and Laura Doyle and Laura Winkiel, *Geomodernisms: Race, Modernism, Modernity*.

4. Many of the key studies of modernism focus on urban spaces, including the following examples: Shari Benstock, *Women of the Left Bank*; Raymond Quinones, *Mapping Literary Modernism*; Robert Alter, *Imagined Cities*; Desmond Harding, *Writing the City*; David Harvey, *Paris, Capital of Modernity*; and Richard Lehan, *Literary Modernism and Beyond*.

5. See Stephen Kern, *The Culture of Time and Space*; Peter Osborne, *The Politics of Time*; and David Harvey, *The Condition of Postmodernity*.

6. Marjorie Perloff traces the vectors of futurism in relation to technology, art, and war in *The Futurist Moment*. Writing before the war, Marinetti claimed that the futurists would glorify war, and he fought for Italy during World War I.

7. Regionalism has been the subject of several important studies, including Robert Dainotto's *Place in Literature*, Robert Dorman's *Revolt of the Provinces*, and Judith Fetterley and Marjorie Pryse's *Writing Out of Place*. For a comprehensive overview, see *A Companion to the Regional Literatures of America*, edited by Charles L. Crow.

8. I am grateful to Scott Klein and Michael Valdez Moses for their contributions to this list.

9. The critical consensus, as Vincent Sherry states, is that World War I was "the signal event of artistic modernism" ("The Great War," 113). For European writers, the war's impact was direct and immediate, taking place within the proximal zone and profoundly disrupting everyday life, and its effect on modernist literature has been well documented. Randall Stevenson's *Literature and the Great War*, for example, catalogs the way that numerous writers depicted the war. However, his story mentions no writers from the US South, not even Faulkner. Because of the South's distance from the site of conflict, the war's impact on southern literature has often been overlooked, usually limited to considerations of Faulkner. Pearl James does this in *The New Death*, the most significant work on World War I and American

modernism, and John T. Matthews, a noted scholar of southern literature, does the same in his essay, "American Writing of the Great War," in *The Cambridge Companion to the Literature of the First World War*. Consequently, the war's impact on southern literature has not been thoroughly examined.

10. The unevenness between the South's rate of development and the North's rate of development becomes evident in two works, Ed Ayers's *The Promise of the New South* and Ron Kline's *Consumers in the Country*. Ayers documents the tumultuous history of the South after Reconstruction, and he demonstrates that as the nation modernized, the South retrenched by adapting new technologies, mediums, and political systems to suit the region's retrograde culture. Kline discusses the process of spreading electrification into the nation's rural areas, and he notes that the South lagged behind the rest of the nation. Much of the Midwest electrified after World War I, but the South did not electrify until after World War II.

11. In addition to W. J. Cash's *The Mind of the South* and Daniel J. Singal's *The War Within*, see Michael O'Brien, *The Idea of the American South*, esp. chapter 10; John M. Bradbury, *Renaissance in the South: A Critical History of the Literature*, esp. chapter 1; Richard Gray, *The Literature of Memory: Modern Writers of the American South*, esp. chapter 1; Richard H. King, *A Southern Renaissance: The Cultural Awakening of the American South*, esp. chapter 1; and Lewis P. Simpson, "The Southern Writer and the Great Literary Secession."

CHAPTER ONE

1. For details about Faulkner's experience as an RAF cadet in Canada, see Joseph Blotner, *Faulkner: A Biography*, 203–30; and Michael Millgate, "William Faulkner, Cadet."

2. Keith Gandal argues in *The Gun and the Pen* that Faulkner, Hemingway, and Fitzgerald were inspired by their failure to actively participate in the war.

3. Faulkner dramatized his experience in several early short stories, including "Landing in Luck," "Thrift," and "With Caution and Dispatch." For more on Faulkner's World War I short stories, see Duane J. MacMillan, "Fictional Facts and Factual Fiction: William Faulkner and World War I"; and M. E. Bradford, "The Anomaly of Faulkner's World War I Stories."

4. Pratt employs these ideas in her book *Imperial Eyes: Travel Writing and Transculturation*.

5. The issue of the South's relationship to the greater United States is the subject of many studies of southern culture, but three books in particular influence my understanding of the South as a problematic component of the nation. Barbara Ladd argues in *Nationalism and the Color Line* that some southern writers "construct the southerner as a dangerous border figure, someone who might look like an American and claim to be so but who carries within him or herself traces of the displaced and who might act traitorously to undermine the progressive nation" (36). In *The Nation's Region*, Leigh Anne Duck describes the South as an imaginary projection within nationalist discourse that has allowed simultaneously for the emergence of liberal capitalism, primarily in the North, and the maintenance of traditional (as in nonmodern) racist feudalism. Jennifer Greeson contends in *Our South* that, since the beginning of the American nation, the South has been a site of geographic fantasy, consistently defined as peripheral other to the developing national core.

6. Christopher McKnight Nichols gives a thorough examination of Bourne's ideas about nationalism and pluralism in "Rethinking Randolph Bourne's Trans-National America: How World War I Created an Isolationist Antiwar Pluralism."

7. Anthony Gaughan, in "Woodrow Wilson and the Rise of Militant Interventionism in the South," explains that southerners have been consistently supportive of military intervention since World War I.

8. For more information about the New South movement, see Paul M. Gaston, *The New South Creed*; and Edward Ayers, *The Promise of the New South*.

9. The exception was the chain of beach resorts that catered to wealthy northerners wintering in the warm South in Jekyll Island, Saint Augustine, and Palm Beach.

10. Chad Berry remarks in *Southern Migrants, Northern Exiles* that "after World War I, more and more southerners believed that the opportunity they were seeking did not exist in the South," so many southerners sought their opportunity in the North (17).

11. A detailed historical analysis of these events may be found *The Emergence of the New South, 1913–1945*, by George B. Tindall. Of World War I's impact on the South, Tindall says:

> As Southerners emerged onto the threshold of the 1920s the experience of the war had in many ways altered and enlarged their perspectives.... Above all, the experience of the war years brought a new realization of change, the significance of which touched most keenly the sensitive young writers of a coming revival in Southern letters.... Some Southerners responded eagerly to change, others defensively; but most, like the rising authors, reacted with ambivalence. Whatever their response, the consciousness of change had become one of the abiding facts of the twentieth century South. (69)

12. T. J. Jackson Lears explores "the origins and effects of American antimodernism, particularly its dominant form—the recoil from an 'overcivilized' modern existence to more intense forms of physical or spiritual experience supposedly embodied in medieval or Oriental cultures," in *No Place of Grace: Antimodernism and the Transformation of American Culture, 1880–1920*. His study has obvious analogs in the South, specifically in the appeal to feudalistic antecedents, but he does not directly discuss southern antimodernism (xv). His more recent book, *Rebirth of a Nation: The Making of Modern America, 1877–1920*, gives some attention to the development of southern historical revisionism, but it does not document the South's encounter with modernity.

13. For details about America's mobilization, see Jennifer Keene's *Doughboys, the Great War, and the Remaking of America*, 31–34. She notes that regional tensions were evident not only among white soldiers but also among black soldiers in the segregated army.

14. Michael O'Brien examines the ways in which this assertion has been used to flagellate the South in *Henry Adams and the Southern Question*.

15. C. Vann Woodward discusses Basil Ransom in *The Burden of Southern History*, chapter 6.

16. See John T. Irwin, "Is Fitzgerald a Southern Writer?"

17. For details about Fitzgerald's military service in the South and his courtship of Zelda Sayre, see Matthew J. Bruccoli, *Some Sort of Epic Grandeur*, 79–91; and Wesley Phillips Newton, "'Tenting Tonight on the Old Camp Grounds': Alabama's Military Bases in World War I."

18. Scott Donaldson explores this relationship in "Scott Fitzgerald's Romance with the South."

19. Page citations for the Fitzgerald stories discussed here are taken from *The Short Stories of F. Scott Fitzgerald*, edited by Matthew J. Bruccoli.

20. See C. Hugh Holman, "Fitzgerald's Changes on the Southern Belle"; and P. Keith Gammons, "The South of the Mind."

21. Dos Passos based his portrayal of life in an American training camp on his experience at Camp Crane in Allentown, Pennsylvania, where he met soldiers named Fuselli and Christenfield. See Townsend Ludington, *The Fourteenth Chronicle*, 207–27.

22. *Three Soldiers*, like Henri Barbusse's novel *Le feu*, proved to be highly controversial at the time of its publication. See, for example, reviews collected in Barry Maine, *Dos Passos: The Critical Heritage.*

23. Dos Passos dramatizes his experience as an adolescent in Virginia in the short story "July," which he originally intended to incorporate into *Manhattan Transfer.*

24. The connection between Mahon and the porter prefigures the connection between Quentin Compson and Deacon, the Cambridge train porter, in *The Sound and the Fury.*

25. Jacquelyn Scott Lynch addresses this point in "Postwar Play: Gender Performatives in Faulkner's *Soldiers' Pay.*"

26. Michael Zeitlin discusses Faulkner's early female characters in "The Passion of Margaret Powers: A Psychoanalytic Reading of *Soldiers' Pay.*"

27. For a discussion of Faulkner's manuscript for the novel, see Margaret J. Yonce, "The Composition of *Soldiers' Pay.*"

28. Faulkner actually makes references to James Branch Cabell's *Jurgen*, then a controversial book, in *Soldiers' Pay* (63), and he makes a derisive comment about Henry James that hints at the antagonism between realism and modernism (227).

29. Michael Millgate discusses Faulkner's modernist literary devices in more detail in "Starting Out in the Twenties: Reflections on *Soldiers' Pay.*"

30. Michael Millgate published the recovered essay in "Faulkner on the Literature of the First World War."

31. In his contribution to *I'll Take My Stand*, "Remarks on the Southern Religion," Tate outlines the southern civic religion, "Tradition," and he makes the odd and controversial assertion that southerners may seize hold of Tradition "by violence" (174). I see this statement as more defeatist than militant. Whether Tate is willing to admit it or not, by 1930 southern tradition had already begun to make way for progress, so the violence he proposes is a quixotic last stand.

32. Susan V. Donaldson rightly rebukes Tate for ignoring the significant literary contributions of women and African Americans to southern literature in her essay "Race, Gender, and Allen Tate's Profession of Letters in the South."

CHAPTER TWO

1. Woodrow Wilson, *Congressional Record*, 65th Congress, 2nd Session, 1827–1828.

2. Perhaps the most notable contribution—certainly the most famous—by a single enlisted soldier to the American war effort occurred in October 1918 when Sergeant Alvin York of Tennessee killed 25 Germans and captured 132 more in a single day. Media attention made Sergeant York an immediate folk hero in the United States, and the film *Sergeant York*, directed by Howard Hanks and starring Gary Cooper, has made him an enduring pop-culture icon. For more on the story of Sergeant York, see David D. Lee, *Sergeant York: An American Hero.*

3. Buddy, by the way, is the pastoral antithesis to Bayard's modernism. When Bayard asks Buddy where he served, Buddy responds, "Where them limeys was. . . . Flat country. Don't see how they ever drained it enough to make a crop with all that rain" (366). His concern about farming and the condition of the land even in a combat zone signals that he is completely integrated with the environment.

4. See Tindall, *The Emergence of the New South*, 1.

5. Link, *Wilson: The New Freedom*, 24–26.

6. In *Rich Man's War, Poor Man's Fight: Race, Class, and Power in the Rural South during the First World War*, Jeanette Keith explains that support for the war ran along race and class lines with white middle-class and urban southerners generally supporting the war and rural white and black southerners generally dissenting. These latter groups represented the bulk of southern draft dodgers during the war.

7. A century and a half after the end of the Civil War, the myth of the lost cause continues to define the identities of some white southerners. The acrimonious debates on the placement of the Confederate battle flag on the state capitol grounds in South Carolina and Alabama and the statewide referendums in favor of keeping emblems of the Confederacy on the state flags of Mississippi and Georgia indicate that old times, at least in those states, will not be forgotten. Tony Horwitz, furthermore, documents the fanaticism of Civil War reenactors in *Confederates in the Attic*, and John Shelton Reed's research in *The Enduring South* indicates that white southerners continue to identify themselves according to regional labels.

8. In the minds of some southerners, Wilson's election signified the final triumph of the lost cause. Edwin Alderman, the president of the University of Virginia, for example, wrote that the election of Wilson was "a sort of fulfillment of an unspoken prophecy lying close to the heart of nearly every faithful son of the South that out of this life of dignity and suffering, and out of this discipline of fortitude and endurance there would spring a brave, modern national minded man to whom the whole nation, in some hour of peril and difficulty would turn for succor and for helpfulness." Quoted in Foster, *Ghosts of the Confederacy*, 193.

9. For an analysis of southern attitudes toward American foreign policy in the early twentieth century, see Alexander Deconde, "The South and Isolationism."

10. Senator James K. Vardaman of Mississippi and House Majority Leader Claude Kitchin of North Carolina opposed America's entrance into the war. Both men had been friends of Wilson's secretary of state, William Jennings Bryan, and they admired his conviction and commitment to neutrality, which he demonstrated by resigning from his office when Wilson pursued preparedness policies following the sinking of the *Lusitania*. Their opposition to the war despite their position's political costs indicates that, while patriotism lessened isolationism in the South, isolationism was not vanquished. Dissenting on the war vote cost Vardaman his political career, and even newspapers in his native Mississippi branded him "Herr Von Vardaman." Incidentally, the majority of southern politicians who opposed preparedness also lost wartime elections. The single exception was Claude Kitchin, who remained in office through the end of the war. For more on Vardaman, see William F. Holmes, *The White Chief: James Kimble Vardaman*; and for more on Kitchin, see Alex M. Arnett, *Claude Kitchin and the Wilson War Policies*.

11. Prophetically, a Florida newspaper lamented in 1918 that after World War I all Americans, including southerners, would be known by that hateful epithet, "Yankees." Bailey, *The Man in the Street*, 114.

12. Quoted in Grantham, *The South in Modern America*, 81.

13. The discourse on globalization and the US South originates in the growth of the South as an economic center since the end of the Cold War. James Peacock, Harry Watson, and Carrie Matthews's edited volume *The American South in a Global World*, and James Cobb and William Stueck's edited volume *Globalization and the American South*, examine the international flows of population and capital that led to the emergence of the Sunbelt.

14. Wilson, "Remarks to the Confederate Veterans in Washington," 451.

15. Thomas Dixon, a staunch advocate of military preparedness, made a film in 1916 titled *Fall of a Nation* that depicts a race of obviously Germanic people infiltrating and conquering

the United States. The film apparently flopped, and no copies of the movie survive. For details about the film, see Anthony Slide, *American Racist: The Life and Films of Thomas Dixon*, 89–104.

16. For the context of Wilson's quotations, see *A History of the American People*, vol. 5, *Reunion and Nationalization*, 19–78.

17. Thomas Dixon and Woodrow Wilson knew each other as graduate students at Johns Hopkins University, and they maintained a relationship throughout their careers. Dixon helped to arrange a private screening of *The Birth of a Nation* for the president, making it the first film ever shown in the White House. For more on the relationship between Griffith, Dixon, and Wilson, see Michael P. Rogin, *Ronald Reagan, The Movie, and Other Episodes in Political Demonology*, 192–98.

18. Quoted from the script of *The Birth of a Nation*; published in Lang, *The Birth of a Nation: D. W. Griffith, Director*, 134.

19. In *Race and Reunion*, David Blight comments that "Dixon's vision captured the attitudes of thousands and forged in story form a collective memory of how the war was lost but Reconstruction was won—by the South and by a reconciled nation" (111).

20. For more on the film's reception, see Janet Staiger, "*The Birth of a Nation*: Reconsidering Its Reception."

21. For details about Percy's military service, see Benjamin Wise, *William Alexander Percy: The Curious Life of a Mississippi Planter and Sexual Freethinker.*

22. Quoted in Lewis Baker, *The Percys of Mississippi*, 84.

23. Bertram Wyatt-Brown explains that, in the southern code of honor, war brings esteem to the warrior (*Southern Honor*, 34–42).

24. Quoted in Lewis Baker, *The Percys of Mississippi*, 86.

25. For comparison, see Brooke's poem "The Soldier" and McCrae's poem "In Flanders Fields" in *The Penguin Book of First World War Poetry*, edited by Jon Silkin. In the introduction to this anthology, Silkin usefully describes the arc of European trench poetry from idealistic to utterly disillusioned while highlighting the work of British poets, especially Wilfred Owen.

26. Quoted in Collins, *William Faulkner*, 71.

27. Quoted in Collins, *William Faulkner*, 72.

28. For details about Green's childhood and his later career as a dramatist, see John Herbert Roper, *Paul Green: Playwright of the New South.*

29. John Herbert Roper published Green's war poems, including the poems in *Trifles of Thought*, as *Paul Green's War Songs*. The volume includes a lengthy introduction about Green's war experience.

30. Paul Green to Erma Green, in Avery, *A Southern Life*, 10.

31. Paul Green to Erma Green, in Avery, *A Southern Life*, 11.

32. Quoted in Roper, *Paul Green: Playwright of the Real South*, 41.

33. Paul Green to Erma Green, in Avery, *A Southern Life*, 15.

34. Harold Clurman, a member of the Group Theatre, recounts the company's history in *The Fervent Years: The Group Theatre and the Thirties*. For details about Green's collaboration with the company, see 187–93.

35. In the original production of *Johnny Johnson* presented by the Group Theatre at the Forty-Fourth Street Theatre in New York in 1936, Elia Kazan, later to become famous as a director of Tennessee Williams's plays, played Private Goldberger and a few other minor roles.

36. Quoted in Zachary Perkinson, "The Group Theatre," 26.

37. Green, like Johnny Johnson, greatly admired Woodrow Wilson. In 1964, he wrote to a friend who had sent him a recently published biography of Wilson: "I admired and loved

Wilson long ago, and still venerate and love his memory. . . . [This biography] is one more step in the rehabilitation and reaffirmation of a great man and his rightful vision in a tangled world." See Paul Green to Frances Phillips, in Avery, *A Southern Life*, 632.

38. John Crowe Ransom, Davidson's poetic and intellectual mentor, also served in the military during the war, as an artillery training officer in France. For an account of Ransom's experience during the war and its effect on his aesthetic sensibility, see Davis, "Grace after Battle."

39. Mark Royden Winchell quotes a lengthy passage from Davidson's diary recounting his experiences in combat; see *Where No Flag Flies*, 39.

40. Quoted in Inge, "Donald Davidson's Notes," 210.

41. Quoted in Young and Inge, *Donald Davidson*, 30.

42. Quoted in Jordan, "*The Tall Men*: Davidson's Answer to Eliot," 50.

43. Daniel J. Singal also notes the modernist antimodernism in Davidson's poem. He writes: "Davidson was convinced that he was moving daringly backward [in composing *The Tall Men*], rejecting twentieth-century culture decisively. To the extent that he was countering the threats of skepticism and relativism, this was true. But paradoxically, his glorification of primitivism and attack on cultural elitism sprang directly from the Modernist strain in his thought" (223).

44. Randall Stevenson explains in *Literature of the Great War* that the danger of mechanization was a common theme in writing by European veterans such as Wilfred Owen and Frederic Manning, "reflecting a much accelerated phase in the advance of modernity, and deepening doubts about its consequences" (225).

Chapter Three

1. Richard Slotkin examines the impact of wartime nationalism on two multicultural battalions, the Melting Pot Division, a battalion of ethnic immigrants, and Harlem's Hell Fighters, a battalion of northern blacks, in *Lost Battalions: The Great War and the Crisis of American Nationality*.

2. Houston Baker, Brent Hayes Edwards, Paul Gilroy, Michelle Stephens, and Mark Whalan have already offered explanations of the relationship between African American modernism and transnational identity. But these studies have not factored in the significance of regional identity, which complicates racial identity in important ways.

3. Soon after the war a number of other texts, most transcribed by white writers, were published that borrow from the tradition of local color to portray ignorant black soldiers as amusingly bewildered by their war experience. For examples, see Howard Odum, *Wings on My Feet*; W. Irwin MacIntyre, *Colored Soldiers*; and Charles E. Mack, *Two Black Crows in the A.E.F.*

4. Quoted in Barbeau and Henri, *The Unknown Soldiers: Black American Troops in World War I*, 34.

5. Government monitoring of black organizations was not limited to the World War I period. In addition to *"Investigate Everything,"* also see Kornweibel's *Seeing Red: Federal Campaigns against Black Militancy, 1919–1925*; and William J. Maxwell's *New Negro, Old Left: African American Writing and Communism between the Wars*.

6. For more information on the Great Migration, see Florette Henri, *Black Migration: Movement North, 1900–1920*; Alferdteen Harrison, ed., *Black Exodus: The Great Migration from the American South*; and James Grossman, *Land of Hope: Chicago, Black Southerners, and the Great Migration*.

7. Quoted in Barbeau and Henri, *The Unknown Soldiers: Black American Troops in World War I*, 193.

8. For details on these two incidents, see Elliott Rudwick, *Race Riot at East St. Louis, July 2, 1917*; Robert Haynes, *A Night of Violence: The Houston Riot of 1917*; and Adriane Lentz-Smith, *Freedom Struggles: African Americans and World War I*.

9. For details about the Houston riot, see Arthur Barbeau and Florette Henri, *The Unknown Soldiers*, 26–32; and Garna L. Christian, *Black Soldiers in Jim Crow Texas, 1899–1917*.

10. Quoted in Barbeau and Henri, *The Unknown Soldiers: Black American Troops in World War I*, 199.

11. Richard Wright recollects in his autobiography *Black Boy* one day encountering a column of black soldiers carrying rifles dressed in uniforms and the next day encountering a column of black convicts working on a road dressed in stripes, a juxtaposition that typifies the promise and the reality of black military service (55–58).

12. After the armistice, Du Bois intended to write a full-length history of black soldiers in the war, but he became involved in the Pan-African Conference, which occupied too much of his time to complete the project.

13. Stephen L. Harris, in *Harlem's Hell Fighters*, notes that black troops were rejected from New York's famous Rainbow Division because "black is not a color of the rainbow" (98).

14. For a short time, William Alexander Percy served as a training officer with the Ninety-Second.

15. For details about the postwar movement for civil rights, see Mark Robert Schneider, *"We Return Fighting": The Civil Rights Movement in the Jazz Age*.

16. The New York Post Office held this issue of the *Crisis* for six days because of Du Bios' potentially seditious editorial (W. Jordan, 138).

17. A white man speaking to blacks in New Orleans summarizes the attitude of the southern racial hegemony: "You niggers are wondering how you are going to be treated after the war. Well, I'll tell you, you are going to be treated exactly like you were before the war; this is a white man's country and we expect to rule it" (Barbeau and Henri, 175).

18. For a provocative, contemporary study of the Chicago riot, see Carl Sandburg, *The Chicago Race Riots, July, 1919*.

19. The trope of the black World War I veteran continues to hold cultural capital. Tom, a black veteran, figures indirectly in Richard Wright's story "Long Black Song." In Ernest Gaines's novel *A Gathering of Old Men*, for example, one of the old men, Coot, who claims to be the only veteran in the parish, wears his World War I uniform for apparently the first time since the war. He recalls being told by a white man: "I better not ever wear that uniform or that medal again no matter how long I lived. He told me I was back home now, and they didn't cotton to no nigger wearing medals for killing white folks" (104).

20. Andrew Leiter analyzes the literary trope of the black beast in *In the Shadow of the Black Beast*.

21. The two black soldiers involved in the initial incident were Noble Sissle, who purchased the paper, and James Reese Europe, who quelled the crowd. Europe was a famous bandleader in New York before the war, and during the war he became quite famous throughout France and England for playing jazz. Sissle played in his orchestra. After the war, Europe was considered one of the most prominent black artists in America. For more about his role in the Spartanburg incident and his role in the war, see Stephen Harris, *Harlem's Hell Fighters*, 113–36.

22. Adriane Lentz-Smith describes the experience of black soldiers in France in chapter 3 of *Freedom Struggles*, 121.

23. The French military also employed racist polices targeted toward its colonial African troops. African soldiers were deliberately taught a simplistic French patois called *petit negre* that the French used, as Brent Hayes Edwards explains, "both to infantilize them and to control their modes of interaction with their mainly white French commanding officers" (52).

24. Quoted in Williams, *Torchbearers of Democracy*, 268.

25. The ending of *Not Only War* may draw from Joseph Seamon Cotter Jr.'s play *On the Fields of France*, published in the *Crisis* in 1920.

26. After a few years of investigating lynchings for the NAACP, White wrote one of the most provocative and insightful studies of race relations in the South, *Rope and Faggot: A Biography of Judge Lynch.*

27. Kenneth Robert Janken notes that Central City appears to be based primarily on Albany, Georgia, the city that W. E. B. Du Bois explored in *The Souls of Black Folk*; see Janken, *White: The Biography of Walter White*, 106.

28. Castronovo argues in "Beauty along the Color Line" that Dr. Harper's preoccupation with literature marks him as queer. "Art jeopardizes black masculinity by inviting suspicions that the doctor in *The Fire in the Flint*, an avid reader, is not only 'decadent' and 'effete' but also 'a little queer in the head,' disposed to 'moral turpitude and perversion'" (1455).

29. For details on the emerging black labor movement, see Beth Tompkins Bates, *Pullman Porters and the Rise of Protest Politics in Black America, 1925-1945.*

30. Richard Wright briefly lived with his aunt and uncle in Elaine, Arkansas, the seat of Phillips County, until his uncle was murdered by a white mob in 1916. He describes his life there in his autobiography, *Black Boy.*

31. For details about the Phillips County riot, see Grif Stockley, *Blood in the Eyes: The Elaine Race Massacres of 1919*; Nan Elizabeth Woodruff, *American Congo: The African American Freedom Struggle in the Delta*; and Philip Dray, *At the Hands of Persons Unknown: The Lynching of Black America*, 237-45.

32. White describes his experience in Phillips County in his autobiography, *A Man Called White*, 46-51.

33. White narrates his escape in "I Investigate Lynchings," an article originally published in *American Mercury* in 1929.

34. The ending of *The Fire in the Flint* borrows heavily from the ending of Charles Chesnutt's *The Marrow of Tradition.*

35. In *Rope and Faggot*, White explores the sexualized rationale for lynching (54-81).

36. For additional studies of lynching in the South, see W. Fitzhugh Brundage, ed., *Under Sentence of Death*; Stewart E. Tolnay and E. M. Beck, *A Festival of Violence*; and James Allen, *Without Sanctuary.*

37. I make a more extended version of this argument in Davis, "Not Only War Is Hell: World War I and African American Lynching Narratives."

38. For a discussion of McKay's experience in Harlem as a form of exile, see Carl Pedersen, "'The Tropics in New York: Claude McKay and the New Negro Movement."

Chapter Four

1. Several feminist scholars have elaborated on the construction and function of the southern patriarchy, including Catherine Clinton, *The Plantation Mistress*; Jean Friedman, *The Enclosed Garden*; Hazel V. Carby, *Reconstructing Womanhood*; Laura F. Edwards, *Gendered*

Strife and Confusion; Minrose Gwin, *Black and White Women of the Old South*; and Lucinda MacKethan, *Daughters of Time*.

2. Quoted in Anne Firor Scott, *The Southern Lady*, 5.

3. Histories of women in the labor force during World War I include Susan Zeiger, *In Uncle Sam's Service: Women Workers with the American Expeditionary Force, 1917–1919*; Carrie Brown, *Rosie's Mom: Forgotten Women Workers of the First World War*; and Maurine Weiner Greenwald, *Women, War, and Work: The Impact of World War I on Women Workers in the United States*.

4. For more on women in the military, see Lettie Gavin, *American Women in World War I*; and Kimberly Jensen, *Mobilizing Minerva*.

5. In *The Weight of Their Votes*, Lorraine Gates Schulyer documents that southern women, both white and black, did have a significant impact on electoral politics after the passage of the Nineteenth Amendment.

6. Specific histories of the New Woman in southern states can be found in Mary Martha Thomas, *The New Woman in Alabama*; and Judith N. McArthur, *Creating the New Woman*.

7. Many studies of British women's writing and World War I have been published in recent years. A partial list includes Sharon Oudit, *Fighting Forces, Writing Women: Identity and Ideology in the First World War*; Claire Tylee, *The Great War and Women's Consciousness*; Debra Rae Cohen, *Remapping the Home Front*; Angela K. Smith, *The Second Battlefield: Women, Modernism, and the First World War*; Trudi Tate, *Modernism, History, and the First World War*; *Women Writers and the Great War*, edited by Dorothy Goldman; and *Women's Fiction and the Great War*, edited by Suzanne Raitt and Trudi Tate.

8. For a sense of the range of women's literary responses to the war, see Margaret R. Higonnet's anthology *Lines of Fire: Women Writers of World War I*.

9. Carol S. Manning argues that southern women writers initiated a period of artistic and social change before World War I. She claims in "The Real Beginning of the Southern Renaissance" that masculinist critics have arbitrarily marked World War I as the beginning of the Southern Renaissance, overlooking the artistic advances of southern women writers, including Kate Chopin, Ellen Glasgow, Anna Julia Cooper, and Belle Kearney, who were actively writing about and criticizing the South in the decades before the war. All of these writers critique southern patriarchy, and they were in that way predecessors for the modernist writers who would follow them.

10. Jennifer Haytock explores the intersection of the domestic novel and the war novel during World War I in *At Home, At War*.

11. For details about Alice Dunbar Nelson's war work and literary work, see Nikki Brown, *Private Politics and Public Voices*; and Gloria T. Hull, *Color, Sex, and Poetry*.

12. For discussions of Hurston's combination of modernism with African American folklore, see Eric Sundquist, *The Hammers of Creation*; John Lowe, *Jump at the Sun*; and Anthony Wilson, "The Music of God, Man, and Beast: Spirituality and Modernity in *Jonah's Gourd Vine*."

13. Catherine G. Peaslee recounts Glasgow's role in the suffrage movement in "Novelist Ellen Glasgow's Feminist Rebellion in Virginia—the Suffragist."

14. For details about Glasgow's changing political opinions, see Ellen M. Caldwell, "Ellen Glasgow and the Southern Agrarians."

15. For a feminist analysis of *Virginia*, see Anne Goodwyn Jones, *Tomorrow Is Another Day*, chapter 6.

16. Pamela R. Matthews explores Glasgow's representation of feminism in "From Joan of Arc to Lucy Dare: Ellen Glasgow on Southern Womanhood."

17. For a discussion of urbanization in the South, see David Goldfield, *Cotton Fields and Skyscrapers.*

18. For a brilliant analysis of Glasgow's contentious relationship with feminism and feminist criticism, see Pamela R. Matthews, *Ellen Glasgow and a Woman's Traditions.*

19. At the end of the book, Ada returns to the family home on the mountain, which Mary Weaks-Baxter sees as a rejection of "the encroaching industrialization, mechanization, and commercialism of the modern world" (33).

20. The critical discourse on Roberts has developed slowly. Until two recent essay collections edited by H. R. Stoneback, the most significant examples are a pair of monographs—Earl Rovit's *Herald to Chaos* and Frederick McDowell's *Elizabeth Madox Roberts*—and a special issue of the *Southern Review* in 1984.

21. George Brosi offers a brief estimation of Roberts's literary technique and her contribution to southern literature in his chapter "Elizabeth Madox Roberts" in the collection *The History of Southern Women's Literature.* Catherine Rainwater discusses Glasgow's relationship to modernism in the essay "'That Abused Word, Modern' and Ellen Glasgow's 'Literature of Revolt.'" Also see Helen Fiddyment Levy's essay on Glasgow's technique, "Mining the *Vein of Iron*: Ellen Glasgow's Later Communal Voice."

22. I discuss this story more fully in the essay "The Forgotten Apocalypse: Katherine Anne Porter's 'Pale Horse, Pale Rider,' Traumatic Memory, and the Influenza Pandemic of 1918."

23. For a history of the New Woman in America, see *The Rise of the New Woman: The Women's Movement in America, 1875–1930,* by Jean V. Matthews.

24. Newman's review of F. Scott Fitzgerald's *This Side of Paradise,* for example, prompted Fitzgerald to write her an outraged letter. She paraded the letter before James Branch Cabell, saying that she felt like she had "pulled a spoiled baby's curls and made him cry." The exchange can be found in *Frances Newman's Letters,* edited by Hansell Baugh, 40–45.

25. Matthew Bruccoli describes the critical response to the novel in his introduction to *Save Me the Waltz* in *Zelda Fitzgerald: The Collected Writings.*

26. Although Zelda Fitzgerald grew up in Alabama, she has not been heavily incorporated into the criticism of southern women's literature. In fact, she merits only a passing mention in Carolyn Perry and Mary Louise Weaks's *The History of Southern Women's Literature.* Lisa Nanney's essay "Zelda Fitzgerald's *Save Me the Waltz* as Southern Novel and *Künstelerroman*" is the only work that claims Fitzgerald as a southern writer. Her position within the criticism of American modernism is also problematic. Some feminist critics have reclaimed her work, but most treatments of her novel approach it as a curious appendage to *Tender Is the Night.*

27. For a description of American soldiers in Montgomery, see Nancy Milford, *Zelda: A Biography,* 19–23. While still in high school, Zelda wrote a patriotic poem called "Over the Top with Pershing" that reflects the jingoism of the day.

28. F. Scott Fitzgerald insisted that a number of revisions be made to the novel before he would allow his editor, Maxwell Perkins, to publish it. Because the novel is based closely on their marriage and because he based *Tender Is the Night* on the same material, he saw Zelda's novel as a threat to his own. In the original version, the character David Knight is named Amory Blaine, which also happens to be the name of Fitzgerald's doppelgänger in *This Side of Paradise.* Fitzgerald requested this change and the omission of several passages describing Alabama's affair in France. For details about the tension between Scott and Zelda over

these revisions, see *Dear Scott, Dearest Zelda*, edited by Jackson R. Bryer and Cathy W. Barks, 144–71, especially F. Scott Fitzgerald's note to Zelda's doctor, 164–65.

Chapter Five

1. That Wolfe's novels are based closely on his personal experience is no secret. For details about Wolfe's experience during the war, see David Herbert Donald, *Look Homeward: A Life of Thomas Wolfe*, 42–48.

2. Duchamp's cubist, mechanical representations of the human form caused a sensation when first exhibited at the New York Armory in 1913. That particular show, whose spectators included Wallace Stevens and William Carlos Williams, propelled avant-garde literary experimentation by northeastern writers; see Milton Brown, *American Painting from the Armory Show to the Depression*. Henry Adams, a medieval historian, realized while examining exhibits at the 1893 Chicago exposition that the dynamo would be as powerful a symbol of force in the twentieth century as the image of the Virgin Mary had been in the twelfth century, thus indicating a change in social values that privileged technology over spirituality and presaging a debate that would play out in southern literature following World War I; see his autobiography, *The Education of Henry Adams*.

3. For a study of the economic and cultural impact of the boll weevil infestation, see James Giesen, *Boll Weevil Blues: Cotton, Myth, and Power in the American South*.

4. From a sermon by Baptist minister M. Ashby Jones of Augusta, Georgia, quoted in George Tindall, *The Emergence of the New South, 1913–1945*, 39.

5. In *Agricultural Progress in the Cotton Belt since 1920*, John Leonard Fulmer explains that, in fact, cotton would not become a consistently profitable crop until after World War II, when southern farmers finally diversified their land distribution, adopted schemes of crop rotation, and invested in tractors and other mechanical labor devices; curiously, as more southerners moved to urban areas, fewer farmers were left to do more work (170–78). For statistics related to agricultural development and production during the war, see *Effects of the Great War upon Agriculture in the United States and Great Britain* by Benjamin H. Hibbard.

6. For details about federal programs and the economic development of the South through the 1920s into the era of the New Deal, see D. Clayton Brown, *Electricity for Rural America: The Fight for the REA*; Walter L. Creese, *TVA's Public Planning: The Vision, The Reality*; and David Conrad, *The Forgotten Farmers: The Story of Sharecroppers in the New Deal*. For works by the Chapel Hill Regionalists, see Howard Odum, *Southern Regions of the United States*; and Rupert Vance, *Human Factors in Cotton Culture*.

7. In *No Place of Grace: Antimodernism and the Transformation of American Culture, 1880–1920*, T. J. Jackson Lears documents a strong current of antimodernism among American intellectuals, many of whom worried about the dehumanizing effects of corporate capitalism. Incidentally, of the sixty-five figures Lears examines in the book, including Henry Adams, Charles Eliot Norton, and Edith Wharton, only one, James Branch Cabell, lived his entire adult life in the South.

8. W. J. Cash labels this commitment to orthodoxy the "savage ideal" in *The Mind of the South*. But many other scholars have described the same tendency. One perceptive observation comes from Hortense Powdermaker's *After Freedom*, in which she documents that the white members of the southern community she studied "display a marked unanimity of background, education, outlook, life mode. If you know that a white person lives in Cottonville and you know his approximate age, you know a great deal about what he does, thinks, and feels" (14).

9. In *The War Within*, Daniel J. Singal, who presents Glasgow as a late Victorian southern writer, says of *Barren Ground* specifically that "what this book really entails is not Modernism at all, but nineteenth-century theology got up in stoic dress" (106).

10. For a discussion of Dorinda's dedication from a Spenglerian perspective, see Peter Nicolaisen, "Rural Poverty and the Heroics of Farming."

11. In *"Tractorization,"* Sargen tracks the diffusion of tractor consumption in the United States from 1900 to 1965, and his analysis indicates that tractors were not commonly in use until after World War II and that the South was the slowest region in the country to adopt tractors, largely because early tractors were ill suited to harvesting cotton. Sargen's analysis of farm mechanization reinforces Ronald Kline's analysis of the spread of electrical and mechanical products through rural areas in *Consumers in the Country: Technology and Social Change in Rural America*.

12. Tanya Ann Kennedy, in "The Secret Properties of Southern Regionalism," offers an insightful reading of the ways that Glasgow negotiates gender roles in *Barren Ground*.

13. Quoted in Caldwell, "Ellen Glasgow and the Southern Agrarians," 210.

14. In *The Fugitive Group*, Louise Cowan documents that the foreword to the first issue of the *Fugitive* famously states: "Official exception having been taken by the sovereign people to the mint julep, a literary phase known rather euphemistically as Southern Literature has expired, like any other stream whose source is stopped up. The demise is not untimely: among other advantages *The Fugitive* is enabled to come to birth in Nashville, Tennessee, under a star not entirely unsympathetic. *The Fugitive* flees from nothing faster than from the high-caste Brahmins of the Old South" (48).

15. The extent of scholarly sources devoted to analyzing the impact of the Southern Agrarians is startling. All or a significant part of more than a dozen books discuss the Agrarians, including *The Fugitive Group* by Louise Cowan, *The Burden of Time* by John L. Stewart, *Tillers of a Myth* by Alexander Karanikas, *The Wary Fugitives* by Louis D. Rubin Jr., *A Southern Renaissance* by Richard King, *The Idea of the American South* by Michael O'Brien, *The War Within* by Daniel J. Singal, *The Southern Agrarians* by Paul Conkin, *The Southern Tradition* by Eugene Genovese, *Inventing Southern Literature* by Michael Kreyling, *The Unregenerate South* by Mark Malvasi, *Fugitive Theory* by Christopher Duncan, and *The Rebuke of History* by Paul Murphy. The Agrarian movement has also been commemorated in three collections of essays and interviews: *A Band of Prophets*, edited by William C. Havard and Walter Sullivan; *Fugitives' Reunion*, edited by Rob Roy Purdy; and *The Southern Agrarians and the New Deal*, edited by Emily S. Bingham and Thomas A. Underwood. A seventy-fifth-anniversary edition of *I'll Take My Stand* with a new introduction by Susan V. Donaldson was published in 2006.

16. Andrew Lytle, himself a Fugitive turned Agrarian, explains his perspective of the transition from poetry to social criticism as follows: "It seems to me in this [Fugitive] stage, when they were trying to purify the word in terms of poems and discussion, their flight was from that spurious word which defined the cultural tradition and its history, and that historical circumstance of the First World War, which gave this affluent kind of release into which all things seemed to be extravagantly enlarged. Then suddenly, as always, you come back to the domestic scene, into the local situation; and the trial at Dayton focused it—as a concrete instance always does. And then what you got was a poet operating at various levels of interest" (quoted in Purdy, *Fugitives' Reunion*, 178).

17. For a discussion of the debate between the Southern Agrarians and the New Humanists, particularly Allen Tate's role in the exchange, see *The New Humanism: A Critique of Modern America, 1900–1940*, by David J. Hoeveler.

18. Donald Davidson to Herman Clarence Nixon, quoted in Shouse, *Hillbilly Realist*, 52.

19. Twelve Southerners, *I'll Take My Stand*, xlvii. In *The War Within*, Daniel J. Singal describes the Agrarian agenda as an sign of cultural change: "the Agrarians, in their resort to Old South symbolism, were attempting to recapture the unified structure of belief that had characterized Victorian culture, and with it the capacity for religious faith they had lost—all the while preserving the intellectual advances of Modernism" (202).

20. In *Radical Visions and American Dreams: Culture and Social Thought in the Depression Years*, Richard Pells notes that, ironically, the Agrarians use the same means and methods to reach their audience that the communists used to reach their audience (103).

21. Mark Jancovich argues that this ideology evolved into the New Criticism, an aesthetic theory based on capitalist principles. See *The Cultural Politics of the New Criticism*, esp. 33–66.

22. Ransom's debate with Calverton appeared in *Scribner's* magazine in 1936 and has been reprinted as "The South Is a Bulwark" in *The Southern Agrarians and the New Deal*, edited by Emily S. Bingham and Thomas A. Underwood. For an insider's slightly revisionist history of the Agrarian movement, see *Southern Writers in the Modern World* by Donald Davidson.

23. For details about Nixon's personal and intellectual life, see *Hillbilly Realist: Herman Clarence Nixon of Possum Trot* by Sarah N. Shouse.

24. For details about Couch's role in the editing and publication of *Culture in the South*, see Singal, *The War Within*, 281–84.

25. For descriptions of the lives of sharecroppers in the South during the 1930s, see *Let Us Now Praise Famous Men* by James Agee and Walker Evans; *You Have Seen Their Faces* by Erskine Caldwell and Margaret Bourke-White; and *Forty Acres and Steel Mules* by Herman Clarence Nixon. Nixon's book is especially significant because it signifies his break with conservative agrarianism.

26. In *The Southern Agrarians*, Paul Conkin calls Owlsey's article "the closest the group ever came to endorsing specific remedies for agricultural distress in the South" (113).

27. Quoted in Purdy, *Fugitives' Reunion*, 209.

28. Jacquelyn Dowd Hall and others construct an eloquent account of life in southern mill villages in *Like a Family: The Making of a Southern Cotton Mill World*. The book captures the movement of white tenant families into the mills, where they earned consistent wages. During World War I, they received significant bonuses, but after the war, hours and wages were cut, leading to strikes in 1929 and 1934.

29. For a critique of Cash's economic analysis, see Gavin Wright, "Economic Progress and the Mind of the South."

30. Details of Cash's life can be found in *W. J. Cash: A Life* by Bruce Clayton.

31. David L. Carlton explains the uniqueness and history of the textile industry in the Gaffney area in *Mill and Town in South Carolina, 1880–1920*.

32. For a discussion of *Flags in the Dust* specifically within the context of modernist technique, see Barry Atkins, "Yoknapatawpha, History and the Matter of Origins: Locating *Flags in the Dust* within Faulkner's Modernist Project."

33. Bayard shows signs of shell shock, the psychological disorder that was ubiquitous in World War I literature. In *Shell Shock, Memory, and the Novel in the Wake of World War I*, Trevor Dodman argues that "shell shock novels are about what it means to live with dead who will not return, about how to persevere in the persistent company of scars and wounds, about ways of surviving in the midst of 'broken' men, shattered communities, and devastated landscapes" (6).

34. Faulkner personally opposed the paving of streets in Oxford in 1927 because, as Thomas Hines writes in *William Faulkner and the Tangible Past*, "he saw it as the breaking of another link with the past" (118).

35. For an interesting explanation of both Faulkner's fascination with flying and his use of aircraft terminology, see *Aviation Lore in Faulkner* by Robert Harrison.

Conclusion

1. While on the train from Eastrod, in an episode that recalls Mahon's journey back to Charlestown, Motes has an encounter with a porter who he assumes is a member of the Parrum family from Eastrod, and he disbelieves the porter's assertion that he is from Chicago. This shift indicates the effects of the Great Migration, and it signals a white writer portraying a confrontational rather than subservient relationship between blacks and whites.

2. In *Selling the South*, James Cobb describes the often duplicitous strategies that southern politicians have used to court economic development, and the essays in Phillip Scranton's *The Second Wave* examine specific elements of southern industrialization.

3. Sosna has argued that World War II had a greater impact on the South than the Civil War; see "More Important than the Civil War? The Impact of World War II on the South."

4. Lawrence Schwartz explains the political dynamics of Faulkner's cultural ascendency in *Creating Faulkner's Reputation*.

5. The essays in the collection *The Myth of Southern Exceptionalism* argue that, since the civil rights movement, southern political and racial values have become mainstream in the United States. Rather than the South shifting toward progressivism following integration, Matthew Lassiter and Joseph Crespino explain that racism underlies the nation's political landscape.

6. In *The Southern Writer in the Postmodern World*, Fred Hobson asserts that southern writers born since World War II "have various and conflicting attitudes toward the South and the contemporary world" and disavow the work of southern modernists (9), and Matthew Guinn argues in *After Southern Modernism* that southern writers since the 1970s have intentionally broken with southern literary tradition.

7. Bruce Schulman explains the emergence of the Sunbelt in *From Cotton Belt to Sunbelt*.

8. Kevin Kruse documents the racial politics of suburbanization in the South in *White Flight*.

9. For a discussion of World War II and race relations, see John Egerton, *Speak Now against the Day*; Harvard Sitkoff, "African American Militancy in the World War II South"; and Jacquelyn Dowd Hall, "The Long Civil Rights Movement and the Political Uses of the Past."

BIBLIOGRAPHY

Abbott, Emory Reginald. "A Southern Lady Still: A Reinterpretation of Frances Percy Newman's *The Hard-Boiled Virgin*." *Southern Quarterly* 27 (Summer 1989).

Adams, Henry. *The Education of Henry Adams*. Boston: Houghton Mifflin, 1918.

Agee, James, and Walker Evans. *Let Us Now Praise Famous Men*. Boston: Houghton Mifflin, 1941.

Aiken, Charles. *The Cotton Plantation South since the Civil War*. Baltimore: Johns Hopkins University Press, 1998.

Allen, James. *Without Sanctuary: Lynching Photography in America*. Santa Fe, NM: Twin Palms, 2000.

Alter, Robert. *Imagined Cities: Urban Experience and the Language of the Novel*. New Haven, CT: Yale University Press, 2005.

Anderson, Benedict. *Imagined Communities: Reflections on the Origin and Spread of Nationalism*. Rev. ed. New York: Verso, 1991.

Anderson, Charles R. "James's Portrait of the Southerner." *American Literature* 27, no. 1 (November 1955): 309–31.

Andrews, William L. "In Search of a Common Identity: The Self and the South in Four Mississippi Autobiographies." *Southern Review* 24, no. 1 (Winter 1988): 47–64.

Armstrong, Tim. *Modernism: A Cultural History*. New York: Polity, 2005.

Arnett, Alex Mathews. *Claude Kitchin and the Wilson War Policies*. Boston: Little, Brown, 1937.

Arnow, Harriette. *The Dollmaker*. New York: Macmillan, 1954.

Atkins, Barry. "Yoknapatawpha, History and the Matter of Origins: Locating *Flags in the Dust* within Faulkner's Modernist Project." *Renaissance and Modern Studies* 41 (1998): 86–100.

Avery, Laurence G., ed. *A Southern Life: Letters of Paul Green, 1916–1981*. Chapel Hill: University of North Carolina Press, 1994.

Ayers, Edward L. *The Promise of the New South: Life after Reconstruction*. New York: Oxford University Press, 1992.

Bailey, Thomas A. *The Man in the Street: The Impact of American Public Opinion on Foreign Policy*. New York: Macmillan, 1948.

Baker, Houston A., Jr. *Modernism and the Harlem Renaissance*. Chicago: University of Chicago Press, 1987.

———. *Turning South Again: Re-thinking Modernism/Re-reading Booker T.* Durham, NC: Duke University Press, 2001.

Baker, Lewis. *The Percys of Mississippi: Politics and Literature in the New South*. Baton Rouge: Louisiana State University Press, 1983.

Baldwin, Kate A. *Beyond the Color Line and the Iron Curtain: Reading Encounters between Black and Red, 1922–1963.* Durham, NC: Duke University Press, 2002.

Balibar, Etienne. "Racism and Nationalism." In *Race, Nation, and Class,* edited by Etienne Balibar and Immanuel Wallerstein. London: Verso, 1991.

Barbeau, Arthur E., and Florette Henri. *The Unknown Soldiers: Black American Troops in World War I.* Philadelphia: Temple University Press, 1974.

Bates, Beth Tompkins. *Pullman Porters and the Rise of Protest Politics in Black America, 1925–1945.* Chapel Hill: University of North Carolina Press, 2001.

Baudelaire, Charles. *The Painter of Modern Life and Other Essays.* Translated by Jonathan Mayne. New York: Phaidon Press, 1995.

Bauman, Zygmunt. *Liquid Modernity.* London: Polity, 2000.

Baym, Nina. "The Myth of the Myth of Southern Womanhood." In *Feminism and American Literary History,* 183–96. New Brunswick, NJ: Rutgers University Press, 1992.

Beck, Charlotte. *The Fugitive Legacy.* Baton Rouge: Louisiana State University Press, 2001.

Benson, Melanie. *Disturbing Calculations: The Economics of Identity in Postcolonial Southern Literature, 1912–2002.* Athens: University of Georgia Press, 2008.

Benstock, Shari. *Women of the Left Bank: Paris, 1900–1940.* Austin: University of Texas Press, 1986.

Berman, Jessica. *Modernism, Cosmopolitanism, and the Politics of Community.* Cambridge: Cambridge University Press, 2001.

Berman, Marshall. *All That Is Solid Melts into Air: The Experience of Modernity.* New York: Simon and Schuster, 1982.

Berry, Chad. *Southern Migrants, Northern Exiles.* Urbana: University of Illinois Press, 2000.

Bingham, Emily S., and Thomas A. Underwood, eds. *The Southern Agrarians and the New Deal: Essays after "I'll Take My Stand."* Charlottesville: University Press of Virginia, 2001.

Blair, Arthur H. "Bayard Sartoris: Suicidal or Foolhardy?" *Southern Literary Journal* 15, no. 1 (Fall 1982): 55–60.

Blight, David. *Race and Reunion: The Civil War in American Memory.* Cambridge, MA: Belknap Press of Harvard University Press, 2001.

Blotner, Joseph. *Faulkner: A Biography.* New York: Random House, 1974.

———. *Selected Letters of William Faulkner.* New York: Random House, 1977.

Bonadeo, Alfredo. *Mark of the Beast: Death and Degradation in the Literature of the Great War.* Lexington: University Press of Kentucky, 1989.

Bone, Martyn. *The Postsouthern Sense of Place in Contemporary Fiction.* Baton Rouge: Louisiana State University Press, 2005.

Booth, Allyson. *Postcards from the Trenches: Negotiating the Space between Modernism and the First World War.* New York: Oxford University Press, 1996.

Bourne, Randolph. "Trans-National America." In *Randolph Bourne: The Radical Will; Selected Writings, 1911–1918,* 248–65. Berkeley: University of California Press, 1992.

Bradbury, John M. *Renaissance in the South: A Critical History of the Literature, 1920–1960.* Chapel Hill: University of North Carolina Press, 1963.

Bradbury, Malcolm, and James McFarlane, eds. *Modernism, 1890–1930.* New York: Penguin, 1976.

Bradford, M. E. "The Anomaly of Faulkner's World War I Stories." *Mississippi Quarterly* 36, no. 3 (Summer 1983): 243–61.

Brickell, Herschel. "The Literary Awakening in the South." 1927. In *Defining Southern Literature: Perspectives and Assessments, 1831–1952,* edited by John E. Bassett. Teaneck, NJ: Fairleigh Dickinson University Press, 1997.

Brinkmeyer, Robert. *The Fourth Ghost: White Southern Writers and European Fascism, 1930–1950*. Baton Rouge: Louisiana State University Press, 2009.

Brittain, Joan T. *Laurence Stallings*. Boston: Twayne, 1975.

Brooks, Cleanth. *William Faulkner: Toward Yoknapatawpha and Beyond*. New Haven, CT: Yale University Press, 1978.

———. *William Faulkner: The Yoknapatawpha Country*. New Haven, CT: Yale University Press, 1963.

Brosi, George. "Elizabeth Madox Roberts." In *The History of Southern Women's Literature*, edited by Carolyn Perry and Mary Louise Weaks, 349–53. Baton Rouge: Louisiana State University Press, 2002.

Brown, Carrie. *Rosie's Mom: Forgotten Women Workers of the First World War*. Boston: Northeastern University Press, 2002.

Brown, D. Clayton. *Electricity for Rural America: The Fight for the REA*. Westport, CT: Greenwood Press, 1980.

Brown, Milton. *American Painting from the Armory Show to the Depression*. Princeton, NJ: Princeton University Press, 1955.

Brown, Nikki. *Private Politics and Public Voices: Black Women's Activism from World War I to the New Deal*. Bloomington: Indiana University Press, 2006.

Bruccoli, Matthew J. Introduction to *Save Me the Waltz*. In *Zelda Fitzgerald: The Collected Writings*, edited by Matthew J. Bruccoli. New York: Charles Scribner's Sons, 1991.

———. *Some Sort of Epic Grandeur: The Life of F. Scott Fitzgerald*. 2nd ed. Columbia: University of South Carolina Press, 2002.

Brundage, W. Fitzhugh, ed. *Under Sentence of Death: Lynching in the South*. Chapel Hill: University of North Carolina Press, 1997.

Bryer, Jackson R., and Cathy W. Barks, eds. *Dear Scott, Dearest Zelda: The Love Letters of F. Scott and Zelda Fitzgerald*. New York: St. Martin's Press, 2002.

Buell, Lawrence. "Faulkner and the Claims of the Natural World." In *Faulkner and the Natural World*, edited by Donald M. Kartiganer and Ann J. Abadie, 1–18. Jackson: University Press of Mississippi, 1999.

Burrill, Mary. *Aftermath*. 1919. In *Strange Fruit: Plays on Lynching by American Women*, edited by Kathy A. Perkins and Judith L. Stephens, 79–98. Bloomington: Indiana University Press, 1998.

Caldwell, Ellen M. "Ellen Glasgow and the Southern Agrarians." *American Literature* 56, no. 2 (May 1984): 203–13.

Caldwell, Erskine, and Margaret Bourke-White. *You Have Seen Their Faces*. New York: Modern Age Books, 1937.

Carby, Hazel V. *Reconstructing Womanhood: The Emergence of the Afro-American Woman Novelist*. New York: Oxford University Press, 1987.

Carlton, David L. *Mill and Town in South Carolina, 1880–1920*. Baton Rouge: Louisiana State University Press, 1982.

Cash, W. J. *The Mind of the South*. 1941. New York: Vintage, 1991.

Cason, Clarence. *90° in the Shade*. 1935. Tuscaloosa: University of Alabama Press, 2001.

Castronovo, Russ. "Beauty along the Color Line: Lynching, Aesthetics, and the *Crisis*." *PMLA* 121, no. 5 (2006): 1443–59.

Christian, Garna L. *Black Soldiers in Jim Crow Texas, 1899–1917*. College Station: Texas A&M University Press, 1995.

Clayton, Bruce. *W. J. Cash: A Life*. Baton Rouge: Louisiana State University Press, 1991.

Clifford, Carrie Williams. "The Black Draftee from Dixie." 1922. In *Witnessing Lynching: American Writers Respond*, edited by Anne P. Rice. New Brunswick, NJ: Rutgers University Press, 2003.

Clinton, Catherine. *The Plantation Mistress: Woman's World in the Old South*. New York: Pantheon, 1982.

Clurman, Harold. *The Fervent Years: The Group Theatre and the Thirties*. 1945. New York: Harvest, 1975.

Cobb, James C. *Away Down South: A History of Southern Identity*. New York: Oxford University Press, 2005.

———. *Industrialization and Southern Society, 1877–1984*. Lexington: University Press of Kentucky, 1984.

———. *Selling the South: The Southern Crusade for Industrial Development, 1936–1990*. Urbana: University of Illinois Press, 1993.

Cobb, James C., and William Stueck, eds. *Globalization and the American South*. Athens: University of Georgia Press, 2005.

Cohen, Debra Rae. *Remapping the Home Front: Locating Citizenship in British Women's Great War Fiction*. Boston: Northeastern University Press, 2002.

Collins, Carvel, ed. *William Faulkner: Early Prose and Poetry*. Boston: Little, Brown, 1962.

Conkin, Paul K. *The Southern Agrarians*. Knoxville: University of Tennessee Press, 1988.

Conlogue, William. "'Passion Transfigured': *Barren Ground* and the New Agriculture." *Mississippi Quarterly* 52, no. 1 (Winter 1998): 17–31.

Connelly, Thomas L., and Barbara L. Bellows. *God and General Longstreet: The Lost Cause and the Southern Mind*. Baton Rouge: Louisiana State University Press, 1982.

Conrad, David. *The Forgotten Farmers: The Story of Sharecroppers in the New Deal*. Urbana: University of Illinois Press, 1965.

Cooper, Wayne F. *Claude McKay: Rebel Sojourner in the Harlem Renaissance*. Baton Rouge: Louisiana State University Press, 1987.

Cooperman, Stanley. *World War I and the American Novel*. Baltimore: Johns Hopkins University Press, 1967.

Couch, William Terry, and Howard Mumford Jones. Preface to *Culture in the South*, edited by William Terry Couch, vii–xi. Chapel Hill: University of North Carolina Press, 1934.

Cowan, Louise. *The Fugitive Group*. Baton Rouge: Louisiana State University Press, 1959.

Cowley, Malcolm. *Exile's Return: A Literary Odyssey of the 1920s*. New York: Viking 1951.

———. Introduction to *The Portable Faulkner*, edited by Malcolm Cowley. New York: Penguin, 2003.

Cox, Karen L. *Dixie's Daughters: The United Daughters of the Confederacy and the Preservation of Confederate Culture*. Gainesville: University Press of Florida, 2003.

Creese, Walter L. *TVA's Public Planning: The Vision, The Reality*. Knoxville: University of Tennessee Press, 1990.

Crow, Charles L., ed. *A Companion to the Regional Literatures of America*. Oxford: Blackwell, 2003.

Dabney, Virginius. *Liberalism in the South*. 1932. New York: AMS Press, 1970.

Dainotto, Roberto. *Place in Literature: Region, Culture, and Communities*. Ithaca, NY: Cornell University Press, 2000.

Daly, Victor. *Not Only War: A Story of Two Great Conflicts*. 1932. Charlottesville: University of Virginia Press, 2010.

Daniel, Pete. *Lost Revolutions: The South in the 1950s.* Chapel Hill: University of North Carolina Press, 2000.

Davidson, Donald. *Southern Writers in the Modern World.* Athens: University of Georgia Press, 1958.

——. *The Spyglass: Views and Reviews, 1924–1930.* Edited by John Tyree Fain. Nashville: Vanderbilt University Press, 1963.

——. "Still Rebels, Still Yankees." In *Regionalism and Nationalism in the United States: The Attack on Leviathan.* Chapel Hill: University of North Carolina Press, 1938.

——. *The Tall Men.* New York: Houghton Mifflin, 1927.

Davis, David A. "The Forgotten Apocalypse: Katherine Anne Porter's 'Pale Horse, Pale Rider,' Traumatic Memory, and the Influenza Pandemic of 1918." *Southern Literary Journal* 43, no. 2 (Spring 2011): 55–74.

——. "Grace after Battle: World War One and the Poetry of John Crowe Ransom." *Kentucky Review* 15, no.2 (Fall 2003): 57–70.

——. "Not Only War Is Hell: World War I and African American Lynching Narratives." *African American Review* 42, nos. 3–4 (Fall–Winter 2008): 477–91.

Deconde, Alexander. "The South and Isolationism." In *The South and the Sectional Image,* edited by Dewey Grantham, 117–26. New York: Harper and Row, 1967.

DeSantis, Vincent P. *The Shaping of Modern America, 1877–1920.* 2nd ed. Wheeling, IL: Forum Press, 1993.

Dixon, Thomas. *The Way of a Man: A Story of the New Woman.* New York: Appleton, 1919.

Dodman, Trevor. *Shell Shock, Memory, and the Novel in the Wake of World War I.* New York: Cambridge University Press, 2015.

Donald, David Herbert. *Look Homeward: A Life of Thomas Wolfe.* New York: Little, Brown, 1987.

Donaldson, Scott. "Scott Fitzgerald's Romance with the South." *Southern Literary Journal* 5, no. 2 (Spring 1973): 3–17.

Donaldson, Susan V. "Gender, Race, and Allen Tate's Profession of Letters in the South." In *Haunted Bodies: Gender and Southern Texts,* edited by Anne Goodwyn Jones and Susan V. Donaldson, 492–518. Charlottesville: University Press of Virginia, 1997.

Donaldson, Susan V., and Anne Goodwyn Jones. "Haunted Bodies: Rethinking the South Through Gender." In *Haunted Bodies: Gender and Southern Texts,* edited by Anne Goodwyn Jones and Susan V. Donaldson. Charlottesville: University Press of Virginia, 1997.

Dorman, Robert L. *Revolt of the Provinces: The Regionalist Movement in America, 1920–1945.* Chapel Hill: University of North Carolina Press, 1993.

Dos Passos. John. "July." *Transatlantic Review* 2 (September 1924): 154–79.

——. *Three Soldiers.* 1921. New York: Penguin, 1997.

Douglas, Ellen. *Can't Quit You, Baby.* New York: Penguin, 1989.

Doyle, Laura, and Laura Winkiel. *Geomodernisms: Race, Modernism, Modernity.* Bloomington: Indiana University Press, 2005.

Dray, Philip. *At the Hands of Persons Unknown: The Lynching of Black America.* New York: Random House, 2002.

Du Bois, W. E. B. "The African Roots of the War." 1916. In *W. E. B. Du Bois: A Reader,* edited by David Levering Lewis, 642–51. New York: Henry Holt, 1995.

——. "Awake America." 1917. In *The Oxford W. E. B. Du Bois Reader,* edited by Eric J. Sundquist, 379. New York: Oxford University Press, 1996.

———. "Close Ranks." 1917. In *W. E. B. Du Bois: A Reader*, edited by David Levering Lewis, 697. New York: Henry Holt, 1995.

———. "Documents of the War." *Crisis* 18, no. 1 (May 1919): 16–21.

———. "An Essay toward the History of the Black Man in the Great War." 1919. In *W. E. B. Du Bois: A Reader*, edited by David Levering Lewis, 698–733. New York: Henry Holt, 1995.

———. "Returning Soldiers." 1919. In *The Oxford W. E. B. Du Bois Reader*, edited by Eric J. Sundquist, 380–81. New York: Oxford University Press, 1996.

———. *The Souls of Black Folk*. 1903. New York: Library of America, 1990.

Duck, Leigh Anne. *The Nation's Region: Southern Modernism, Segregation, and U.S. Nationalism*. Athens: University of Georgia Press, 2006.

Dunbar-Nelson, Alice. "I Sit and Sew." In *The Works of Alice Dunbar-Nelson*. Vol. 2, edited by Gloria T. Hull, 84. New York: Oxford University Press, 1988.

———. *Mine Eyes Have Seen*. In *The Works of Alice Dunbar-Nelson*. Vol. 3, edited by Gloria T. Hull, 239–49. New York: Oxford University Press, 1988.

———. "Negro Women and War Work." In *Scott's Official History of the American Negro in the World War*, by Emmett J. Scott. Privately published, 1919.

Duncan, Christopher M. *Fugitive Theory: Political Theory, the Southern Agrarians, and America*. New York: Lexington Books, 2000.

Edwards, Brent Hayes. *The Practice of Diaspora: Literature, Translation, and the Rise of Black Internationalism*. Cambridge, MA: Harvard University Press, 2003.

Edwards, Laura F. *Gendered Strife and Confusion: The Political Culture of Reconstruction*. Urbana: University of Illinois Press, 1997.

Egerton, John. *The Americanization of Dixie: The Southernization of America*. New York: Harper's Magazine Press, 1974.

———. *Speak Now against the Day: The Generation before the Civil Rights Movement in the South*. Chapel Hill: University of North Carolina Press, 1995.

Eksteins, Modris. *Rites of Spring: The Great War and the Birth of the Modern Age*. New York: Anchor Books, 1989.

Ellmann, Richard, and Charles Feidelson Jr., eds. *The Modern Tradition: Backgrounds of Modern Literature*. New York: Oxford University Press, 1965.

Eysteinsson, Astradur. *The Concept of Modernism*. Ithaca, NY: Cornell University Press, 1990.

Faulkner, William. *Flags in the Dust*. New York: Random House, 1974.

———. *Requiem for a Nun*. 1950. New York: Vintage, 1975.

———. *Soldiers' Pay*. 1926. New York: Boni and Liveright, 1997.

———. *The Sound and the Fury*. 1929. New York: Vintage, 1997.

Fauset, Jesse Redmon. *There Is Confusion*. New York: Boni and Liveright, 1924.

Felski, Rita. *The Gender of Modernity*. Cambridge, MA: Harvard University Press, 1995.

Fetterley, Judith, and Marjorie Pryse. *Writing Out of Place: Regionalism, Women, and American Literary Culture*. Urbana: University of Illinois Press, 2003.

Filene, Peter G. *Him/Her/Self: Gender Identities in Modern America*. Baltimore: Johns Hopkins University Press, 1998.

Fite, Gilbert C. *Cotton Fields No More: Southern Agriculture, 1865–1980*. Lexington: University Press of Kentucky, 1984.

Fitzgerald, F. Scott. *The Short Stories of F. Scott Fitzgerald*. Edited by Matthew J. Bruccoli. New York: Charles Scribner's Sons, 1989.

Fitzgerald, Zelda. *Save Me the Waltz*. 1932. Carbondale: Southern Illinois University Press, 1967.

Fleming, Robert E. *James Weldon Johnson*. Boston: Twayne, 1987.

Foley, Barbara. *Specters of 1919: Class and Nation in the Making of the New Negro*. Urbana: University of Illinois Press, 2003.

Foster, Gaines M. *Ghosts of the Confederacy: Defeat, the Lost Cause, and the Emergence of the New South, 1865 to 1913*. New York: Oxford University Press, 1987.

Franklin, John Hope. *From Slavery to Freedom: A History of Negro Americans*. 5th ed. New York: Alfred A. Knopf, 1980.

Friedman, Jean E. *The Enclosed Garden: Women and Community in the Evangelical South, 1830–1900*. Chapel Hill: University of North Carolina Press, 1985.

Friedman, Susan Stanford. "Definitional Excursions: The Meanings of Modern/Modernity/Modernism." *Modernism/Modernity* 8, no. 3 (2001): 493–513.

Fullilove, Maggie Shaw. *Who Was Responsible?* 1918. New York: G. K. Hall and Company, 1996.

Fulmer, John Leonard. *Agricultural Progress in the Cotton Belt since 1920*. Chapel Hill: University of North Carolina Press, 1950.

Fussell, Paul. *The Great War and Modern Memory*. New York: Oxford University Press, 1975.

Gaines, Ernest. *A Gathering of Old Men*. New York: Alfred A. Knopf, 1983.

Gallagher, Gary W., and Alan T. Nolan, eds. *The Myth of the Lost Cause and Civil War History*. Bloomington: Indiana University Press, 2000.

Gammons, P. Keith. "The South of the Mind: The Changing Myth of the Lost Cause in the Life and Work of F. Scott Fitzgerald." *Southern Quarterly* 36, no. 4 (Summer 1998): 106–12.

Gandal, Keith. *The Gun and the Pen: Hemingway, Fitzgerald, Faulkner, and the Fiction of Mobilization*. New York: Oxford University Press, 2008.

Gardner, Sarah. *Blood and Irony: Southern White Women's Narratives of the Civil War, 1861–1937*. Chapel Hill: University of North Carolina Press, 2004.

Gaston, Paul M. *The New South Creed: A Study in Southern Myth-Making*. 1970. Baton Rouge: Louisiana State University Press, 1992.

Gaughan, Anthony. "Woodrow Wilson and the Rise of Militant Interventionism in the South." *Journal of Southern History* 65, no. 4 (November 1999): 771–807.

Gavin, Lettie. *American Women in World War I: They Also Served*. Niwot: University Press of Colorado, 1997.

Gellner, Ernest. *Nations and Nationalism*. 2nd ed. Ithaca, NY: Cornell University Press, 2006.

Genovese, Eugene. *Roll, Jordan, Roll: The World the Slaves Made*. New York: Random House, 1972.

———. *The Southern Tradition: The Achievement and Limitations of an American Conservatism*. Cambridge, MA: Harvard University Press, 1994.

Giddens, Anthony. *The Consequences of Modernity*. Stanford, CA: Stanford University Press, 1990.

———. *Modernity and Self-Identity*. Stanford, CA: Stanford University Press, 1991.

Giesen, James. *Boll Weevil Blues: Cotton, Myth, and Power in the American South*. Chicago: University of Chicago Press, 2011.

Gilbert, Sandra M., and Susan Gubar. Introduction to *The Female Imagination and the Modernist Aesthetic*, edited by Sandra M. Gilbert and Susan Gubar, 1–10. New York: Gordon and Breach, 1986.

———. *No Man's Land: The Place of the Woman Writer in the Twentieth Century*. Vol. 2, *Sexchanges*. New Haven, CT: Yale University Press, 1989.

Gilroy, Paul. *The Black Atlantic: Modernity and Double Consciousness*. Cambridge, MA: Harvard University Press, 1993.

Glasgow, Ellen. *Barren Ground*. 1925. New York: Harvest, 1985.

———. *A Certain Measure*. New York: Harcourt, Brace and Company, 1938.

———. "The Novel in the South." In *Ellen Glasgow's Reasonable Doubts: A Collection of Her Writings*, edited by Julius R. Raper. Baton Rouge: Louisiana State University Press, 1988.

———. *The Romance of a Plain Man*. New York: Macmillan, 1909.

———. *Vein of Iron*. 1935. Charlottesville: University Press of Virginia, 1995.

———. *The Woman Within*. New York: Harcourt, Brace and Company, 1954.

Godden, Richard. *Fictions of Capital: The American Novel from James to Mailer*. New York: Cambridge University Press, 1990.

———. *Fictions of Labor: William Faulkner and the South's Long Revolution*. New York: Cambridge University Press, 1997.

Goldfield, David. *Cotton Fields and Skyscrapers: Southern City and Region, 1607–1980*. Baton Rouge: Louisiana State University Press, 1982.

———. *Still Fighting the Civil War: The American South and Southern History*. Baton Rouge: Louisiana State University Press, 2002.

Goldman, Dorothy, ed. *Women Writers and the Great War*. New York: Twayne, 1995.

Goodman, Susan. *Ellen Glasgow: A Biography*. Baltimore: Johns Hopkins University Press, 1998.

Grantham, Dewey. *The South in Modern America: A Region at Odds*. New York: HarperCollins, 1994.

———. *Southern Progressivism: The Reconciliation of Progress and Tradition*. Knoxville: University of Tennessee Press, 1983.

Gray, Richard. *The Literature of Memory: Modern Writers of the American South*. Baltimore: Johns Hopkins University Press, 1976.

———. *Writing the South: Ideas of an American Region*. Baton Rouge: Louisiana State University Press, 1986.

Green, Elna C. *Southern Strategies: Southern Women and the Woman Suffrage Question*. Chapel Hill: University of North Carolina Press, 1996.

Green, Paul. *Home to My Valley*. Chapel Hill: University of North Carolina Press, 1970.

———. *Johnny Johnson: Biography of a Common Man*. New York: Samuel French, 1937.

Greene, J. Lee. *Blacks in Eden: The African American Novel's First Century*. Charlottesville: University Press of Virginia, 1996.

Greenfeld, Liah. *Nationalism: Five Roads to Modernity*. Cambridge, MA: Harvard University Press, 1992.

Greenwald, Maurine Weiner. *Women, War, and Work: The Impact of World War I on Women Workers in the United States*. Westport, CT: Greenwood Press, 1980.

Greeson, Jennifer. *Our South: Geographic Fantasy and the Rise of National Literature*. Cambridge, MA: Harvard University Press, 2010.

Gregory, James N. *The Southern Diaspora: How the Great Migrations of Black and White Southerners Transformed America*. Chapel Hill: University of North Carolina Press, 2005.

Grossman, James. *Land of Hope: Chicago, Black Southerners, and the Great Migration*. Chicago: University of Chicago Press, 1989.

Guinn, Matthew. *After Southern Modernism: Fiction of the Contemporary South*. Jackson: University Press of Mississippi, 2000.

Gwin, Minrose. *Black and White Women of the Old South: The Peculiar Sisterhood in American Literature*. Knoxville: University of Tennessee Press, 1985.

Haferkamp, Hans, and Neil J. Smelser, eds. *Social Change and Modernity*. Berkeley: University of California Press, 1992.

Hale, Grace Elizabeth. *Making Whiteness: The Culture of Segregation in the South, 1890–1940*. New York: Random House, 1999.

Hall, Jacquelyn Dowd. "The Long Civil Rights Movement and the Political Uses of the Past." *Journal of American History* 91, no. 4 (March 2005): 1233–63.

———. *Revolt against Chivalry: Jessie Daniel Ames and the Women's Campaign against Lynching*. New York: Columbia University Press, 1979.

Hall, Jacquelyn Dowd, James Leloudis, Robert Korstad, Mary Murphy, LuAnn Jones, and Christopher Daly. *Like a Family: The Making of a Southern Cotton Mill World*. New York: W. W. Norton, 1987.

Hamilton, C. Horace. "The Social Effects of Recent Trends in the Mechanization of Agriculture." 1939. In *The Social Consequences and Challenges of New Agricultural Technologies*, edited by Gigi M. Berardi and Charles C. Geisler, 63–72. Boulder, CO: Westview Press, 1984.

Harding, Desmond. *Writing the City: Urban Visions and Literary Modernism*. New York: Routledge, 2003.

Harrell, David E., ed. *Varieties of Southern Evangelicalism*. Macon, GA: Mercer University Press, 1981.

Harris, Joel Chandler. *Uncle Remus and His Legends of the Old Plantation*. London: David Bogue, 1881.

Harris, Marvin. *Cultural Materialism: The Struggle for a Science of Culture*. Updated ed. New York: Altamira Press, 2001.

Harris, Stephen L. *Harlem's Hell Fighters: The African-American 369th Infantry in World War I*. Washington, DC: Brassey's, 2003.

Harris, Trudier. *Exorcising Blackness: Historical and Literary Lynching and Burning Rituals*. Bloomington: Indiana University Press, 1984.

Harrison, Alferdteen, ed. *Black Exodus: The Great Migration from the American South*. Jackson: University Press of Mississippi, 1991.

Harrison, Robert L. *Aviation Lore in Faulkner*. Philadelphia: John Benjamins, 1985.

Harvey, David. *The Condition of Postmodernity: An Enquiry into the Origins of Cultural Change*. Cambridge: Blackwell, 1990.

———. *Paris, Capital of Modernity*. New York: Routledge, 2005.

Havard, William C., and Walter Sullivan, eds. *A Band of Prophets: The Vanderbilt Agrarians after Fifty Years*. Baton Rouge: Louisiana State University Press, 1982.

Haynes, Robert V. *A Night of Violence: The Houston Riot of 1917*. Baton Rouge: Louisiana State University Press, 1976.

Haytock, Jennifer. *At Home, At War: Domesticity and World War I in American Literature*. Columbus: Ohio State University Press, 2003.

Hemingway, Ernest. *A Moveable Feast*. New York: Charles Scribner's Sons, 1964.

Henri, Florette. *Black Migration: Movement North, 1900–1920*. Garden City, NY: Anchor Press, 1975.

Herring, Harriet L. *Southern Industry and Regional Development*. Chapel Hill: University of North Carolina Press, 1941.

Hibbard, Benjamin H. *Effects of the Great War upon Agriculture in the United States and Great Britain*. New York: Oxford University Press, 1919.

Higonnet, Margaret R., ed. *Lines of Fire: Women Writers of World War I*. New York: Plume, 1999.

Higonnet, Margaret R., and Patrice Higonnet. "The Double Helix." In *Behind the Lines: Gender and the Two World Wars*, edited by Margaret Higonnet et al., 31–47. New Haven, CT: Yale University Press, 1987.

Hildebidle, John. "Neither Worthy nor Capable: The War Memoirs of Graves, Blunden, and Sassoon." In *Modernism Reconsidered*, edited by Robert Kiely, 101–21. Cambridge, MA: Harvard University Press, 1983.

Hines, Thomas. *William Faulkner and the Tangible Past: The Architecture of Yoknapatawpha*. Berkeley: University of California Press, 1996.

Hobsbawm, Eric. "Inventing Traditions." In *The Invention of Tradition*, edited by Eric Hobsbawm and Terrence Ranger. New York: Cambridge University Press, 1983.

———. *Nations and Nationalism since 1870*. New York: Cambridge University Press, 1990.

Hobson, Fred. "The New South, 1880–1940." In *The Literature of the American South: A Norton Anthology*, edited by William L. Andrews et al., 245–33. New York: W. W. Norton, 1998.

———. *Serpent in Eden: H. L. Mencken and the South*. Chapel Hill: University of North Carolina Press, 1974.

———. *The Southern Writer in the Postmodern World*. Athens: University of Georgia Press, 1991.

———. *Tell about the South: The Southern Rage to Explain*. Baton Rouge: Louisiana State University Press, 1982.

Hodgin, Katherine C. "Horace Benbow and Bayard Sartoris: Two Romantic Figures in Faulkner's *Flags in the Dust*." *American Literature* 50, no. 4 (1979): 647–52.

Hoeveler, David J. *The New Humanism: A Critique of Modern America, 1900–1940*. Charlottesville: University Press of Virginia, 1976.

Holman, C. Hugh. "Fitzgerald's Changes on the Southern Belle: The Tarleton Trilogy." In *The Short Stories of F. Scott Fitzgerald: New Approaches in Criticism*, edited by Jackson R. Bryer, 53–64. Madison: University of Wisconsin Press, 1982.

Holmes, William F. *The White Chief: James Kimble Vardaman*. Baton Rouge: Louisiana State University Press, 1970.

Horwitz, Tony. *Confederates in the Attics: Dispatches from the Unfinished Civil War*. New York: Pantheon, 1998.

Hubbell, Jay. *The South in American Literature, 1607–1900*. Durham, NC: Duke University Press, 1954.

Huggins, Nathan Irvin. *Harlem Renaissance*. New York: Oxford University Press, 1971.

Hull, Gloria T. *Color, Sex, and Poetry: Three Women Writers of the Harlem Renaissance*. Bloomington: Indiana University Press, 1987.

Hunton, Addie W., and Kathryn M. Johnson. *Two Colored Women with the American Expeditionary Forces*. 1920. New York: G. K. Hall and Company, 1997.

Hurston, Zora Neale. *Jonah's Gourd Vine*. 1934. New York: Harper Perennial, 1990.

———. *Their Eyes Were Watching God*. 1937. New York: Harper Perennial, 1990.

Hurt, R. Douglas. Introduction to *The Rural South since World War II*, edited by R. Douglas Hurt, 1–7. Baton Rouge: Louisiana State University Press, 1998.

Hutchinson, George. "Aftermath: African American Literary Responses to the Great War." In *Reconstructing Societies in the Aftermath of War*, edited by Flavia Brizio-Skov, 188–99. Boca Raton, FL: Bordighera, 2004.

———. *The Harlem Renaissance in Black and White*. Cambridge, MA: Belknap Press of Harvard University Press, 1995.

Inge, Thomas. "Donald Davidson's Notes for an Autobiography: The Early Years." In *The Vanderbilt Tradition: Essays in Honor of Thomas Daniel Young*, edited by Mark Royden Winchell, 199–210. Baton Rouge: Louisiana State University Press, 1991.

Inness, Sherrie, and Diana Royer. *Breaking Boundaries: New Perspectives on Women's Regional Writing*. Iowa City: University of Iowa Press, 1997.

Irwin, John T. *Doubling and Incest, Repetition and Revenge: A Speculative Reading of Faulkner*. Baltimore: Johns Hopkins University Press, 1975.

———. "Is Fitzgerald a Southern Writer?" *Raritan* 16, no. 3 (Winter 1997): 1–24.

James, Henry. *The American Scene*. 1905. New York: St. Martin's Press, 1987.

———. *The Bostonians*. 1886. New York: Penguin, 2000.

James, Jennifer C. *A Freedom Bought with Blood: African American War Literature from the Civil War to World War II*. Chapel Hill: University of North Carolina Press, 2007.

James, Pearl. *The New Death: American Modernism and World War I*. Charlottesville: University of Virginia Press, 2013.

Jancovich, Mark. *The Cultural Politics of the New Criticism*. New York: Cambridge University Press, 1993.

Janken, Kenneth Robert. *White: The Biography of Walter White, Mr. NAACP*. New York: New Press, 2003.

Jensen, Kimberly. *Mobilizing Minerva: American Women in the First World War*. Urbana: University of Illinois Press, 2008.

Johnson, Georgia Douglas. "Soldier." In *Selected Works of Georgia Douglas Johnson*, edited by Claudia Tate, 144. New York: G. K. Hall and Company, 1997.

Johnson, James Weldon. "Why Should a Negro Fight?" In *James Weldon Johnson: Writings*, edited by William L. Andrews, 632–36. New York: Library of America, 2004.

Jones, Anne Goodwyn. "Every Woman Loves a Fascist: Writing World War II on the Southern Home Front." In *Remaking Dixie: The Impact of World War II on the U.S. South*, edited by Neil R. McMillen, 111–30. Jackson: University Press of Mississippi, 1997.

———. Foreword to *Dead Lovers Are Faithful Lovers*, by Frances Newman, vii–xxxvi. Athens: University of Georgia Press, 1994.

———. "Gender and the Great War: The Case of Faulkner and Porter." In *The Female Imagination and the Modernist Aesthetic*, edited by Sandra M. Gilbert and Susan Gubar, 135–148. New York: Gordon and Breach, 1986.

———. *Tomorrow Is Another Day: The Woman Writer in the South, 1859–1936*. Baton Rouge: Louisiana State University Press, 1981.

———. "Women Writers and the Myths of Southern Womanhood." In *The History of Southern Women's Literature*, edited by Carolyn Perry and Mary Louise Weaks, 275–89. Baton Rouge: Louisiana State University Press, 2002.

———. "The Work of Gender in the Southern Renaissance." In *Southern Writers and Their Worlds*, edited by Christopher Morris and Steven G. Reinhardt, 41–56. College Station: Texas A&M University Press, 1996.

Jordan, Michael M. "*The Tall Men*: Davidson's Answer to Eliot." *South Carolina Review* 26 (Fall 1993): 50–70.

Jordan, William G. *Black Newspapers and America's War for Democracy, 1914–1920*. Chapel Hill: University of North Carolina Press, 2001.

Karanikas, Alexander. *Tillers of a Myth: Southern Agrarians as Social and Literary Critics.* Madison: University of Wisconsin Press, 1966.

Kartiganer, Donald. "'So I, Who Never Had a War . . .': William Faulkner, War, and the Modern Imagination." In *William Faulkner: Six Decades of Criticism,* edited by Linda Wagner-Martin, 3–28. East Lansing: Michigan State University Press, 2002.

Kasson, John. *Civilizing the Machine: Technology and Republican Values in America, 1776–1900.* New York: Grossman, 1976.

Keene, Jennifer D. *Doughboys, the Great War, and the Remaking of America.* Baltimore: Johns Hopkins University Press, 2001.

Keith, Jeanette. *Rich Man's War, Poor Man's Fight: Race, Class and Power in the Rural South during the First World War.* Chapel Hill: University of North Carolina Press, 2004.

Kennedy, David. *Over Here: The First World War and American Society.* New York: Oxford University Press, 1980.

Kennedy, Tanya Ann. "The Secret Properties of Southern Regionalism: Gender and Agrarianism in Ellen Glasgow's *Barren Ground.*" *Southern Literary Journal* 38, no. 2 (Spring 2006): 40–63.

Kenner, Hugh. *The Mechanic Muse.* New York: Oxford University Press, 1987.

Kenny, Vincent. *Paul Green.* New York: Twayne, 1971.

Kern, Stephen. *The Culture of Time and Space, 1880–1918.* Cambridge, MA: Harvard University Press, 1983.

Killens, John Oliver. *And Then We Heard the Thunder.* 1963. Washington, DC: Howard University Press, 1984.

King, Richard H. "Mourning and Melancholia: Will Percy and the Southern Tradition." *Virginia Quarterly Review* 53, no. 2 (Spring 1977): 248–64.

———. *A Southern Renaissance: The Cultural Awakening of the American South, 1930–1955.* New York: Oxford University Press, 1980.

Kirby, Jack Temple. *Rural Worlds Lost: The American South, 1920–1960.* Baton Rouge: Louisiana State University Press, 1987.

Klein, Marcus. *Foreigners: The Making of American Literature, 1900–1940.* Chicago: University of Chicago Press, 1981.

Kline, Ronald R. *Consumers in the Country: Technology and Social Change in Rural America.* Baltimore: Johns Hopkins University Press, 2000.

Kornweibel, Theodore, Jr. *"Investigate Everything": Federal Efforts to Compel Black Loyalty during World War I.* Bloomington: Indiana University Press, 2002.

———. *Seeing Red: Federal Campaigns against Black Militancy, 1919–1925.* Bloomington: Indiana University Press, 1998.

Kreyling, Michael. *Inventing Southern Literature.* Jackson: University Press of Mississippi, 1998.

Kruse, Kevin. *White Flight: Atlanta and the Making of Modern Conservatism.* Princeton, NJ: Princeton University Press, 2005.

Ladd, Barbara. *Nationalism and the Color Line in George W. Cable, Mark Twain, and William Faulkner.* Baton Rouge: Louisiana State University Press, 1996.

———. *Resisting History: Gender, Modernity, and Authorship in William Faulkner, Zora Neale Hurston, and Eudora Welty.* Baton Rouge: Louisiana State University Press, 2007.

Lang, Robert, ed. *The Birth of a Nation: D. W. Griffith, Director.* New Brunswick, NJ: Rutgers University Press, 1994.

Larkin, Philip. "MCMXIV." In *Collected Poems*, edited by Anthony Thwaite, 127. London: Faber and Faber, 1988. 127.

Larson, Edward J. *Summer for the Gods: The Scopes Trial and America's Continuing Debate over Science and Religion*. New York: Basic Books, 1997.

Lassiter, Matthew. *The Silent Majority: Suburban Politics in the Sunbelt South*. Princeton, NJ: Princeton University Press, 2006.

Lassiter, Matthew, and Joseph Crespino, eds. *The Myth of Southern Exceptionalism*. New York: Oxford University Press, 2010.

Latour, Bruno. *We Have Never Been Modern*. Cambridge, MA: Harvard University Press, 1993.

Lears, T. J. Jackson. *No Place of Grace: Antimodernism and the Transformation of American Culture, 1880–1920*. New York: Pantheon, 1981.

———. *Rebirth of a Nation: The Making of Modern America, 1877–1920*. New York: HarperCollins, 2009.

Lee, David D. *Sergeant York: An American Hero*. Lexington: University Press of Kentucky, 1985.

Lehan, Richard. *Literary Modernism and Beyond*. Baton Rouge: Louisiana State University Press, 2009.

Leiter, Andrew. *In the Shadow of the Black Beast: African American Masculinity in the Harlem and Southern Renaissances*. Baton Rouge: Louisiana State University Press, 2010.

Lemmon, Sarah. *North Carolina's Role in the First World War*. Raleigh: North Carolina State Department of Archives and History, 1966.

Lentz-Smith, Adriane. *Freedom Struggles: African Americans and World War I*. Cambridge, MA: Harvard University Press, 2009.

Leuchtenburg, William E. *The Perils of Prosperity, 1914–1932*. 2nd ed. Chicago: University of Chicago Press, 1993.

Levenson, Michael. *Modernism*. New Haven, CT: Yale University Press, 2011.

Levy, Helen Fiddyment. "Mining the *Vein of Iron*: Ellen Glasgow's Later Communal Voice." In *Regarding Ellen Glasgow*, edited by Welford Dunaway Taylor and George C. Longest, 43–54. Richmond: Library of Virginia, 2001.

Lewis, David Levering. *W. E. B. Du Bois: Biography of a Race, 1868–1919*. New York: Henry Holt, 1993.

———. *When Harlem Was in Vogue*. New York: Penguin, 1997.

Lewis, Sinclair. *Cheap and Contented Labor: The Picture of a Southern Mill Town in 1929*. New York: United Textile Worker's Union, 1929.

Link, Arthur. *Wilson: The New Freedom*. Princeton, NJ: Princeton University Press, 1956.

———. *Woodrow Wilson and the Progressive Era*. New York: Harper and Brothers, 1954.

Locke, Alain, ed. *The New Negro: Voices of the Harlem Renaissance*. 1925. New York: Simon and Schuster, 1992.

Lowe, John. *Jump at the Sun: Zora Neale Hurston's Cosmic Comedy*. Urbana: University of Illinois Press, 1994.

Ludington, Townsend, ed. *The Fourteenth Chronicle: The Letters and Diaries of John Dos Passos*. Boston: Gambit, 1973.

———. *John Dos Passos: A Twentieth-Century Odyssey*. New York: E. P. Dutton, 1980.

Lumpkin, Katherine Du Pre. *The Making of a Southerner*. 1946. Athens: University of Georgia Press, 1991.

Lynch, Jacquelyn Scott. "Postwar Play: Gender Performatives in Faulkner's *Soldiers' Pay*." *Faulkner Journal* 14, no. 1 (Fall 1998): 3–20.

Lytle, Andrew. "The Small Farm Secures the State." In *Who Owns America? A New Declaration of Independence*, edited by Herbert Agar and Allen Tate, 309–26. 1936. Wilmington, DE: ISI Books, 1999.

MacIntyre, W. Irwin. *Colored Soldiers*. Macon, GA: J. W. Burke, 1923.

Mack, Charles E. *Two Black Crows in the A. E. F.* Indianapolis: Bobbs-Merrill, 1928.

Mackaman, Douglas, and Michael Mays, eds. *World War I and the Cultures of Modernity*. Jackson: University Press of Mississippi, 2000.

MacKethan, Lucinda. *Daughters of Time: Creating Woman's Voice in Southern Story*. Athens: University of Georgia Press, 1990.

———. "Restoring Order: Matriarchal Design in *The Battle-Ground* and *Vein of Iron*." In *Ellen Glasgow: New Perspectives*, edited by Dorothy M. Scura, 89–105. Knoxville: University of Tennessee Press, 1995.

MacMillan, Duane J. "Fictional Facts and Factual Fiction: William Faulkner and World War I." *Faulkner Journal* 2, no. 2 (Spring 1987): 47–54.

Maine, Barry. *Dos Passos: The Critical Heritage*. New York: Routledge, 1988.

Malvasi, Mark. *The Unregenerate South: The Agrarian Thought of John Crowe Ransom, Allen Tate, and Donald Davidson*. Baton Rouge: Louisiana State University Press, 1997.

Manning, Carol S. "The Real Beginning of the Southern Renaissance." In *The Female Tradition in Southern Literature*, edited by Carol S. Manning, 37–56. Urbana: University of Illinois Press, 1993.

Mao, Douglas, and Rebecca L. Walkowitz. "Introduction: Modernisms Bad and New." In *Bad Modernisms*, edited by Douglas Mao and Rebecca Walkowitz, 2–16. Durham, NC: Duke University Press, 2006.

Marx, Leo. *The Machine in the Garden: Technology and the Pastoral Ideal in America*. New York: Oxford University Press, 1964.

Matthews, Jean V. *The Rise of the New Woman: The Women's Movement in America, 1875–1930*. Chicago: Ivan R. Dee, 2003.

Matthews, John T. "American Writing of the Great War." In *The Cambridge Companion to the Literature of the First World War*, edited by Vincent Sherry, 217–42. New York: Cambridge University Press, 2005.

Matthews, Pamela R. *Ellen Glasgow and a Woman's Traditions*. Charlottesville: University Press of Virginia, 1994.

———. "From Joan of Arc to Lucy Dare: Ellen Glasgow on Southern Womanhood." In *Regarding Ellen Glasgow*, edited by Welford Dunaway Taylor and George C. Longest, 35–42. Richmond: Library of Virginia, 2001.

Maxwell, William J. *New Negro, Old Left: African American Writing and Communism between the Wars*. New York: Columbia University Press, 1999.

McArthur, Judith N. *Creating the New Woman: The Rise of Women's Progressive Culture in Texas, 1893–1918*. Urbana: University of Illinois Press, 1998.

McDowell, Frederick. *Elizabeth Madox Roberts*. New York: Twayne, 1963.

McKay, Claude. *Banjo: A Story without a Plot*. 1929. New York: Harvest, 1957.

———. *Complete Poems*. Edited by William J. Maxwell. Urbana: University of Illinois Press, 2004.

———. *Home to Harlem*. New York: Harper and Brothers, 1928.

———. *A Long Way from Home*. 1937. New York: Harcourt, Brace and World, 1969.

——. *The Negroes in America.* Translated by Robert J. Winter. Port Washington, NY: Kennikat Press, 1979.

——. "The Soldier's Return." In *Trial by Lynching: Stories about Negro Life in North America.* Translated by Robert J. Winter. Mysore, India: Centre for Commonwealth Literature and Research, 1977.

Mencken, H. L. "The Sahara of the Bozart." In *Prejudices: Second Series.* London: Jonathan Cape, 1921.

Merritt, Russell. "Dixon, Griffith, and the Southern Legend." *Cinema Journal* 12, no. 1 (Fall 1972): 26–45.

Milford, Nancy. *Zelda: A Biography.* New York: Harper and Row, 1970.

Mill, Jerry Leath. "Equine Gothic: The Dead Mule as Generic Signifier in Southern Literature of the Twentieth Century." *Southern Literary Journal* 29, no. 1 (Fall 1996): 2–17.

Millgate, Michael. "Faulkner on the Literature of the First World War." *Mississippi Quarterly* 26 (1973): 387–93.

——. "Starting Out in the Twenties: Reflections on *Soldiers' Pay.*" *Mosaic* 7, no. 1 (Fall 1973): 1–14.

——. "William Faulkner, Cadet." *University of Toronto Quarterly* 35 (1966): 117–32.

Mims, Edwin. *The Advancing South.* Garden City, NY: Doubleday, Page and Company, 1926.

Minter, David. *A Cultural History of the American Novel.* Cambridge: Cambridge University Press, 1994.

Mitchell, Broadus. *The Industrial Revolution in the South.* Baltimore: Johns Hopkins University Press, 1930.

Mixon, Wayne. *Southern Writers and the New South Movement, 1865–1913.* Chapel Hill: University of North Carolina Press, 1980.

Moore, Harry T. Foreword to *Save Me the Waltz,* by Zelda Fitzgerald. Carbondale: Southern Illinois University Press, 1967.

Murphy, Paul V. *The Rebuke of History: The Southern Agrarians and American Conservative Thought.* Chapel Hill: University of North Carolina Press, 2001.

Nanney, Lisa. "Zelda Fitzgerald's *Save Me the Waltz* as Southern Novel and *Künstelerroman.*" In *The Female Tradition in Southern Literature,* edited by Carol S. Manning, 220–32. Urbana: University of Illinois Press, 1993.

Neverdon-Morton, Cynthia. *Afro-American Women of the South and the Advancement of the Race, 1895–1925.* Knoxville: University of Tennessee Press, 1989.

Newman, Frances. *Dead Lovers Are Faithful Lovers.* 1928. Athens: University of Georgia Press, 1994.

——. *Frances Newman's Letters.* Edited by Hansell Baugh. New York: Horace Liveright, 1929.

——. *The Hard-Boiled Virgin.* 1926. Athens: University of Georgia Press, 1980.

——. *The Short Story's Mutations.* New York: B. W. Huebsch, 1924.

Newton, Wesley Phillips. "'Tenting Tonight on the Old Camp Grounds': Alabama's Military Bases in World War I." In *The Great War in the Heart of Dixie,* edited by Martin Olliff, 41–65. Tuscaloosa: University of Alabama Press, 2008.

Nichols, Christopher McKnight. "Rethinking Randolph Bourne's Trans-National America: How World War I Created an Isolationist Antiwar Pluralism." *Journal of the Gilded Age and Progressive Era* 8, no. 2 (April 2009): 217–57.

Nicolaisen, Peter. "Rural Poverty and the Heroics of Farming: Elizabeth Madox Roberts's *The Time of Man* and Ellen Glasgow's *Barren Ground.*" In *Reading Southern Poverty between the Wars, 1918–1939*, edited by Richard Godden and Martin Crawford, 192–205. Athens: University of Georgia Press, 2006.

Nixon, Herman Clarence. *Forty Acres and Steel Mules*. Chapel Hill: University of North Carolina Press, 1938.

———. "Whither the Southern Economy?" In *I'll Take My Stand: The South and the Agrarian Tradition*, by Twelve Southerners, 176–200. 1930. Baton Rouge: Louisiana State University Press, 1995.

O'Brien, Michael. *Henry Adams and the Southern Question*. Athens: University of Georgia Press, 2005.

———. "A Heterodox Note on the Southern Renaissance." In *Rethinking the South: Essays in Intellectual History*, 157–78. Baltimore: Johns Hopkins University Press, 1988.

———. *The Idea of the American South, 1920–1941*. Baltimore: Johns Hopkins University Press, 1979.

O'Connor, Flannery. *Wise Blood*. In *Collected Works*. New York: Library of America, 1988.

Odum, Howard. *Southern Regions of the United States*. Chapel Hill: University of North Carolina Press, 1936.

———. *Wings on My Feet: Black Ulysses at the Wars*. Indianapolis: Bobbs-Merrill,1929.

Osborne, Peter. *The Politics of Time: Modernity and Avant-Garde*. New York: Verso, 1995.

Oudit, Sharon. *Fighting Forces, Writing Women: Identity and Ideology in the First World War*. New York: Routledge, 1994.

Owsley, Frank Lawrence. "The Pillars of Agrarianism." 1935. In *The Southern Agrarians and the New Deal: Essays after I'll Take My Stand*, edited by Emily S. Bingham and Thomas A. Underwood, 199–211. Charlottesville: University Press of Virginia, 2001.

Page, Thomas Nelson. *In Ole Virginia*. 1887. Chapel Hill: University of North Carolina Press, 1969.

Painter, Nell Irvin. *Southern History across the Color Line*. Chapel Hill: University of North Carolina Press, 2002.

Payne, James Robert. "A *MELUS* Interview: Victor R. Daly." *MELUS* 12, no. 2 (Summer 1985): 87–92.

Peacock, James L. *Grounded Globalism: How the U.S. South Embraces the World*. Athens: University of Georgia Press, 2007.

Peacock, James L., Harry L. Watson, and Carrie R. Matthews, eds. *The American South in a Global World*. Chapel Hill: University of North Carolina Press, 2005.

Peaslee, Catherine G. "Novelist Ellen Glasgow's Feminist Rebellion in Virginia—the Suffragist." In *Regarding Ellen Glasgow*, edited by Welford Dunaway Taylor and George C. Longest, 55–62. Richmond: Library of Virginia, 2001.

Pedersen, Carl. "The Tropics in New York: Claude McKay and the New Negro Movement." In *Temples for Tomorrow: Looking Back at the Harlem Renaissance*, edited by Geneviève Fabre and Michel Feith, 259–69. Bloomington: Indiana University Press, 2001.

Pells, Richard H. *Radical Visions and American Dreams: Culture and Social Thought in the Depression Years*. 1973. Urbana: University of Illinois Press, 1998.

Percy, William Alexander. *The Collected Poems of William Alexander Percy*. New York: Alfred A. Knopf, 1943.

———. *Lanterns on the Levee: Recollections of a Planter's Son*. 1941. Baton Rouge: Louisiana State University Press, 1973.

Perkinson, Zachary. "The Group Theatre." *North Carolina Literary Review* 2, no. 1 (Spring 1994): 26.

Perloff, Marjorie. *The Futurist Moment: Avant-Garde, Avant Guerre, and the Language of Rupture*. Chicago: University of Chicago Press, 2003.

Perry, Carolyn, and Mary Louise Weaks, eds. *The History of Southern Women's Literature*. Baton Rouge: Louisiana State University Press, 2002.

Peterson, H. C., and Gilbert C. Fite. *Opponents of War, 1917–1918*. Madison: University of Wisconsin Press, 1957.

Poe, Clarence. "The Farmer and His Future." In *Culture in the South*, edited by William Terry Couch, 319–43. Chapel Hill: University of North Carolina Press, 1934.

Polk, Noel. "Faulkner and World War II." In *Remaking Dixie: The Impact of World War II on the U.S. South*, edited by Neil R. McMillen, 131–45. Jackson: University Press of Mississippi, 1997.

Powdermaker, Hortense. *After Freedom: A Cultural Study of the Deep South*. 1939. New York: Russell and Russell, 1968.

Powell, Douglas Reichert. *Critical Regionalism: Connecting Politics and Culture in the American Landscape*. Chapel Hill: University of North Carolina Press, 2007.

Pratt, Mary Louise. "Arts of the Contact Zone." *Profession* (1991): 33–40.

———. *Imperial Eyes: Travel Writing and Transculturation*. New York: Routledge, 1992.

Purdy, Rob Roy, ed. *Fugitives' Reunion: Conversations at Vanderbilt*. Nashville: Vanderbilt University Press, 1959.

Quinones, Raymond. *Mapping Literary Modernism: Time and Development*. Princeton, NJ: Princeton University Press, 1985.

Rainwater, Catherine. "'That Abused Word, Modern' and Ellen Glasgow's 'Literature of Revolt.'" *Mississippi Quarterly* 49, no. 2 (Spring 1996): 345–61.

Raitt, Suzanne, and Trudi Tate. *Women's Fiction and the Great War*. Oxford: Clarendon Press, 1997.

Ransom, John Crowe. "Reconstructed but Unregenerate." In *I'll Take My Stand: The South and the Agrarian Tradition*, by Twelve Southerners, 1–27. 1930. Baton Rouge: Louisiana State University Press, 1995.

———. "The South Is a Bulwark." 1936. In *The Southern Agrarians and the New Deal: Essays after I'll Take My Stand*, edited by Emily S. Bingham and Thomas A. Underwood, 257–69. Charlottesville: University Press of Virginia, 2001.

———. "What Does the South Want?" In *Who Owns America? A New Declaration of Independence*, edited by Herbert Agar and Allen Tate, 233–52. 1936. Wilmington, DE: ISI Books, 1999.

Raper, Julius R. "*Barren Ground* and the Transition to Southern Modernism." In *Ellen Glasgow: New Perspectives*, edited by Dorothy M. Scura, 146–61. Knoxville: University of Tennessee Press, 1995.

———. *Without Shelter: The Early Career of Ellen Glasgow*. Baton Rouge: Louisiana State University Press, 1971.

Reed, John Shelton. *The Enduring South: Subcultural Persistence in Mass Society*. Chapel Hill: University of North Carolina Press, 1974.

Reidy, Joseph P. *From Slavery to Agrarian Capitalism in the Cotton Plantation South: Central Georgia, 1800–1880*. Chapel Hill: University of North Carolina Press, 1992.

Rhode, Robert. *Setting in the American Short Story of Local Color, 1865–1900*. Paris: De Gruyter Mouton, 1975.

Richardson, Riché. *Black Masculinity and the U.S. South: From Uncle Tom to Gangsta*. Athens: University of Georgia Press, 2007.

Ring, Natalie J. *The Problem South: Region, Empire, and the New Liberal State, 1880–1930*. Athens: University of Georgia Press, 2012.

Roberts, Elizabeth Madox. *He Sent Forth a Raven*. New York: Viking, 1935.

Robertson, Ben. *Red Hills and Cotton: An Upcountry Memory*. 1942. Columbia: University of South Carolina Press, 1991.

Rocks, James E. "The Art of *Lanterns on the Levee*." *Southern Review* 12 (1976): 814–23.

Rogers, Daniel T. *Atlantic Crossings: Social Politics in a Progressive Age*. Cambridge, MA: Harvard University Press, 1998.

Rogin, Michael Paul. *Ronald Reagan, the Movie, and Other Episodes in Political Demonology*. Berkeley: University of California Press, 1987.

Romine, Scott. *The Narrative Forms of Southern Community*. Baton Rouge: Louisiana State University Press, 1999.

———. *The Real South: Southern Narrative in the Age of Cultural Reproduction*. Baton Rouge: Louisiana State University Press, 2008.

Roosevelt, Franklin Delano. *The Continuing Struggle for Liberalism: 1938; The Public Papers and Addresses of Franklin D. Roosevelt*. New York: Macmillan, 1941.

Roper, John Herbert. *Paul Green: Playwright of the Real South*. Athens: University of Georgia Press, 2003.

———, ed. *Paul Green's War Songs: A Southern Poet's History of the Great War, 1917–1920*. Rocky Mount: North Carolina Wesleyan College Press, 1993.

Rovit, Earl H. *Herald to Chaos: The Novels of Elizabeth Madox Roberts*. Lexington: University of Kentucky Press, 1960.

Royce, Edward. *The Origins of Southern Sharecropping*. Philadelphia: Temple University Press, 1992.

Rubin, Louis D., Jr. *The Wary Fugitives: Four Poets and the South*. Baton Rouge: Louisiana State University Press, 1978.

———. *Writers of the Modern South: The Faraway Country*. Seattle: University of Washington Press, 1966.

Rubin, Louis D., Jr., and Robert Jacobs, eds. *Southern Renascence: The Literature of the Modern South*. Baltimore: Johns Hopkins University Press, 1953.

Rudwick, Elliott M. *Race Riot at East St. Louis, July 2, 1917*. Carbondale: Southern Illinois University Press, 1964.

Russell, Francis. *The Shadow of Blooming Grove: Warren G. Harding in His Times*. New York: McGraw-Hill, 1968.

Sahlins, Marshall. *Culture and Practical Reason*. Chicago: University of Chicago Press, 1976.

Salmond, John. *Gastonia, 1929: The Story of the Loray Mill Strike*. Chapel Hill: University of North Carolina Press, 1995.

Sandburg, Carl. *The Chicago Race Riots, July, 1919*. New York: Harcourt, Brace and Howe, 1919.

Sargen, Nicholas Peter. *"Tractorization" in the United States and Its Relevance for the Developing Countries*. New York: Garland, 1979.

Sassoon, Siegfried. *The Complete Memoirs of George Sherston*. London: Faber and Faber, 1972.

Schneider, Mark Robert. *"We Return Fighting": The Civil Rights Movement in the Jazz Age*. Boston: Northeastern University Press, 2002.

Schulman, Bruce. *From Cotton Belt to Sunbelt: Federal Policy, Economic Development, and the Transformation of the South, 1938–1990*. Durham, NC: Duke University Press, 1994.

Schulyer, Lorraine Gates. *The Weight of Their Votes: Southern Women and Political Leverage in the 1920s*. Chapel Hill: University of North Carolina Press, 2006.

Schwartz, Lawrence. *Creating Faulkner's Reputation: The Politics of Modern Literary Criticism*. Knoxville: University of Tennessee Press, 1990.

Scott, Anne Firor. Foreword to *The Hard-Boiled Virgin*, by Frances Newman, v–xix. Athens: University of Georgia Press, 1980.

———. *The Southern Lady: From Pedestal to Politics, 1830–1930*. Chicago: University of Chicago Press, 1970.

Scott, Emmett J. *Scott's Official History of the American Negro in the World War*. Privately published, 1919.

Scranton, Phillip, ed. *The Second Wave: Southern Industrialization from the 1940s to the 1970s*. Athens: University of Georgia Press, 2001.

Seidel, Kathryn Lee. *The Southern Belle in the American Novel*. Tampa: University of South Florida Press, 1985.

Sherry, Vincent. *The Great War and the Language of Modernism*. New York: Oxford University Press, 2003.

———. "The Great War and Literary Modernism in England." In *The Cambridge Companion to the Literature of the First World War*, edited by Vincent Sherry, 113–37. New York: Cambridge University Press, 2005.

Shockley, Ann Allen. "Afro-American Women Writers: The New Negro Movement, 1924–1933." In *Rereading Modernism: New Directions in Feminist Criticism*, edited by Lisa Rado, 123–36. New York: Garland, 1994.

Shouse, Sarah N. *Hillbilly Realist: Herman Clarence Nixon of Possum Trot*. Tuscaloosa: University of Alabama Press, 1986.

Silber, Nina. *The Romance of Reunion: Northerners and the South, 1865–1900*. Chapel Hill: University of North Carolina Press, 1993.

Silkin, Jon, ed. *The Penguin Book of First World War Poetry*. London: Penguin, 1979.

Simpson, Claude M. *The Local Colorists*. New York: Harper and Brothers, 1960.

Simpson, Lewis P. *The Dispossessed Garden: Pastoral and History in Southern Literature*. Athens: University of Georgia Press, 1975.

———. Foreword to *The Literary Correspondence of Donald Davidson and Allen Tate*, edited by John T. Fain and Thomas D. Young. Athens: University of Georgia Press, 1974.

———. "The Southern Writer and the Great Literary Secession." In *The Man of Letters in New England and the South: Essays on the Literary Vocation in America*, 229–55. Baton Rouge: Louisiana State University Press, 1973.

Singal, Daniel J. *The War Within: From Victorian to Modernist Thought in the South, 1919–1945*. Chapel Hill: University of North Carolina Press, 1982.

Sitkoff, Harvard. "African American Militancy in the World War II South: Another Perspective." In *Toward Freedom Land: The Long Struggle for Racial Equality in America*, 93–128. Lexington: University Press of Kentucky, 2010.

Slide, Anthony. *American Racist: The Life and Films of Thomas Dixon*. Lexington: University Press of Kentucky, 2004.

Slotkin, Richard. *Lost Battalions: The Great War and the Crisis of American Nationality*. New York: Henry Holt, 2005.

Smith, Angela K. *The Second Battlefield: Women, Modernism, and the First World War*. Manchester: Manchester University Press, 2000.

Smith, Jon, and Deborah Cohn, eds. *Look Away: The U.S. South in New World Studies*. Durham, NC: Duke University Press, 2004.

Smith, Neil. *Uneven Development: Nature, Capital, and the Production of Space*. Athens: University of Georgia Press, 2008.

Sosna, Morton. Introduction to *Remaking Dixie: The Impact of World War II on the U.S. South*, edited by Neil R. Mcmillen, xiii–xix. Jackson: University Press of Mississippi, 1997.

———. "More Important than the Civil War? The Impact of World War II on the South." In *Perspectives on the American South*, edited by James C. Cobb and Charles Reagan Wilson. New York: Gordon and Breach, 1987.

Staiger, Janet. "*The Birth of a Nation*: Reconsidering Its Reception." In *The Birth of a Nation: D. W. Griffith, Director*, edited by Robert Lang, 195–213. New Brunswick, NJ: Rutgers University Press, 1994.

Stallings, Laurence. *The Doughboys: The Story of the AEF, 1917–1918*. New York: Harper and Row, 1963.

———. "Faulkner in Hollywood." In *Conversations with William Faulkner*, edited by M. Thomas Inge, 27–29. Jackson: University Press of Mississippi, 1999.

———. *The First World War: A Photographic History*. New York: Simon and Schuster, 1933.

———. *Plumes*. 1924. Columbia: University of South Carolina Press, 2006.

Stephens, Michelle. *Black Empire: The Masculine Global Imaginary of Caribbean Intellectuals in the United States, 1914–1962*. Durham, NC: Duke University Press, 2005.

———. "Black Transnationalism and the Politics of National Identity: West Indian Intellectuals in Harlem in the Age of War and Revolution." *American Quarterly* 50, no. 3 (September 1998): 592–608.

Stevenson, Randall. *Literature and the Great War*. Oxford: Oxford University Press, 2013.

Stewart, John L. *The Burden of Time: The Fugitives and Agrarians*. Princeton, NJ: Princeton University Press, 1965.

Stockley, Grif. *Blood in Their Eyes: The Elaine Race Massacres of 1919*. Fayetteville: University of Arkansas Press, 2001.

Sullivan, Walter. *A Requiem for the Renascence: The State of Fiction in the Modern South*. Athens: University of Georgia Press, 1976.

Sundquist, Eric J. *The Hammers of Creation: Folk Culture in Modern African-American Fiction*. Athens: University of Georgia Press, 1992.

Tate, Allen. *Collected Essays*. Denver: Alan Swallow, 1959.

———. *Mr. Pope and Other Poems*. New York: Minton, Balch and Company, 1928.

———. "The New Provincialism: With an Epilogue on the Southern Novel." *Virginia Quarterly Review* 21, no. 2 (Spring 1945).

———. "Remarks on the Southern Religion." In *I'll Take My Stand: The South and the Agrarian Tradition*, by Twelve Southerners, 155–75. 1930. Baton Rouge: Louisiana State University Press, 1995.

Tate, Claudia. Introduction to *Selected Works of Georgia Douglas Johnson*, edited by Claudia Tate, xvii–lxxx. New York: G. K. Hall and Company, 1997.

Tate, Trudi. *Modernism, History, and the First World War*. Manchester: Manchester University Press, 1998.

Terborg-Penn, Rosalyn. *African American Women in the Struggle for the Vote, 1850–1920*. Bloomington: Indiana University Press, 1998.

Thomas, Mary Martha. *The New Woman in Alabama: Social Reforms and Suffrage, 1890–1920*. Tuscaloosa: University of Alabama Press, 1992.

Tichi, Cecelia. *Shifting Gears: Technology, Literature, Culture in Modernist America*. Chapel Hill: University of North Carolina Press, 1987.

Tindall, George B. *The Emergence of the New South, 1913–1945*. Baton Rouge: Louisiana State University Press, 1967.

Tippett, Thomas. *When Southern Labor Stirs*. New York: Cape and Smith, 1931.

Tolnay, Stewart E., and E. M. Beck. *A Festival of Violence: An Analysis of Southern Lynchings, 1882–1930*. Urbana: University of Illinois Press, 1995.

Toth, Emily. *Kate Chopin*. New York: William Morrow, 1990.

Toulmin, Stephen. *Cosmopolis: The Hidden Agenda of Modernity*. Chicago: University of Chicago Press, 1990.

Twelve Southerners. *I'll Take My Stand: The South and the Agrarian Tradition*. 1930. Baton Rouge: Louisiana State University Press, 1995.

Tylee, Claire M. *The Great War and Women's Consciousness: Images of Militarism and Womanhood in Women's Writings, 1914–64*. Iowa City: University of Iowa Press, 1990.

———. "Womanist Propaganda, African-American Great War Experience, and Cultural Strategies of the Harlem Renaissance: Plays by Alice Dunbar-Nelson and Mary P. Burrill." *Women's Studies International Forum* 20, no. 1 (1997): 153–63.

Underwood, Thomas. *Allen Tate: Orphan of the South*. Princeton, NJ: Princeton University Press, 2000.

Vance, Rupert. *Human Factors in Cotton Culture: A Study in the Social Geography of the American South*. Chapel Hill: University of North Carolina Press, 1929.

Vickers, Kenneth. *T. S. Stribling: A Life of the Tennessee Novelist*. Knoxville: University of Tennessee Press, 2004.

Wade, Barbara Ann. *Frances Newman: Southern Satirist and Literary Rebel*. Tuscaloosa: University of Alabama Press, 1998.

Wagner-Martin, Linda. *The Modern American Novel, 1914–1945*. Boston: Twayne, 1990.

Walkowitz, Rebecca. *Cosmopolitan Style: Modernism beyond the Nation*. New York: Columbia University Press, 2006.

Wallerstein, Immanuel. "What Can One Mean by Southern Culture?" In *Geopolitics and Geoculture: Essays on the Changing World-System*, 200–214. New York: Cambridge University Press, 1991.

Warren, Robert Penn. "The Circus in the Attic." In *The Circus in the Attic and Other Stories*, 3–62. New York: Harcourt, Brace and Company, 1947.

———. "Literature as Symptom." In *Who Owns America? A New Declaration of Independence*, edited by Herbert Agar and Allen Tate, 342–62. 1936. Wilmington, DE: ISI Books, 1999.

———. "Mad for Poetry." Interview with Bill Ferris. *Southern Cultures* 10, no. 4 (Winter 2004): 8–32.

Watts, Trent, ed. *White Masculinity in the Recent South*. Baton Rouge: Louisiana State University Press, 2008.

Weaks-Baxter, Mary. *Reclaiming the American Farmer: The Reinvention of a Regional Mythology in Twentieth-Century Southern Writing*. Baton Rouge: Louisiana State University Press, 2006.

Weaver, Richard M. *The Southern Tradition at Bay: A History of Postbellum Thought*. 1968. Washington, DC: Regnery Gateway, 1989.

Webb, George Ernest. *The Evolution Controversy in America*. Lexington: University Press of Kentucky, 1994.

Whalan, Mark. *The Great War and the Culture of the New Negro*. Gainesville: University Press of Florida, 2008.

Wheeler, Marjorie Spruill. *New Women of the New South: The Leaders of the Woman Suffrage Movement in the Southern States*. New York: Oxford University Press, 1993.

White, Walter. *The Fire in the Flint*. 1924. Athens: University of Georgia Press, 2001.

———. "I Investigate Lynchings." 1929. In *Witnessing Lynching: American Writers Respond*, edited by Anne P. Rice, 252–60. New Brunswick, NJ: Rutgers University Press, 2003.

———. *A Man Called White: The Autobiography of Walter White*. 1948. Bloomington: Indiana University Press, 1970.

———. *Rope and Faggot: A Biography of Judge Lynch*. 1929. Notre Dame, IN: Notre Dame University Press, 2001.

Williams, B. O. "The Impact of Mechanization of Agriculture on the Farm Population of the South." 1939. In *The Social Consequences and Challenges of New Agricultural Technologies*, edited by Gigi M. Berardi and Charles C. Geisler, 73–82. Boulder, CO: Westview Press, 1984.

Williams, Chad L. *Torchbearers of Democracy: African American Soldiers in the World War I Era*. Chapel Hill: University of North Carolina Press, 2010.

Williamson, Joel. *The Crucible of Race: Black-White Relations in the American South since Emancipation*. New York: Oxford University Press, 1984.

Wilson, Anthony. "The Music of God, Man, and Beast: Spirituality and Modernity in *Jonah's Gourd Vine*." *Southern Literary Journal* 35, no. 2 (Spring 2003): 64–78.

Wilson, Charles Reagan. *Baptized in Blood: The Religion of the Lost Cause, 1865–1920*. Athens: University of Georgia Press, 1980.

———, ed. *Religion in the South*. Jackson: University Press of Mississippi, 1985.

Wilson, Edmund. *Axel's Castle: A Study of the Imaginative Literature of 1870–1930*. New York: Charles Scribner's Sons, 1931.

Wilson, Woodrow. *Congressional Record*. 65th Congress, 2nd Session, 1827–1828.

———. *A History of the American People*. Vol. 5, *Reunion and Nationalization*. New York: Harper and Brothers, 1902.

———. "Remarks to the Confederate Veterans in Washington." In *The Papers of Woodrow Wilson*, vol. 42, edited by Arthur S. Link, 451–53. Princeton, NJ: Princeton University Press, 1983.

Winchell, Mark Royden. *Where No Flag Flies: Donald Davidson and the Southern Resistance*. Columbia: University of Missouri Press, 2000.

Winter, Jay. *Sites of Memory, Sites of Mourning: The Great War in European Cultural History*. New York: Cambridge University Press, 1995.

Wise, Benjamin E. "On Naïve and Sentimental Poetry: Nostalgia, Sex, and the Souths of William Alexander Percy." *Southern Cultures* 14, no. 1 (Spring 2008): 54–79.

———. *William Alexander Percy: The Curious Life of a Mississippi Planter and Sexual Freethinker*. Chapel Hill: University of North Carolina Press, 2012.

Wittenburg, Judith Bryant. "Vision and Re-Vision: Bayard Sartoris." In *Critical Essays on William Faulkner: The Sartoris Family*, edited by Arthur F. Kinney, 323–31. Boston: G. K. Hall and Company, 1985.

Wolfe, Thomas. *Look Homeward, Angel*. 1929. New York: Charles Scribner's Sons, 1995.

Wood, Amy. *Lynching and Spectacle: Witnessing Racial Violence in America, 1890–1940*. Chapel Hill: University of North Carolina Press, 2009.

Woodruff, Nan Elizabeth. *American Congo: The African American Freedom Struggle in the Delta*. Cambridge, MA: Harvard University Press, 2003.

Woodward, C. Vann. *The Burden of Southern History*. Baton Rouge: Louisiana State University Press, 1960.

———. *Origins of the New South, 1877–1913*. Baton Rouge: Louisiana State University Press, 1951.

———. *The Strange Career of Jim Crow*. New York: Oxford University Press, 1957.

——. "Why the Southern Renaissance?" *Virginia Quarterly Review* 51 (1975): 222–39.

Woolf, Virginia. "Mr. Bennett and Mrs. Brown." In *Selected Essays*, edited by David Bradshaw, 32–36. New York: Oxford University Press, 2009.

Wright, Gavin. "Economic Progress and the Mind of the South." In *W. J. Cash and the Minds of the South*, edited by Paul D. Escott, 187–206. Baton Rouge: Louisiana State University Press, 1992.

Wright, Richard. *Black Boy*. 1945. New York: HarperCollins, 1998.

——. "Long Black Song." In *Uncle Tom's Children*, 124–52. New York: Harper and Brothers, 1936.

Wyatt-Brown, Bertram. *The House of Percy: Honor, Melancholy, and Imagination in a Southern Family*. New York: Oxford University Press, 1994.

——. *Southern Honor: Ethics and Behavior in the Old South*. New York: Oxford University Press, 2007.

Yonce, Margaret J. "The Composition of *Soldiers' Pay*." *Mississippi Quarterly* 33, no. 3 (Summer 1980): 291–326.

Young, Thomas Daniel. "The Southern Renascence, 1920–1950." In *The History of Southern Literature*, edited by Louis D. Rubin Jr. et al., 261–63. Baton Rouge: Louisiana State University Press, 1985.

Young, Thomas Daniel, and M. Thomas Inge. *Donald Davidson*. New York: Twayne, 1990.

Zeiger, Susan. *In Uncle Sam's Service: Women Workers with the American Expeditionary Force, 1917–1919*. Ithaca, NY: Cornell University Press, 1999.

Zeitlin, Michael. "The Passion of Margaret Powers: A Psychoanalytic Reading of *Soldiers' Pay*." *Mississippi Quarterly* 46, no. 3 (Summer 1993): 351–72.

INDEX

CPSIA information can be obtained
at www.ICGtesting.com
Printed in the USA
BVHW030248290319
544024BV00003B/5/P